The Quick-Reference Guide to

SEXUALITY & RELATIONSHIP COUNSELING

DR. TIM CLINTON
AND DR. MARK LAASER

BakerBooks

a division of Baker Publishing Group
Grand Rapids, Michigan

© 2010 by Tim Clinton

Published by Baker Books
a division of Baker Publishing Group
P.O. Box 6287, Grand Rapids, MI 49516-6287
www.bakerbooks.com

Printed in the United States of America

Library of Congress Cataloging-in-Publication Data
Clinton, Timothy E., 1960–
    The quick-reference guide to sexuality & relationship counseling / Tim Clinton, Mark Laaser.
       p. cm.
    Includes bibliographical references.
    ISBN 978-0-8010-7236-9 (pbk. : alk. paper)
    1. Sex—Religious aspects—Christianity—Handbooks, manuals, etc. 2. Pastoral counseling—Handbooks, manuals, etc. 3. Counseling—Handbooks, manuals, etc. I. Laaser, Mark R. II. Title.
    BT708.C64 2010
    259′.14—dc22   2009053568

10 11 12 13 14 15 16   7 6 5 4 3 2 1

Contents

Acknowledgments

Dr. Laaser and I would like to say a special thank-you to all involved in helping build a resource that we pray will be used by Christian leaders and people helpers all over the world to foster hope and healing for those who are searching for wisdom, direction, and understanding.

A note of deep appreciation goes to Robert Hosack at Baker Books for believing in the project and to Mary Suggs and Mary Wenger for their excellence in editing.

Likewise, we extend sincere gratitude to the entire AACC team, who helped in the writing, editing, and research for this project:

Pat Springle, MA

Joshua Straub, PhD

Amy Feigel, MA, LMFT

Anthony Centore, PhD

George Ohlschlager, JD

Laura Faidley

We would also like to thank our wives, Julie and Deb, and our families for their love and support through the years. We could not enter into the work we do without you.

And to the entire AACC team and tens of thousands of pastors and Christian counselors who are literally entering into the darkness of the lives of hurting people, may this resource help you bring the light and hope of Jesus in every situation. To you we dedicate this series.

Introduction

Comedian Phyllis Diller once complained, "A terrible thing happened to me last night again: nothing."

We live in an incredibly sexualized society, but many people who come to us for counseling are like Phyllis—disappointed about their sex lives. A few come to us with sexual problems at the top of their list of things they want to talk about, but even in our sex-saturated culture (and perhaps because of it), some people are ashamed to bring up their sexual problems in counseling.

Since the beginning of the American Association of Christian Counselors (AACC), we have been consistently asked to catalog and provide "quick-reference" materials that pastors and counselors could easily access for the variety of issues they face. This third volume on sexuality and relationship counseling—and all the volumes in this series—is our response to that legitimate call. The topics for the quick-reference guides are:

Personal and emotional issues

Marriage and family issues

Sexuality and relationship issues

Teenager issues

Women's issues

Singles issues

Money issues

We are delighted to deliver to you this volume, *The Quick-Reference Guide to Sexuality and Relationship Counseling*, and trust that God will use it to bring His hope and life to millions of believers throughout America and the world to whom the continually growing membership in the AACC ministers.

Everywhere we look in this new millennium, we find people who desperately need God's touch, who cry out constantly for His gracious care. The mind-boggling advances in every professional and scientific field, along with a multibillion-dollar advertising blitz, have stoked the false expectation that we can "have it all, and have it all now." If you look at the latest advertising tactics, you'll quickly see that sex sells.

All of these factors only reinforce the aching "hole in the soul" that so many suffer in the midst of material abundance and relational brokenness, thus intensifying the stress that we all live under in our 24-7 sociocultural landscape. It begs the question, Does an authentic remedy really exist?

We believe the answer is a resounding yes. And it starts with you. Since you are reading the introduction to this book, you have likely been called to counseling ministry, to a work of authentic caregiving. You have been called and are likely trained to some degree to deliver care and consolation to the many broken-down and brokenhearted souls living in your church and community. You will find this book and this entire series most helpful if you have been called to remind others that "the LORD is close to the brokenhearted; he rescues those whose spirits are crushed" (Ps. 34:18 NLT). He has chosen you as a vessel for delivery of His special grace; you have both the privilege and the responsibility to deliver that care in the most excellent and ethical way possible.

When it comes to the issues of sexuality and relationship counseling, one of the most important things we can do for people is to normalize discussions about sex. If they can learn to talk more openly and candidly to us in a safe environment, they will probably have more courage and confidence to talk to their spouse or doctor to find solutions to their problems. Over the course of a life, and in a long-lasting marriage, every aspect of the relationship ebbs and flows—including sexual satisfaction. Pregnancy and childbirth, the pressures of moving to a new city or changing jobs, the stress of having too many bills and too little money, illness, boredom, and the physical limitations that come with age are normal parts of life.

Quite often a client comes to us with a single presenting problem, but a few questions uncover a tangled web of emotional, relational, spiritual, financial, and sexual difficulties. The counselor's task is to uncover the most pressing issues, prioritize them, and address them in a way that offers a process of change and hope that life can be better.

While all problems impact all dimensions of a person's life in some manner, a quick glance at the table of contents of this book shows that some of the problems clients face are primarily *medical*, such as infertility, sexually transmitted diseases, and HIV; some are *psychological* and are the result of traumatic events, addictions, compulsions, or inordinate fears; some are *spiritual* with roots in the person's relationship with God; and some deal with *communication* between spouses. In many (if not most) cases, the problem results from a combination of causes. If there is any question about a medical condition causing or contributing to the problem, refer the client to a gynecologist or urologist or perhaps a family physician.

A wide array of Christian approaches has proven effective for people with sexual problems, including cognitive therapy to help clients identify and replace destructive thought patterns, behavior therapy to teach exercises in caressing and other meaningful touching, therapy groups and support groups for dealing with abuse or addiction, and various sexual coaching strategies that are beginning to be recognized and used.

Counselors and pastors sometimes overlook sexual issues because people who meet with them fail to bring up these concerns. For this reason, we recommend that counselors make sure their intake form includes a simple question about sexual function and satisfaction. In addition to other elements on the form (such as stating the primary concern for the visit, family history, education, employment, spiritual interests, substance use and abuse history, and physical health), include something like: "Sexual function and satisfaction: Is this an area of concern for you? If so, please explain." In your initial assessment with the client, look for signs that the person may want or need to talk more freely about his sex life.

SEX IS GOD'S INVENTION

When Adam first saw Eve, he must have been amazed (see Gen. 2:23)! Have you ever thought how he must have felt the first time he touched her—had sex with her? He had every reason to enjoy life to the fullest with the woman God gave him. The Bible says, "They were both naked, the man and his wife, and were not ashamed" (Gen. 2:25 NKJV). Jesus reaffirmed intimacy and sexual delight as the adhesive in marriage relationships. He repeated what was said in Genesis: "The two will become one flesh" (Matt. 19:5). The writer of the book of Hebrews claimed the marital bed as undefiled (Heb. 13:4 NKJV), and Paul wrote that married couples could withhold sex from each other only for a time and only for the purpose of fasting and prayer (1 Cor. 7:5). Certainly the commandment fulfilled with the most pleasure in all of recorded history was God's order to Adam and Eve: "Be fruitful and increase in number" (Gen. 1:28). In the safety and security of marriage, sex can be experienced with unguarded hearts, creativity, and joy.

Throughout this guide, you will see that we refer often to one of the most beautiful love stories ever written—the Song of Solomon—the story of the Shulamite bride and her beloved husband. It's an amazing testimony to pure love—the desire and passion between a man and woman, the bond God created to set the stage for the kind of sexuality couples can and should engage in today, thousands of years later!

Yet anything that has that much predictive value for good can also be perverted and destroyed. You don't have to read very far in the Bible before you find sexual sin and relational brokenness. There are nine sexual issues in the book of Genesis alone!

Christians vary widely in their sexual beliefs and practices. Today people seeking help come with a wide range of sexual perceptions, experiences, and desires. Although rare, a few still cling to the old concept that sex is somehow beneath those who are fully devoted to Christ, and they feel tremendous shame when they have sex with their spouse. Others use sex to take advantage of others in relationships by being demeaning or demanding or by withholding sex to punish and manipulate.

Whether clients come from a highly oppressive and restrictive background, have been promiscuous, or have experienced abuse, they need to understand God's way—His beautiful design and plan for sex. He created us as sexual beings, with sexual urges and needs, and He desires that we find true sexual freedom, passion, and satisfaction in our loving relationship.

WHO CAN USE THIS GUIDE

Because of the nature of sex therapy, this *Quick-Reference Guide* is designed primarily for professional counselors, but pastors and lay counselors can use it as a valuable resource too. "Sex therapy" should be left to trained professionals who are equipped to handle the often complex, titillating, and explosive issues inherent to human sexuality.

Many people who struggle with their sexuality are in difficult relationships. They—and many untrained caregivers who try to help them—are vulnerable to temptations and the damage from any unethical boundary crossing that the subject of sex inevitably offers. As a result, pastors and even lay counselors should use the guide to gain information about topics brought to the surface in conversations, and they can then use this information to make accurate and effective referrals to physicians and professional counselors.

THE THREE LEGS OF HELPING MINISTRY

We have written these books to apply to every leg of our three-legged stool metaphor. We advance the idea that the helping ministry of the church is made up of *pastors*, who serve in a central case-managing role, as the client nearly always returns to the role of parishioner; of *professional Christian counselors*, who often serve many churches in a given geographic area; and of *lay helpers*, who have been trained and serve in the church in individual or group leadership roles.

People serving at all three levels must develop both the character and the servant qualities that reflect the grace and truth of Christ Himself. God has also distributed His gifts liberally throughout the church to perform the various ministry tasks that are central to any healthy church operation. For no matter how skilled or intelligent or caring we are, unless we directly rely on the Spirit of God to work in us to do the ministry of God, our service will not bear kingdom fruit. He will bring to us the people He wants us to help, and we must learn to depend on Him to touch others in a supernatural way—so that people exclaim, "God showed up (and miracles happened) in that counseling session today!"

Pastor or Church Staff

If you are a pastor or church staff member, virtually everyone sitting in your pews today has been (or soon will be) touched by addiction, divorce, violence, depression, grief, confusion, loneliness, and a thousand other evidences of living as broken people in a fallen world. This guidebook will help you:

- deliver effective counseling and short-term help to those who come to you with their issues
- teach others and construct sermons about the leading issues of the day with which people struggle
- provide essential resources and materials for staff and lay leaders in your church to advance their helping and teaching ministries

Professional Clinician

If you are a professional clinician, licensed or certified in one of the six major clinical disciplines, you are likely already familiar with most of the topics in this book. This book will assist you best to:

- review the definitions and assessment questions to use in your initial session with a new client
- understand and incorporate a biblical view of the client's problem
- shape your treatment plans with some of the best principles and resources available
- deliver information to your clients that best helps them get unstuck and move forward more resolutely with the right thinking and focused action of this treatment process

Lay Helper or Minister

If you are a lay helper or minister, this book will guide you in planning and delivering the best care you can from beginning to end. We recommend that you read through the entire book, highlighting the material most useful to you in either individual or group formats. This guide will best help you to:

- understand and accurately assess the person's problem
- guide your discussions and delivery of helpful suggestions without assuming too much control or yielding too little influence
- remind you of key principles and guide you in the process of moving from problem to resolution more effectively
- remind you of the limits of lay ministry and assist you in making constructive referrals to others more trained and able to help

USING *THE QUICK-REFERENCE GUIDE TO SEXUALITY AND RELATIONSHIP COUNSELING*

You will see that we have divided each topic into an outline format that follows the logic of the counseling process. The goal and purpose of each of the eight parts are as follows:

1. **Portraits.** Each topic begins with a number of short vignettes that tell a common story about people struggling with the issue at hand. We have tried to deliver stories that you will most often encounter with the people you serve.
2. **Definitions and Key Thoughts.** This section begins with a clear definition of the issue in nontechnical language. Then we add a variety of ideas and data points to help you gain a fuller understanding of the issue and how it impacts lives and may harm the people who struggle with it.

3. **Assessment Interview.** Usually this section begins by suggesting a framework with which to approach assessment and is followed by a series of specific questions for gaining a more complete understanding of the client's problem.

4. **Wise Counsel.** One or more key ideas are presented here that should serve as an overarching guide to your intervention—wise counsel will help you frame your interventions in a better way. These key insights may be directed to the clinician or pastor, but they are useful to all three types of helpers we have noted above and will give you an edge in understanding and working with the person(s) in front of you.

5. **Action Steps.** This section—along with wise counsel—will guide you in what to do in your counseling interventions. It helps you construct a logical map that can guide you and your client from problem identification to resolution in a few measured steps—always client action steps. Without a good action plan, it is too easy to leave clients confused and drifting rather than moving in a determined way toward some concrete goals for change. Most Action Steps will be directed to the counselee. Those addressed to the counselor will be in italics.

6. **Biblical Insights.** Here we provide relevant Bible passages and commentary to assist you in your counseling work from beginning to end. Embedding the entire process in a biblical framework and calling on the Lord's power to do many things we cannot do solely in our own strength are essential to authentic Christian counseling. You may choose to give your clients some of these verses as homework—ask them to meditate on them and/or memorize them—or you may want to use them as guides for the intervention process.

7. **Prayer Starter.** While not appropriate with every client, many Christians want—and even expect—prayer to be an integral part of your helping intervention. You should ask each client for his consent to prayer interventions. Every client can and should be prayed for, even if he does not join you and you must pray silently or in pre- or post-session reflection. Prayer is usually the most common spiritual intervention used in Christian counseling, and we prompt a few lines of good prayer that can serve, in whole or part, as effective introductions to taking counseling vertically and inviting God directly into the relationship.

8. **Recommended Resources.** We list here some of the best-known Christian resources and the best secular resources for further reading and study. By no means an exhaustive list, it will direct you to resources that will also reference additional works, allowing you to go as deep as you want in further study of an issue.

One additional note: to avoid the cumbersome use of "he or she" throughout this guide, we have chosen to alternate the use of the male and female pronouns, using only one in a chapter. In most cases these are alternated from one chapter to the next, unless the topic of a chapter is gender specific.

We appreciate your desire to help people walk with God. Christian counseling is a strong, effective case-based form of discipleship. In fact, it is often the door through which people walk to break through years of pain, misperceptions, and destructive habits that have kept them from being fully alive to God. We are honored to be partners with you in your work, and we trust that God will continue to use you in powerful ways to touch people's lives.

ADDITIONAL RESOURCES

The American Association of Christian Counselors is a ministry and professional organization of nearly fifty thousand members in the United States and around the world. We are dedicated to providing and delivering the finest resources available to pastors, professional counselors, and lay helpers in whatever role or setting such services are delivered. With our award-winning magazine, *Christian Counseling Today*, we also deliver a comprehensive range of education, training, ethical direction, consulting, books, and conference events to enhance the ministry of Christian counseling worldwide.

The AACC provides additional books, curricula, training, and conferences to equip you fully for the work of helping ministry in whatever form you do it. While some of these are noted in section 8 in every chapter of this book, some additional resources for your growth include:

The Bible for Hope: Caring for People God's Way by Tim Clinton and many leading contributors (Thomas Nelson, 2006).

Competent Christian Counseling: Foundations and Practice of Compassionate Soul Care by Tim Clinton, George Ohlschlager, and many other leading contributors (WaterBrook, 2002).

Caring for People God's Way (and *Marriage and Family Counseling* and *Healthy Sexuality*—books in the same series) by Tim Clinton, Arch Hart, and George Ohlschlager (Thomas Nelson, 2009).

AACC's Light University also provides various biblical counselor video-based training programs on:

Caring for People God's Way	Caring for Kids God's Way
Breaking Free	Caring for Teens God's Way
Marriage Works	Sexual Addiction
Healthy Sexuality	Nathan Project
Extraordinary Women	

Please come online at either http://www.aacc.net or at http://www.ecounseling .com to consider other resources and services delivered by AACC for the growth and betterment of the church.

PART 1

Sex and Relationships

1 Sexual Intimacy and Delight

1 PORTRAITS

- You have ravished my heart, my sister, my spouse; you have ravished my heart with one look of your eyes, with one link of your necklace. How fair is your love, my sister, my spouse! How much better than wine is your love, and the scent of your perfumes than all spices! Your lips, O my spouse, drip as the honeycomb; honey and milk are under your tongue; and the fragrance of your garments is like the fragrance of Lebanon. A garden enclosed is my sister, my spouse.

  Solomon to his Shulamite bride
  Song of Solomon 4:9–12 NKJV

- Awake, O north wind, and come, O south! Blow upon my garden, that its spices may flow out. Let my beloved come to his garden and eat its pleasant fruits.

  the Shulamite bride, yearning for her loving husband, Solomon
  Song of Solomon 4:16 NKJV

- For this reason a man will leave his father and mother and be united to his wife, and they will become one flesh. The man and his wife were both naked, and they felt no shame.

  Genesis 2:24–25

2 DEFINITIONS AND KEY THOUGHTS

- One of the best definitions for *sexual intimacy and delight* is in Genesis 2:25, where the Bible says that Adam and Eve "were both naked, and they felt no shame." *They were free, safe, valued, sexually expressive, loving, and loved.*
- Sexual intimacy and delight offer deep joy to a husband and wife. *When sex is experienced, as designed by God, nothing comes close to its expression of love.* It is an elusive love, however, one that is very fragile and easy to despoil. But when a man and woman in love honor God and one another in marriage, *sexual intimacy in its purest form is a blessing* that God Himself will provide to the faithful couple.
- Contrary to the lie of the world that God is a big sexual prude who frowns on sexual pleasure and delight, *God is the Creator of our sexuality*. It is His purpose for us to know, by our love and sexual delight with our mate, a piece of the love and delight that exists eternally in relations between the Father, Son, and Holy Spirit.

- Genesis 2:24–25 reveals *God's intended design* for a married man and woman. That is to be united as one flesh—in every way. This union, including sexual union, occurred before mankind fell into sin, so we can conclude that people were created *to be free to share their bodies openly with their spouse, delight in each other sexually, and honor God with their pleasure.*

ASSESSMENT INTERVIEW : 3

Early in counseling, and certainly on your intake forms, ask a few focused questions that will give you some indication of your client's beliefs about sex. Questions along this line will help your clients think about and address the beliefs they bring into counseling.

1. Do you have any ideas about what God intends for you—if He intends anything at all—regarding your sex life?
2. Some Christians believe that God frowns on sex and has no interest at all in your enjoyment of sexual pleasure. Were you ever taught this growing up? Do you believe that these ideas about God and sex are true?
3. Are there any ideas or beliefs—whether good or bad—that you see being played out in your own sexual relations with which you are uncomfortable? Are there any that you like and want to maintain?
4. Are you as free and comfortable about sex with your spouse as you want to be? What ideas or issues are blocking you from having a full and contented sex life?
5. How do you discuss—if you discuss at all—sex with your children? How do you show love and physical affection to your spouse in front of your children?
6. Many parents struggle to find an artful balance between revealing God's good design for human sexuality and challenging the excesses of a thoroughly sexualized culture. Is this an issue for you in your parenting? How are you doing with it?

WISE COUNSEL : 4

As a Christian counselor, in whatever role you serve, view the connection with a client—voluntary or involuntary—as an act of God. Believe that *God has brought you together and wants you to pour out His grace and truth on the needy person sitting before you* and on her marriage and family.

Furthermore, *never compartmentalize God and His grace.* Believe that God can work through physicians, clinicians, pastors, lawyers, anyone who will be called on to help and advise the counselee in your care. Pray that God will give wisdom to these experts.

Use a *cognitive-restructuring approach* to changing a client's false beliefs and assumptions.

- Raise questions with your client when you hear statements and beliefs that reflect false assumptions she may have brought into counseling.
- Ask what it would mean in her behavior or emotional life to adopt truths more in line with Scripture or that are drawn from more logical thinking.
- Challenge the client to adopt a new belief or worldview on a specific issue and practice it during the week as if it were true. Ask her to report what happens during your next counseling session.
- Praise and reinforce any changes for the better or consider a different or more narrow path to change if what she tried was not successful. Also ask whether the spouse and/or children saw and liked the changes. Sometimes family members notice changes sooner than the client.

The Bible is not silent on sexual desire and intimacy. In fact, it is *forthright about the act of marriage*. Have spouses consider these specific passages:

> I belong to my lover,
>   and his desire is for me.
> Come, my lover, let us go to the countryside,
>   let us spend the night in the villages.
> Let us go early to the vineyards
>   to see if the vines have budded,
> if their blossoms have opened,
>   and if the pomegranates are in bloom—
>   there I will give you my love.
> The mandrakes send out their fragrance,
>   and at our door is every delicacy,
> both new and old,
>   that I have stored up for you, my lover.
>
> Song of Songs 7:10–13

> The public image of sex in America bears virtually no relationship to the truth . . . in real life, the unheralded, seldom discussed world of married sex is actually the one that satisfies people the most.
>
> R. T. Michael et al.,
> Sex in America

To place love truly as the highest of all values, we must *treasure it more than our own life or our possessions. True love begets freedom.* It reflects the relationship we have with the Lord God—a mutual, exclusive, pure, absolute, and unconditional love that has no limits or boundaries within it. When we love God only and no other gods before Him, we are free to dance in His grace, love, mercy, and forgiveness.

The *marital relationship should reflect this same kind of love—pure, absolute, and unconditional.* When a husband and wife are joined together, having left their parents, they can become so close and intimate that their desire is solely for each other, united as one flesh.

> The husband should fulfill his marital duty to his wife, and likewise the wife to her husband. The wife's body does not belong to her alone but also to her husband. In the same way, the husband's body does not belong to him alone but also to his wife. Do not deprive each other except by mutual consent and for a time, so that you may devote yourselves to prayer. Then come together again so that Satan will not tempt you because of your lack of self-control.

1 Corinthians 7:3–5

Paul is straightforward on the issue of sex in marriage—a lack of desire or intimacy can lead to other temptations both inside and outside of the marriage relationship. Paul points out specifically that both husband and wife do not belong to themselves alone but to one another. Therefore, when either husband or wife is deliberately withholding sexual relations out of spite or if one of them demands sex without respect or affection, the unfortunate result may be that *the deprived or victimized spouse begins looking elsewhere for love and intimacy*. This is where temptation comes into play. Paul understood the temptation of outside influences. Any relationship that has the potential for good, Satan will be out to destroy (John 10:10). The Bible says, "The lips of a strange woman drop as an honeycomb, and her mouth is smoother than oil" (Prov. 5:3 KJV). Paul's warning about the susceptibility to temptation is based on the inevitable outcome, "But her end is bitter as wormwood, sharp as a twoedged sword. Her feet go down to death; her steps take hold on hell" (Prov. 5:4–5 KJV). Encourage spouses to understand that their sexual relationship matters.

ACTION STEPS 5

1. Listen and Talk

- Lack of communication, stresses at work, money problems, and any current fears or anger you are harboring can negatively affect sexual desire. Other common problems couples face that affect sexual desire include destructive arguments, current or past affairs, financial and career stressors, and a lack of quality time together. Emotional issues from your past—such as pain from past sexual abuse or feelings of betrayal—also have profound influence.

- Great lovers are great communicators. Good sex speaks clearly and gently about caring for, accepting, and valuing your spouse. Be sure to express your heartfelt needs and feelings. Share your love openly before, during, and after lovemaking. While many people struggle with telling their feelings to their spouse, honesty about what you're *really* feeling is the best foundation for having fun together in bed.

2. Get Alone Together

- Make time for just the two of you to get away from the fast pace of life and just enjoy each other. Often this means saying no to other commitments and planning ahead to get a sitter.

- Typically, sexual intimacy and sexual satisfaction increase when a couple starts dating again—even dating around the simplest of fun tasks, such as going to dinner and seeing a movie. Planning weekend getaways by jumping on a plane or driving a few hours to a vacation spot for a one- or two-day rendezvous can go far in revitalizing a busy or empty marriage.

Of all sexually active people, married people with only one lifetime partner are most likely to report they are "extremely" or "very" satisfied with the amount of physical and emotional pleasure they experience in their sex lives.

R. T. Michael et al., Sex in America .

3. Take Your Time

- African writer Ernestine Banyolak illustrates beautifully the need for time in lovemaking.

  > A man's experience is like a fire of dry leaves. It is easily kindled, flaring up suddenly and dying down just as quickly. A woman's experience, on the other hand, is like a fire glowing charcoal. Her husband has to tend to these coals with loving patience. Once the blaze is burning brightly, it will keep on glowing and radiating warmth for a long time."[1]

  Husbands and wives must take the time—not just during sex—to show their spouse they care and love him or her.

4. Show Some Heart

- Noted author Ingrid Trobisch says, "The greatest erogenous zone in a woman's body is her heart."[2] This should be true of women and men alike. Sex was never meant to be a single act of expression or feeling. On the contrary, gentleness, understanding, acts of kindness, and self-sacrifice all combine to form the building blocks of sexual satisfaction. Sex is about joining with your partner as God designed, for warmth, intimacy, and bonding.

5. Touch Each Other

- Most sex therapists agree that meaningful touching is the gateway to helping couples bond emotionally and physically. Unfortunately, after the marriage vows, many forget or don't take time simply to touch one another—give back rubs, hold hands, kiss, hug, and caress. These acts, if done often, will only serve to draw you closer and enhance intimacy.

6. Talk about Sex

- Read the Song of Solomon to each other and use the expressions Solomon and his bride use as a pattern for expressing your love for and physical admiration of your spouse. Tell each other what you like and don't like when making love. (Use words like *hot* and *sexy*—pull out all the good words!)

7. Explore Each Other

- Proverbs 5:19 says to let her breasts satisfy you wholly and completely. There is nothing wrong with deep sexual satisfaction. One thing is for sure—it doesn't just happen. Relax and explore new ways of making love with your spouse (see chapter 4). You were created *for each other*, so being sexually confident together brings glory to God.

BIBLICAL INSIGHTS : 6

May your fountain be blessed, and may you rejoice in the wife of your youth. A loving doe, a graceful deer—may her breasts satisfy you always, may you ever be captivated by her love.

Proverbs 5:18–19

Meaningful and delightful sex is enjoyed in the context of a rich, rewarding marriage in which both people feel valued and respected. This is the core of God's design for human sexuality.

But for Adam no suitable helper was found. So the LORD God caused the man to fall into a deep sleep; and while he was sleeping, he took one of the man's ribs and closed up the place with flesh. Then the LORD God made a woman from the rib he had taken out of the man, and he brought her to the man.

The man said, "This is now bone of my bones and flesh of my flesh; she shall be called 'woman,' for she was taken out of man." For this reason a man will leave his father and mother and be united to his wife, and they will become one flesh.

The man and his wife were both naked, and they felt no shame.

Genesis 2:20–25

> Married couples in a loving, long-term relationship report greater satisfaction with sexual intimacy than any other group of individuals.
>
> G. T. Stanton, 1998 South Carolina Marital Health Index

No doubt, Adam was thrilled to see the woman God created and gave to him. And we can assume she was excited to see him too. Marriage is so important that God instructed couples, even before generations had been born, to leave their parents and be physically, spiritually, and emotionally bonded with one another.

Marriage is honorable among all, and the bed undefiled.
Hebrews 13:4 NKJV

Sex is a gift from God, and marriage is its frame of expression. He created us as sexual beings, and He wants us to enjoy the full expression of His gift in the secure, strong relationship of marriage. Before God, the marriage bed is undefiled—meaning that there is nothing inherently wrong or dirty about mutual, consensual sexual expression between husband and wife.

Like an apple tree among the trees of the forest is my lover among the young men. I delight to sit in his shade, and his fruit is sweet to my taste. He has taken me to the banquet hall, and his banner over me is love.

Song of Songs 2:3–4

My lover is mine and I am his; he browses among the lilies. Until the day breaks and the shadows flee, turn, my lover, and be like a gazelle or like a young stag on the rugged hills.

Song of Songs 2:16–17

Song of Solomon is a beautiful depiction of marital love and sensual, sexual expression. The lover and the beloved speak to each other of desire and fulfillment. In the passage above, the bride delights in her husband "browsing among the lilies," exploring her body in all its beauty. The metaphors for foreplay, desire, sensual touching, and intercourse show the pleasure, exhilaration, and creativity of a rich sexual life in the context of a committed relationship.

7 PRAYER STARTER

Lord, we come to You asking for redeemed hearts and minds on the subject of Your design for marriage and marital sexuality. Reveal to us how pleased You are that we come seeking to know Your delight in our sex lives. Reveal to us the holy boundaries in which You have revealed sex to be enjoyed to the maximum. Thank You that You created us as sexual beings and have revealed to us in Your Scriptures Your design and purposes for good and healthy sexual living . . .

8 RECOMMENDED RESOURCES

Dillow, Linda, and Lorraine Pintus. *Intimate Issues: 21 Questions Christian Women Ask about Sex*. Random House, 1999.

Farrel, Bill, and Pam Farrel. *Red Hot Monogamy: Making Your Marriage Sizzle*. Harvest House, 2006.

Gardner, Tim Alan. *Sacred Sex: A Spiritual Celebration of Oneness*. Random House, 2002.

Leman, Kevin. *Sheet Music: Uncovering the Secrets of Sexual Intimacy in Marriage*. Tyndale, 2003.

———. *Turn Up the Heat: A Couple's Guide to Sexual Intimacy*. Revell, 2009.

Wheat, Ed, and Gaye Wheat. *Intended for Pleasure: Sex Technique and Sexual Fulfillment in Christian Marriage*. 4th ed. Revell, 2010.

Sexual Desire and Expectations   2

PORTRAITS : 1

- A few years ago Paul and Laura had a wonderful sex life—even after having their third child. But two years later Paul's company downsized, and he lost his job. He tried for months to find a similar position but finally gave up and went through extensive training for a new career. He despises his new job, and the ordeal shattered his ego. He used to be full of energy and creativity but now drifts through life, including his relationships, with little enthusiasm. He seldom initiates sex with Laura, and when she initiates, he just seems to go through the motions. She's sad and irritated, and he feels like more of a failure than ever.
- The pregnancy certainly cut into Phyllis and John's sex life, but he hoped it would return in a few weeks after their child was born. It didn't. Months later Phyllis kept making excuses. She was always "still too sore" or "too tired" or "too busy" for lovemaking. John's attention started to wander to other women, and Phyllis noticed.
- Sandra was never known as a "wild woman," but she wanted more creativity in her sex life with Richard. Doing the same things in the same way at the same time bored her, but when she suggested new techniques (or acted on them without suggesting them), Richard recoiled. He thought she was going "over the line," and he wouldn't have any of it.

DEFINITIONS AND KEY THOUGHTS : 2

- *Sex is a gift from God.* He created us to be sexual beings, and *He created the act of sex for married couples.* Sex is best seen as a continuing desire, an appetite that is fulfilled on an ongoing basis. Part of being human is to enjoy a rich, fulfilling sexual life, but as is often the case, the desire for sexual contact is different for each spouse in a marriage.
- Therefore sex, like most other issues, becomes *a matter of negotiation between the two partners* (with *negotiation* implying that each partner's desires and wishes regarding sex are given equal weight. It should not be presumed that, due to a couple's adherence to a theology of male headship, the man has any right to impose his sexual will on the woman—as many religious men presume).
- It may be necessary to remind the couple—especially the man—that *no one has ever died from not having sex!* Sex is not essential to life like oxygen and water,

in spite of the perceived notion that being cut off from sex is a crazy-maker or a death sentence—it is neither. Sexual abstinence or learning alternative ways to be sexual is almost required in any long marriage—due to pregnancy, illness, family emergencies, separations for business or work, attaining desired spiritual goals, or any number of situations that demand it.

- In 1 Corinthians Paul writes, "Do not deprive each other except by mutual consent and for a time, so that you may devote yourselves to prayer. Then come together again so that Satan will not tempt you because of your lack of self-control" (7:5). God intended for sexual intimacy to be *a vital part of a healthy marriage relationship*, but sensitivity to one's spouse is essential. Sexual intimacy was created to delight both husband *and* wife, not merely as a marital obligation.

- One barrier to mutual sexual satisfaction is that the frequency of having sex is often dictated by contradictory desires and reasons—attributable to both the differences in men and women as well as their unique life experiences. Though it may be somewhat simplistic to assert, it is largely true that *men tend to want sex for physical pleasure and release, while women want sex more to reinforce the relationship and be assured again of their husband's desire and their primary place in his life.* These and other differences are important for both men and women to understand about each other.

- As couples begin to look at their sexual expectations and desires in the marriage, it's important to consider that barriers to sexual intimacy may be *a symptom of a much bigger and broader communication problem* in the marriage. Sometimes couples can exist in the same house and live in their own worlds, seldom talking about anything more meaningful than their work and schedules. But some couples talk openly and honestly about everything in their lives—everything, that is, except sex—a subject taboo for far too many couples.

- *Building and rebuilding trust* is an important feature of sexual communication. Quite often married people have been hurt or they feel misunderstood. After months or years these hurts may have festered into deep resentments that cloud every part of the relationship. *Trust can't be demanded; it must be earned over time by honesty, patience, integrity, and kindness.*

- As in all topics of communication, one of the most important steps forward is for *both parties to feel understood*, not just to understand the other person's point of view. Connecting on an emotional level takes time, but it tears down barriers and builds strong bonds of trust, creating a relational environment in which sexual expectations can be safely discussed.

3 ASSESSMENT INTERVIEW

Couples may come in together to talk about their sexual desires and expectations, but frequently only one partner comes for help because the other is too embarrassed or too angry to join the discussion. If you sense that the couple or one spouse is reluctant to talk openly about sexual desires and expectations, consider going through a list of topics and asking them to pick the one (or several of them) about which they feel most frustrated. (A strength-based approach to intervention would be to have them list what's going right and to build on that.) You may want to have a written list of topics and ask the couple or person to check the ones that are most troubling to the relationship. The list might include:

- frequency of sexual contact
- quality of foreplay
- smells, sounds, and preparation for sex
- places where you have sex
- her frequency and quality of orgasms (sexual climax)
- premature ejaculation
- creativity in positions and techniques
- sex that's "over the line" (for example, it may seem too rough or too kinky)
- the barriers of stress, worry about finances or kids, and busyness
- shame or disgust over body image
- distrust because of the partner's past sexual experiences
- distrust because of other irresponsible behavior
- health issues that block sexual performance
- breaking patterns of passivity
- learning to talk openly about sexual desires

> On average, 18–29-year-olds have sex 112 times per year; 30–39-year-olds, an average of 86 times per year; and 40–49-year-olds an average of 69 times per year.
>
> L. J. Piccinino and W. D. Mosher, Family Planning Perspectives

Questions for a Couple

1. How would you describe a wonderful and satisfying sex life for each of you?
2. What did you hear the other person saying they enjoy?
3. When was a time in your relationship when sex was at its best? Describe your relationship during that time. What made sex so good at that point?
4. Describe what attracted you to each other and brought you together. Which of these things are still part of your relationship?
5. What are some sexual experiences you enjoy (or want to enjoy) that you find to be creative and full of passion? Please face and directly tell your spouse these sexual experiences.
6. What do you find easy to talk about? What topics are hard to discuss? What might be some reasons these are difficult topics?
7. To you, what's "over the line" sexually?
8. What do you hear your spouse saying about his limits?
9. How would you describe your level of trust in your spouse?
10. What would it mean for your spouse to respect your sexual desires in your relationship?
11. What might be some genuine (if small) steps forward in setting healthy expectations for your sexual relationship?

Questions for an Individual

You can ask many of the same questions that apply to couples, understanding that you have only half of the equation. Here are some other questions to ask:

1. (*Before asking any other questions*) Why is your spouse not with you today to talk about improving your communication about sex? Is sex the only thing that is difficult for the two of you to talk about?
2. If your spouse were here, how would he describe your desires and expectations? Which ones are compatible, and which are different?

4 : WISE COUNSEL

Help each person grasp the fact that men and women are *fundamentally different* in how they approach many aspects of life, including sex. Often men need to be told what their wives want—sometimes even as they are having sex together. If women expect their husband to pick up on signals or read their mind, they'll often be very disappointed. Men need to understand that foreplay lasts all day long for women, and they don't "flip a sexual switch" in an instant as men can. Having men attend to and prepare their wives emotionally by extra kindness and respect during the day goes a long way to mutually satisfying sexual adventure that night.

Watch for the *big picture issue of trust* in a couple's relationship as the context for communication about their sexual lives. If they can't trust each other, they'll feel used and, often, abused. Easily resolved misunderstandings and hurts can become resentments if they are not dealt with quickly, and then bitterness sets in, and the relationship suffers in every area.

Help each person feel understood by staying with the Assessment Interview questions and asking for clarification and reports from the other one (What do you hear him saying?). *If they don't feel understood by their spouse, they'll probably drift back into old habits and attitudes.*

Talking openly about their sexual life will enhance every other part of the couple's relationship. Effective communication lays a foundation for the expression of the couple's desires and expectations about their future, their children, their money, and everything else in their lives.

5 : ACTION STEPS

1. Begin by Talking

- Start where you are in your relationship. Begin talking—about fun times, what's working, and then what isn't. Address the frustrations, disappointments, and other concerns, particularly in regard to your sexual relationship. Honesty and fond memories provide a strong foundation for a satisfying sex life.

2. Expect to Uncover Barriers

- As you communicate, you will uncover barriers and distractions. These might include anger at a spouse's past indiscretions, guilt over your own past sexual sins, shame about body image, resentment about the focus being on children, or a host of other potential problems. If emotional barriers or past behaviors are affecting the level of sexual intimacy in your relationship, they must be talked about and worked through with the help of the counselor. This begins with (1) being honest about the reality of the spouse's feelings and reasons for lack of connectedness; (2) repenting of any behaviors in the relationship that are currently affecting the level of intimacy; (3) the willingness on the part of both spouses to forgive one another as well as themselves for current behaviors, past indiscretions, guilt, shame, or resentment; and (4) seeking reconciliation.

3. Show Respect to Each Other

- Healthy communication about desires and expectations begins with respecting each other. Even if your spouse isn't willing to do everything you desire in your sexual relationship, basic respect is essential. With it, trust can grow, which may create a more positive atmosphere for creativity in the future.

- Discuss creative ways to express sexual desire—explore individual likes and dislikes of sexual relations with each other. Even in an age of freedom for sexual expression, some people are very repressed sexually, so don't be surprised if your spouse does not want to do everything you may want to do. Remember that sex is God's gift to be enjoyed to its fullest, and while you may want to try some new methods, you will need to be sensitive to how your spouse is feeling. Never force sexual experiences. If you do, failure will likely be the result and trust will be shattered. Creativity may need to start small, but it can grow as you both find new techniques you enjoy and as you feel increasingly safe with one another.

- *Train the couple or individual to negotiate and communicate desires and new expectations before urges take over.*

4. Identify Roadblocks

- Identify the roadblocks and distractions in your lives that erode quality time together and provide excuses for your not spending time and energy on your sexual experience.

5. Know God's Perspective on Sex

- Take time to research and read about God's perspective on sex and marital communication. Your counselor will suggest books that will be helpful and will show you how to take steps forward in clarifying your needs, communicating your expectations, and bringing passion and creativity back to your sex lives.

6. Forgive Each Other

- Forgive each other. Pray and ask God for strength to forgive any hurt or miscommunication that has been a part of your marriage up to this point.
- *Don't miss the importance of inviting each person to forgive the other. By the time couples come for counseling, they almost always feel very frustrated if not genuinely angry at each other. Encourage them to forgive each other "just as God in Christ has forgiven" us.*

6 BIBLICAL INSIGHTS

Therefore, as God's chosen people, holy and dearly loved, clothe yourselves with compassion, kindness, humility, gentleness and patience. Bear with each other and forgive whatever grievances you may have against one another. Forgive as the Lord forgave you. And over all these virtues put on love, which binds them all together in perfect unity.

Colossians 3:12–14

Treating one another with love, respect, and kindness is a choice both partners can make. Negotiating desires and expectations begins with this commitment to honor and value one another instead of being selfish.

Forgiveness—of terrible past sins or minor present annoyances—is essential to a strong relationship and a great sex life.

"In your anger do not sin": Do not let the sun go down while you are still angry, and do not give the devil a foothold. . . . Do not let any unwholesome talk come out of your mouths, but only what is helpful for building others up according to their needs, that it may benefit those who listen. And do not grieve the Holy Spirit of God, with whom you were sealed for the day of redemption. Get rid of all bitterness, rage and anger, brawling and slander, along with every form of malice. Be kind and compassionate to one another, forgiving each other, just as in Christ God forgave you.

Ephesians 4:26–32

Unresolved anger, hurt, or bitterness can give the enemy an opportunity to sneak in and distort and eventually destroy the sexual beauty we were designed for with our spouse. Being vigilant and careful about how we talk to and treat our spouse goes a long way when it comes to the sexual pleasure we experience in the marriage relationship.

Once a spouse has worked through the bitterness and anger to a place of forgiveness, he must understand the importance of living out a life of compassion and encouragement that is reflective of the love described in 1 Corinthians 13.

Great sex in marriage begins with mutual respect, forgiveness, and compassion for one another.

How beautiful you are and how pleasing, O love, with your delights! Your stature is like that of the palm, and your breasts like clusters of fruit. I said, "I will climb the palm tree; I will take hold of its fruit." May your breasts be like the clusters of the vine, the fragrance of your breath like apples, and your mouth like the best wine.

Song of Songs 7:6–9

Song of Songs (or Song of Solomon), this beautiful and sensual book of the Bible, portrays the beauty of sex in marriage in poetic language. The metaphors of foreplay, desire, sensual touching, and intercourse show the pleasure, exhilaration, and creativity of a rich sexual life in the context of a committed relationship.

The beauty of loving, joyful, sensual sex deserves time and effort to maximize the pleasure. Poetry, music, flowers, scents, and special times and places can greatly enhance the couple's enjoyment.

PRAYER STARTER 7

Father, thank You that this couple [individual] wants to experience Your gift of joyful sex in their relationship. They've come because they want to grow in this area of their lives. They are committed to You and to each other. Help them, Lord, to take steps to find even more fulfillment. Give them courage to talk openly about their desires and to listen intently to each other. We trust You will be honored and their relationship will grow stronger as they enjoy each other even more . . .

RECOMMENDED RESOURCES 8

Chapman, Gary. *Making Love: The Chapman Guide to Making Sex an Act of Love.* Tyndale, 2008.

Dillow, Linda, and Lorraine Pintus. *Intimate Issues: 21 Questions Christian Women Ask about Sex.* Random House, 1999.

LaHaye, Tim, and Beverly LaHaye. *The Act of Marriage.* Zondervan, 1998.

_____. *The Act of Marriage after 40.* Zondervan, 2000.

Leman, Kevin. *Sheet Music: Uncovering the Secrets of Sexual Intimacy in Marriage.* Tyndale, 2003.

Penner, Clifford L., and Joyce J. Penner. *The Gift of Sex: A Guide to Sexual Fulfillment.* Thomas Nelson, 2003.

Rosenau, Douglas E. *A Celebration of Sex: A Guide to Enjoying God's Gift of Sexual Intimacy.* Thomas Nelson, 2002.

Wheat, Ed, and Gaye Wheat. *Intended for Pleasure: Sex Technique and Sexual Fulfillment in Christian Marriage.* 4th ed. Revell, 2010.

3 Threats to Sexual Intimacy

1 PORTRAITS

- Bill has diabetes and has been gaining weight for several years. Now classified as obese, he's very ashamed of his appearance. His wife, Diane, loves him as much as ever, but their sexual relationship is a casualty of Bill's diabetes and negative self-image. Though he doesn't engage in masturbation, he doesn't take good care of himself, and he just can't believe Diane would want to have sex with him.

- Jim was a great athlete in high school and in college intramurals. He's strong, virile, and handsome, and he had his pick of pretty girls. When he and Pamela got married, he didn't want to talk about his previous sexual exploits, but she assumed there was a lot he wasn't telling her. At first, their sex life was terrific, but soon Pamela's fear and growing distrust clouded every aspect of their relationship. She withdrew sexually and emotionally, and he became angry and frustrated.

- Martin and LeAnn were busy professionals in their early forties. Both worked forty-five to fifty hours weekly at their professions, were raising three active children, were working on various church and community boards, and were spending more and more time with and worrying about aging parents who were losing their health. The last thing they had time for was one another, and it showed in their sex life—they had had sex maybe once or twice in the past six months, and even then it was rushed, allowing no time for cuddling or talking.

2 DEFINITIONS AND KEY THOUGHTS

- *Threats to sexual intimacy include anything that blocks or interferes with a couple experiencing the fullest delight and intimacies* that are afforded to them as a result of a consummate marriage. Some examples of possible barriers include poor health and disabling impediments, psychological distress and conflict, and differing demands, expectations, and beliefs about sex.

Biological Causes

- *Sexual pain disorders* can drastically affect a couple's satisfaction in lovemaking. Research shows that 43 percent of women report some kind of sexual dysfunction, most commonly pain during sexual intercourse,[1] while men report slightly less. Commonly known as *dyspareunia*, genital pain during intercourse occurs in both men and women and can range from uncomfortable to debilitating, depending on its cause.

- In women, sexual pain may involve involuntary muscle cramping, pain on vaginal entry, deep uterine pain, or unusual bleeding following intercourse. The most common female sexual pain disorders include:

  — *vaginismus*, characterized by spasms of the pelvic muscles in the outer third of the vagina that prevent penile penetration or make sex extremely difficult

  — *vulvodinia*, painful burning sensations in the vulva and vaginal area

  — *vaginal dryness*, commonly caused by hormone changes, which can make sex highly uncomfortable for both the woman and the man during intercourse—at least 20 percent of women report vaginal dryness

  — *health conditions*, such as hemorrhoids, endometriosis, or sexually transmitted diseases, which can lead to vaginal discomfort and bleeding

  — *the birth of a baby*, often compromising the strength and flexibility of the vaginal region due to tearing, thus making intercourse impossible until healing occurs

- In men, 5 to 16 percent of all doctor's visits are because of painful sexual dysfunction of some kind. Common causes of pain and dysfunction in males include:

  — *genital lesions or skin disorders*, such as psoriasis and eczema, which may cause irritation

  — *health conditions*, such as kidney stones or sexually transmitted diseases

  — *erectile dysfunction*, otherwise known as impotence, which can make ejaculation impossible

  — *Peyronie's disease*, which causes a bent penis during erection due to the presence of scar tissue

- Aside from these biological causes, sexual intimacy can be impeded by *medication or drug side effects*. A number of medications can cause delayed or absent climax. *Chemicals and/or medications* that can cause orgasmic disorder symptoms, especially in men, include:

  — alcohol

  — high blood pressure medications

  — antidepressants (MAOIs or SSRIs)

  — antianxiety medications (such as benzodiazepines)

  — narcotics or amphetamines

Emotional Issues

- Other threats to sexual intimacy include *emotional pain, such as shame, fear, or guilt,* which are often related to negative sexual experiences in the past.
- *Trauma from sexual, emotional, and physical abuse.* Those who have experienced a *traumatic sexual experience,* such as sexual abuse, are more susceptible to having sexual disorders, including having revulsion toward and avoidance of sex. Numerous studies have also shown that emotional or physical abuse occurring in childhood increases the risk of a person developing paraphilia—a sexual disorder characterized by socially inappropriate sexual conduct.
- *Unrepentant sin.* Unconfessed sins—especially any lingering anger or bitterness or sins that one may be hiding from one's spouse—can produce guilt and shame that impact good sexual relations.
- *Traumatic brain injury.* A number of documented cases have shown that traumatic brain injury (TBI) may increase sexually deviant behavior in persons with no prior history of such offenses.
- *Psycho/social/personality disorder.* All manner of human mental and emotional disorders—from depression to anxiety to self-serving narcissism—interfere with a good sexual experience and performance.
- *Overly sexualized culture.* There is no doubt that in today's culture, sex sells. From billboards, TV commercials and programs, movies, and the internet to magazine and newspaper ads, our culture is inundated with sexual images and powerful messages that "anything goes." God reveals that the last days of history will be characterized by the love of men and women growing cold—and of evil being rampant in the world. This in itself is a huge bath of cold water poured out against love, tenderness, and intimacy in marriage.
- *Sexual addictions.* From pornography to prostitution, addictions to sex steal away the intimacy of healthy sexual relationships. Addictions are selfish acts that inhibit the selfless, altruistic intent of sex.

Hectic Lives

- We cannot forget the issue revealed in the last vignette above: *busy lives and unremitting stress with no margins that allow a couple to care for themselves or one another.* This is far too common for many midlife couples who are very engaged with life at multiple levels of demand, all of which leach vitality or interest from their sexual relationship.

3   ASSESSMENT INTERVIEW

The key challenge here is to help couples identify any impediments that continue to block optimal sexual relations, as well as finding out what the couple does positively to avoid trouble and how they manage the issues that could interfere with good sex.

1. What do you hope we can accomplish together through counseling? Are you committed to follow through and do what may be needed to have and enjoy good sex again?
2. What do you see as blocking your time for or interest in sex? Do you think your desire for sex is abnormally low?
3. How long has it been that you have experienced less sex or desire than you think is normal?
4. Are you able to perform sexually?
5. Are there any problems in your marriage that may be affecting your sexual desire?
6. Are there extenuating circumstances (such as health problems, stress, a painful past, and so on) that might be affecting your sex drive?

WISE COUNSEL : 4

If sex is "glue" that helps keep a marriage bound together in a good and healthy way, then maintaining that bond is an ongoing imperative.

This entire volume is testament to the myriad ways life circumstances, our own sins and selfishness, the many commitments we make, and the work of the enemy can interfere with optimal sexual bonding. Therefore, prevention of these obstacles and enrichment of a couple's life together are key to avoiding threats to their sex life. For those troubles that cannot be avoided—and any long marriage can testify to a large number of them—learning to manage any threats or impediments is critical to marital happiness.

ACTION STEPS : 5

1. Resolve Any Crises

Face and resolve any crisis issues in your marriage and family system. These issues are draining valuable time and energy, which you must refocus and redirect to your marriage.

2. Reduce Stress

The pace, pain, and pressure of our day fuel low-sex and no-sex marriages. Ruthlessly eliminate anything that is preventing you from connecting emotionally, relationally, spiritually, and sexually with your spouse.

3. Plan Your Sex

There is no substitute for good and faithful planning for sex and time together. Our experience tells us that if busy couples don't plan to be sexual, they usually won't be. While you may believe that the best sex is unplanned and spontaneous, it is far better to plan for sex than to have no sex at all—or rushed, heartless sex.

4. Meet Regularly with Other Couples

Some of the stresses in a relationship can be managed or eliminated, but some are quite persistent. Denying the impact of stress doesn't solve the problem. Be honest about the emotional damage that destructive reactions to stresses have on your marriage. A useful way to address and reduce stress is to join an ongoing group of other midlife couples who are dedicated to supporting one another. Though this is an additional commitment of time, it will help you better manage all areas of your life, especially if the group consists of couples who are praying and studying the Bible together. In other words, this commitment is well worth it.

5. Get Medical Help and Professional Counseling

If nothing is working to reduce life stressors and help you reconnect as a couple, consider medical intervention and/or professional counseling with a licensed mental health professional. A primary care physician may be able to diagnose a sexual disorder or prescribe medications that could enhance the sexual relationship with your spouse. Professional counseling can be effective in the treatment of any sexual disorder by addressing the emotional issues behind the problem. By improving your relationship through couple's counseling, threats to sexual intimacy are identified and treated, and often they dissipate.

6 BIBLICAL INSIGHTS

Do not be anxious about anything, but in everything, by prayer and petition, with thanksgiving, present your requests to God. And the peace of God, which transcends all understanding, will guard your hearts and your minds in Christ Jesus.

Philippians 4:6–7

The first step in dealing with threats to sexual intimacy is to turn to God, the source of wisdom, love, and strength. He can give peace that is the platform for rich communication. Nothing is off-limits for prayer, including sexual desires, threats, and expectations. This Scripture passage invites us to ask God for direction and assistance even as we navigate sexual desires and experiences. So often we seek healing on our own, but God wonderfully invites us to embrace Him and His ways to a new and better life.

Husbands, love your wives, just as Christ loved the church and gave himself up for her. . . . However, each one of you also must love his wife as he loves himself, and the wife must respect her husband.

Ephesians 5:25, 33

Frustration may cause people to become passive or aggressive, and neither of these responses builds relationships. The husband's God-given role is to love his wife unconditionally, with tenderness and understanding, patiently listening and caring for her. The wife is to respect her husband and respond to him with love and encouragement.

May your fountain be blessed, and may you rejoice in the wife of your youth. A loving doe, a graceful deer—may her breasts satisfy you always, may you ever be captivated by her love.

Proverbs 5:18–19

The various threats to sexual intimacy don't have to ruin a marriage. Sex is a wonderful gift for couples to enjoy, but they must stay locked in on the goal of mutual pleasure and fun together.

PRAYER STARTER 7

Heavenly Father, You are the creator and giver of each new day, and You have ordained the best way to plan and live out the days You give us. Reveal to us now the chief impediments to being sexual and enjoying that great gift You have given us. Reveal to us Your plan that resolves the issues in ways that exalt You and give honor to one another. Thank You that You have seen this matter and already know the way to resolve it. We trust that You will now reveal Your plan to us . . .

RECOMMENDED RESOURCES 8

Dillow, Linda, and Lorraine Pintus. *Intimate Issues: 21 Questions Christian Women Ask about Sex.* Random House, 1999.

Leman, Kevin. *Sheet Music: Uncovering the Secrets of Sexual Intimacy in Marriage.* Tyndale, 2003.

Penner, Clifford L., and Joyce J. Penner. *The Gift of Sex: A Guide to Sexual Fulfillment.* Thomas Nelson, 2003.

Rosenau, Douglas E. *A Celebration of Sex: A Guide to Enjoying God's Gift of Sexual Intimacy.* Thomas Nelson, 2002.

Wheat, Ed, and Gaye Wheat. *Intended for Pleasure: Sex Technique and Sexual Fulfillment in Christian Marriage.* 4th ed. Revell, 2010.

4 Increasing Sexual Satisfaction

1 PORTRAITS

- Over the past several months, intercourse has become increasingly painful for Suzanne. Her husband, Will, has been understanding and kind and very gentle, but her pain has only grown more intense. Now their sex life is virtually nonexistent.

- Beth went out of her way to avoid Bill's seeing her naked. She made sure he wasn't around when she took showers, and she'd undress in the dark if there was any chance of his seeing her. Beth was ashamed of her body image because she was about one hundred pounds overweight. Her shame affected every aspect of their relationship. Bill tried to make love to her from time to time, and she sometimes allowed herself to endure it.

- John and Sue didn't have any problem with creativity. They tried every position they'd ever read about. Oral sex was a normal part of their sex life, and they experimented with anal sex too. They even thought about inviting some friends to join them in threes or fours to see if that might be fun. But for them, the tolerance effect, or the law of diminishing returns, had set in. No matter what they tried, it didn't satisfy for long.

2 DEFINITIONS AND KEY THOUGHTS

- God has made us *wonderfully creative beings*. Every aspect of our lives, including sex in marriage, can reflect vibrant creativity. Hebrews tells us that the marital bed is undefiled (13:4 KJV). Sex in marriage should be as creative and fulfilling as it can possibly be for both husband and wife.

- Even in a sex-saturated culture of "free love," some individuals believe that full sexual expression is somehow beyond them or beneath them. *Shame, fear, or past hurts may cloud their thinking* and rob them of the joy of sex with their spouse.

- Many people—women as well as men—*harbor secret sexual fantasies* they've never discussed with anyone, especially their spouse. They long for *more creativity and sexual fulfillment*, but they're afraid to talk about their desires, fearful of being considered weird or sinful.

- According to Tim and Beverly LaHaye's *The Act of Marriage after 40* survey:

— 47 percent of men "sometimes" manipulate their wife's clitoris orally.

— 48 percent of women enjoy it.

— 41 percent of women "sometimes" use oral stimulation on their husbands.[1]

- *A variety of stresses, health problems, and other elements of the seasons of life can absorb a couple's attention, sap their energy, and erode their creativity, even their sexual desire.*

- Some couples don't understand *the basic physiology of female sexual arousal.* An understanding of clitoral stimulation and the vaginal "G-spot" often does wonders for a woman's sexual pleasures!

ASSESSMENT INTERVIEW 3

Ask these questions to a couple who comes for counseling:

1. When would you say your sex life was the most creative, fulfilling, and fun? When you think about having the best sex possible, what do you fantasize about?
2. (*If the couple would not respond well to the first question, ask the following.*) What is something you both enjoy doing sexually that you could do slightly differently next time?
3. What do you hear your spouse saying?
4. (*For her*) Describe the quality and frequency of your orgasms (sexual climax). Are you satisfied with this? Why or why not?
5. (*For him*) Do you have any erectile issues or problems with premature ejaculation? How does this affect your creativity and fulfillment in bed?
6. What are some sexual positions you enjoy?
7. Are there any physical concerns (illness, weight, or disability) that limit your enjoyment of sex?
8. What barriers do you face—in yourself or your spouse—in being more creative? (Consider fear, past failures, distrust, shame, and so on.)
9. Which of these concerns do you want to address right now so you can begin to overcome these barriers and set a plan for your next steps?

If an individual comes to you for help, you can ask the following questions; then proceed with variations of the questions above.

1. Why is your spouse not here with you today?
2. How would your spouse describe your sex life together?
3. Has your spouse indicated any desires about finding new, creative techniques to spark your sex life?

4 : WISE COUNSEL

While *predictability* can be a stabilizing force in a relationship, it can also *become a rut and spell disaster for a relationship*: cooking the same meals, eating at the same restaurants, watching the same television programs, hanging out with the same people, and engaging in the same sexual techniques day after day, week after week, and year after year can easily slip into *boring ritualism and laziness*. Boredom leads to a loss of joy or excitement as anticipation begins to wane. Then people become "lukewarm" and lose their first love.

In every area of life, including sex, *communication is essential*. One spouse may be satisfied, but the other isn't; one may be fearful of trying something new, but the other is bold and creative. Without open conversation and patient listening, at least one person will feel very frustrated, and the relationship will suffer.

Though *sexual creativity is to be encouraged within the marriage*, it is important to understand that *if one spouse is uncomfortable in a specific position or with a certain technique, it should not be used*. Only by mutual consent and with utmost respect for one's spouse should any sexual practices be used.

Great Sex: Getting the Most Out of Your Relationship

Creativity

It's *entirely normal* for people, even deeply committed Christians, *to think about enjoying sex* in creative ways. But the level of creativity in the bedroom is *dramatically affected by a host of other factors* in the relationship. *Trust, kindness, gentleness, and patience* add to the bond and create the atmosphere for enjoyable experimentation in sex.

Encourage couples to explore and share their desires with each other and discover common ground for experimentation, but they should set limits. Not only does each partner have limits to his or her willingness to try new things, but certain sexual acts aren't permissible or biblical (for example, group sex or sex that is demeaning or abusive to one or both partners). If one of the individuals pushes an "over-the-top" suggestion, use it as a jumping-off point for discussing desires, expectations, and respect in the relationship.

> My lover is mine and I am his; he browses among the lilies.
> *Song of Songs 2:16*

Stimulation

Sadly, too many women don't have the pleasure of clitoral orgasms because *they don't understand the physiology of their body*, and their husband doesn't grasp the importance of this stimulation to his wife's sexual pleasures. The clitoris has eight thousand nerves all crowded onto that small organ and all designed for pleasure! Gentle stimulation arouses a woman like nothing else and prepares her for sexual ecstasy.

In the 1950s, a doctor named Ernest Grafenberg described a point in a woman's vagina that *provides immense sexual pleasure*. Found near the anterior wall of the vagina, the paraurethral gland is located between the urethra and the vagina. Stimulation of the G-spot generally takes longer than clitoral orgasms, but the effect can be even more powerful—so powerful, in fact, that not all women enjoy it. Encourage couples to learn more about this kind of sexual exploration.

Physical problems such as illness, weight, or disability can cause couples to become frustrated sexually. Help them find creative ways to express their love for each other in sexual techniques that work for them.

Sexual Behaviors

Most couples need only a suggestion or two for new positions to add spice to their lovemaking. Some positions they may want to try include:

- *Wife on top.* As the man lies on his back, the woman sits on top of him with her knees resting on the bed or floor. To control the depth of penetration and range of motion, she can either lean forward to give him better access to fondle her breasts with his hands or lips, stroke her clitoris, and embrace her entire body, or she can sit back at more of a ninety-degree upright position to give him a better view of her body and allowing for more vaginal stimulation for her. To add creativity or to be more comfortable due to physical conditions such as bad knees, she can approach him in this manner on either a sofa or a chair as well.

- *Standing up.* With the woman lying on a table, bed, or any other object that is waist high for him, she positions herself next to the edge and wraps her legs around his waist. This position allows deep thrusting and easy access to stimulate her clitoris. Also, if the couple is of similar height (or if she is considerably shorter, a stool can be used), they can stand face-to-face and she can wrap one leg around him to expose her vagina. In this position, he is able to penetrate her while they look one another in the eyes and caress each other during intercourse. In addition, when both are standing, she bends over and he penetrates her from behind. This is especially fun for a "quickie" in the shower or just having fun in the kitchen.

- *Spoon position.* While lying down, with the woman's buttocks next to the man's groin, she drapes her leg over him, exposing her vagina. From underneath, he inserts his penis. This position is incredibly comfortable for both parties, and it allows him to caress her nipples, clitoris, and the entire front of her body. He also has easy access to her ears for kissing and pillow talk. This position is especially helpful during pregnancy.

- *Side by side.* The couple lies down face-to-face, and the woman drapes her leg over him. He can penetrate her, and they have easy access to kissing and caressing each other.

- *Missionary position.* This is the position most couples use, at least until they learn others that are more satisfying. The woman lies on her back with her legs spread, and he mounts her from the top. One of the most comfortable positions, it offers excellent stimulation. The couple can kiss on the lips, or they may kiss each other's ears or neck.

> A study found that men prefer greater variety of sexual techniques, stimulation, and play, but women want consistency in the techniques and emotional connections through tenderness and intimate conversation.
>
> Louis and Melissa McBurney, "Christian Sex Rules," Christianity Today, September 30, 2008

- *"Doggie style."* With the woman on her hands and knees, the man mounts her from the rear, caressing her breasts, stroking her back, and stimulating her clitoris.
- *Push up.* The woman lies on her back with her buttocks on a pillow, and the man mounts her as he kneels. She puts her feet against his shoulders. This position gives maximum stimulation to her G-spot.

Just Having Fun

- *Showering together.* In the shower, the couple can take turns washing each other, as well as stroking and caressing sensitive areas. While in the shower, they can choose one of the positions previously described, or they can run dripping wet to the bed, the bathroom counter, or the floor for more fun.
- *Mutual stimulation.* Take plenty of time to caress and express affection and tenderness. If a partner has experienced a disability and is unable to enjoy vaginal sex, the couple can stimulate one another manually to orgasm.

5 : ACTION STEPS

1. Identify Ruts

- Identify areas in your life where you feel stuck. Being creative in your sex life is just one area of your life where you need to find meaning and fulfillment. Think of creative changes for other parts of your life as well.
- *Help people look for patterns of ruts in their lives. Identifying and naming them is a first step toward change.*

2. Discuss New Things

- Uncover and communicate your sexual desires and fantasies to each other. Also discuss individual boundaries and God's boundaries about what is appropriate in sexual relations.

3. Try New Things

- With your spouse discuss new positions for lovemaking you might try and the option of lubrication for the wife.
- Remember that all new skills take some practice, so expect to experience a learning curve as you experiment.

4. Talk about What's Working and What Isn't

- Don't be afraid to talk with each other about difficulties that you are having in your sexual relations, including positions you are trying, premature ejaculation, and vaginal dryness. Talk too about what you enjoy, including positions and stimulation of the G-spot and/or clitoris.

- *Ask about concerns that the couple has and discuss as needed. You may need to explain clitoral and G-spot orgasms, give advice about premature ejaculation, and discern any other factors that inhibit or could enhance sexual fulfillment for the couple.*

5. Be Creative

- Many couples enjoy sensual outfits and games. Discuss your ideas and decide on how to add some fun to your relationship.

BIBLICAL INSIGHTS 6

Flee immorality. Every other sin that a man commits is outside the body, but the immoral man sins against his own body. Or do you not know that your body is a temple of the Holy Spirit who is in you, whom you have from God, and that you are not your own? For you have been bought with a price: therefore glorify God in your body.

1 Corinthians 6:18–20 NASB

The Corinthians had a distorted view of sex by believing it was *only* about filling an appetite and no different from the need for food. Paul warned against this viewpoint saying, " 'Food for the stomach and the stomach for food,'—but God will destroy them both. The body is not meant for sexual immorality, but for the Lord, and the Lord for the body" (1 Cor. 6:13).

Glorifying God with our body in this context becomes more about personal conviction than public opinion. Love never degrades another. Marital sex is about purity and the joining of two bodies as one flesh. The marriage bed should be kept pure and undefiled (Heb. 13:4).

Therefore let us stop passing judgment on one another. Instead, make up your mind not to put any stumbling block or obstacle in your brother's way. As one who is in the Lord Jesus, I am fully convinced that no food is unclean in itself. But if anyone regards something as unclean, then for him it is unclean. If your brother is distressed because of what you eat, you are no longer acting in love. Do not by your eating destroy your brother for whom Christ died. Do not allow what you consider good to be spoken of as evil. For the kingdom of God is not a matter of eating and drinking, but of righteousness, peace and joy in the Holy Spirit, because anyone who serves Christ in this way is pleasing to God and approved by men. Let us therefore make every effort to do what leads to peace and to mutual edification. Do not destroy the work of God for the sake of food.

Romans 14:13–20

This passage could very well end with "for the sake of sex" instead of "for the sake of food." If a spouse's convictions are not to engage in a certain technique or practice, then the couple together should support one another in this decision for "mutual edification."

When both spouses are comfortable and consider "clean" what they do together before the Lord in their sexual lives, then creativity is to be encouraged if it brings about a more intimate and fulfilling marital relationship.

His left arm is under my head and his right arm embraces me. Daughters of Jerusalem, I charge you: Do not arouse or awaken love until it so desires. . . . You who dwell in the gardens with friends in attendance, let me hear your voice! Come away, my lover, and be like a gazelle or like a young stag on the spice-laden mountains.
Song of Songs 8:3–4, 13–14

The woman describes a sexual position she enjoys, with her lover's left arm under her head and his right arm embracing her. She sees him as active as a prancing gazelle and as strong and virile as a young buck—he is not a passive lover! His strength is coupled with the fragrance of spices, so their pleasure delights all their senses.

7 PRAYER STARTER

Father, thank You for this couple [individual] who wants to delight in Your gift of sexual pleasure. You give good gifts to enjoy, and their sex life is one they treasure. Give them joy, creativity, and pleasures together beyond anything they can imagine. And in the process, draw them closer to each other and to You . . .

8 RECOMMENDED RESOURCES

Chapman, Gary. *Making Love: The Chapman Guide to Making Sex an Act of Love.* Tyndale, 2008.

Dillow, Linda, and Lorraine Pintus. *Intimate Issues: 21 Questions Christian Women Ask about Sex.* Random House, 1999.

LaHaye, Tim, and Beverly LaHaye. *The Act of Marriage.* Zondervan, 1998.

_____. *The Act of Marriage after 40.* Zondervan, 2000.

Leman, Kevin. *Sheet Music: Uncovering the Secrets of Sexual Intimacy in Marriage.* Tyndale, 2003.

Penner, Clifford L., and Joyce J. Penner. *52 Ways to Have Fun, Fantastic Sex.* Thomas Nelson, 1994.

_____. *The Gift of Sex: A Guide to Sexual Fulfillment.* Thomas Nelson, 2003.

Rosenau, Douglas E. *A Celebration of Sex: A Guide to Enjoying God's Gift of Sexual Intimacy.* Thomas Nelson, 2002.

Wheat, Ed, and Gaye Wheat. *Intended for Pleasure: Sex Technique and Sexual Fulfillment in Christian Marriage.* 4th ed. Revell, 2010.

For sexually stimulating games, manuals, and toys provided by a Christian organization, go to www.covenantspice.com.

Stress and Sex   5

PORTRAITS : 1

- Robert and Anne have three children in junior high and high school, and they spend most of their lives trying to manage their schedules. Attending school events and sports activities and transporting the kids for time with their friends absorb Robert and Anne's time and energy. They have little left for each other, and their sexual life has suffered. They don't feel they can slow down, though, because they don't want their children to miss out on anything. "Maybe in a few years things will change and we'll get our life back," moans Anne.

- For months Cindy had watched the balance in the checkbook steadily decrease. Since their marriage, her salary combined with that of her husband had barely kept their heads above water. Now unforeseen car and medical costs were taking them under financially. As the bills mounted, worry created tension between them. At first, they silently blamed each other, but after a while, they weren't silent any longer. When they went to bed, Rick seemed to find relief from the stress by having sex, but increasingly Cindy felt used.

- Sarah's promotion was a dream come true. She had worked hard for her company, and finally the CEO rewarded her with a huge increase in salary and benefits, along with far greater responsibilities. The new position meant she and Bob had to move across country, but Bob was more than willing because he knew how much this job meant to her. For several months in the new position, Sarah worked about eighty hours a week to prove she could do the job. When she got home, she was so exhausted that she had little energy for spending time with Bob. Both of them became frustrated, and eventually resentment began to poison their relationship.

DEFINITIONS AND KEY THOUGHTS : 2

- *Stress may be the single biggest contributor to decreasing satisfaction in the bedroom.*

- Stress is the common term for "GAS," the *general adaptation syndrome, or the fight-or-flight syndrome.* It is the body's natural response to threatening situations and prepares us to fight or to flee—it arouses us and gives us the GAS needed to resolve or remove ourselves from the stressor. Stress is a normal part of life and *can be both negative and positive*, alerting us to a problem or areas needing attention and giving us the energy to respond to them.

- When a person is constantly stressed without relief or relaxation between challenges, the stress is mostly *negative*. Chronic stress is often a function of the constant negative appraisals a person makes about life, seeing things as more threatening than they really are.

- Sometimes stress comes from a *difficult life situation*, but it may result from *negative perceptions about life situations*, such as worries about failure and perfectionistic tendencies. It is critically important to help clients understand the *difference between stressful events and perceived stress*, as helping is different depending on which kind of stress exists. Some personalities—often referred to as Type A—*cause stress* in themselves and in others. These are people with personalities that are extremely driven or perfectionistic. When people live or work with someone who has such a personality, they feel the stress of the other person's drivenness.

- Stress without relief can lead to *physical symptoms*, such as headaches, upset stomach, elevated blood pressure, chest pain, and problems sleeping. Stress can also *affect a person's relationships* adversely, including a couple's sex life. Stress can *affect the body, mind, and spirit*. Pay attention to each area to reduce the effects of stress on overall well-being.

- If we do not learn to control stress, it will eventually *control us*. Consider the fact that more than 80 percent of physician office visits are associated with unresolved stress issues. In fact, *stress is a big factor in more than 75 percent of all illnesses diagnosed today*, with many studies putting this figure closer to 90 percent.[1]

- People come for help during times when they *feel overwhelmed and out of control*, but these times can be wonderful opportunities to learn important lessons and acquire skills they can use the rest of their lives. Times of stress force a couple to communicate more effectively, listen more attentively, give feedback so their partner feels understood, forgive wrongs, and ask to be forgiven. If addressed with hope and courage, times of stress can draw the couple closer together than they have ever been.

- *Fault lines in relationships become magnified* when the couple is under stress. Those who tend to withdraw from conflict become isolated and uncommunicative; those who might have difficulty accepting responsibility for problems now blame anyone and everyone; while those who have a quick tongue use biting sarcasm to punish and control those who seem to threaten them. Generally, *stress surfaces cracks in a relationship that can remain buried or seem insignificant when people aren't worried and bothered.*

- *We all respond to stress differently*. However, some stressors can have a greater impact than others. In a famous study of the impact of transitions, various events were assigned a numerical "life change unit" (LCU) value. To determine the weight of each event, the research team asked people of different social backgrounds to rate the degree of turmoil each event caused. Then each event was compared to getting married, which was arbitrarily given a score of 50. The research team was surprised to find that people across the spectrum of age, sex, social position, race, culture, and education scored events very similarly.[2]

Note: This *old* work by Thomas Holmes and Richard Rahe, called the Social Readjustment Rating Scale, has been largely modified by factors such as "hardiness." It's more important whether a person sees change as a threat or an opportunity.

- Not surprisingly, negative events and their LCU values include:
  — death of a spouse 100
  — divorce 73
  — death of a close family member 63
  — detention in jail 63
  — major injury or illness 53
  — being fired 47
  — mortgage foreclosure 30
  — trouble with boss 23

But many events commonly considered to be positive also demand significant adjustments, for instance:

  — marriage 50
  — marital reconciliation 45
  — retirement 45
  — pregnancy 40
  — closing a mortgage on a new home 31
  — son or daughter leaving home 29
  — outstanding personal achievement 28
  — start or end of education 26
  — change in residence 20

> All change—even positive changes like promotions, having a baby, or taking a vacation— produces a measure of stress. The accrual of unaddressed and unresolved stresses, even positive ones, can become overwhelming.
>
> *"The Survey of Recent Events"*

- These are just a few of the stresses, both positive and negative, listed in the study. Though people have different capacities for dealing with stress, *the higher the cumulative total of LCUs, the greater the risk of stress-related problems.* People need to pay attention to the effects of the pressure in their lives and take steps to manage their stress. When people endure severe levels of stress, especially for a long period of time, they also *risk the physical, emotional, and spiritual devastation of burnout.*

- Some stresses are *acute and time limited*, but others are *chronic and become normalized in the couple's life.* It's important for people to grasp which kind they are facing because the remedies can be quite different.

- A glimpse at any personality theory gives insight into *the range of possible stress responses*, and we can apply these to the person and the couple's sex life. For example, some may see sex as a way to relieve stress, and some see it as a reward for taking steps forward, but others see sex as an unnecessary (and unwanted) distraction when they are worried about other things.

3 ASSESSMENT INTERVIEW

Ask these questions to an individual or a couple:

1. What kind of stress are you facing? (*Explain that stress can be caused by positive as well as negative factors.*)
2. How is the stress affecting you emotionally, physically, relationally, spiritually, and sexually?
3. How is it affecting you as a couple?
4. What do you hear each other saying?
5. Explain the range of possible stress responses, and then ask: How do you typically try to control life and limit the impact during times of stress?
6. How does your spouse typically respond to stress?
7. What do you hear each other saying?
8. Describe how you view sex when you feel stressed (as a reward, a relief, a distraction, or something else)?
9. How does your spouse view sex when she is stressed?
10. What would be good, healthy goals for communicating, managing stress, and resolving conflict during this time?
11. What are some ways you can negotiate sex that is honoring and pleasant for both of you?

4 WISE COUNSEL

We need not be overwhelmed by stress. Philippians 4:6–7 says, "Do not be anxious about anything, but in everything, by prayer and petition, with thanksgiving, present your requests to God. And the peace of God, which transcends all understanding, will guard your hearts and your minds in Christ Jesus."

People tend to *react in the same ways to the same stress*ors over and over again simply because they don't realize there might be another way to respond. The couple (or individual) may benefit from efforts to identify their "normal stress responses." Identifying and naming these responses is a first step in making changes. Part of this is identifying normal sexual stress responses too. Differences in stress responses in a relationship often *compound and magnify the strain* caused by outside problems. Opposites attract, at least initially, but in times of stress people may deeply resent the other person's way of coping with problems. They need to recognize that they are both coping the best they know how, and you're going to help them find a more effective and helpful way to build bridges between them and support each other.

A primary goal in counseling a couple under stress is to help each person understand the other and *communicate their understanding, love, and acceptance* so that each person genuinely feels understood and supported.

Each person needs to take responsibility for his or her own thoughts, feelings, and behaviors in the stressful situation. Open and honest communication, listening, feedback, forgiving, and asking for forgiveness are essential components in taking strong steps forward.

The *quality of a couple's sexual life is directly related to the depth of their trust, the ability of each to accept influence from the other, and the quality of their communication.* If they aren't communicating, loving, and respecting each other in other parts of their lives, their sex life will suffer. If, however, they address the causes of stress and their reactions to them, and as they learn to respond more positively, they will be drawn closer together in every aspect of their lives, including their lovemaking.

ACTION STEPS 5

1. Explore the Causes

- Explore the stress in your lives—what are the root issues and what are the consequences? They may be worry, confusion, tension, conflict, and anger.
- *Help the couple identify the causes of their stress as clearly as possible. Determine if they are caused by positive or negative factors and whether they are chronic or acute in nature.*

2. Manage the Stressors

- Based on what you have identified, brainstorm ways in which you can begin to reduce these stressors. Stress can drive people apart or draw them together, depending on their understanding, insight into their personality and responses to stress, and their courage to respond positively instead of reacting in anger or fear. If you continue to react to stress only as you have in the past, trust between you and your spouse will be eroded, and your relationship may suffer long-term damage. But if you respond with wisdom and courage, your relationship will grow stronger than ever.

3. Take Responsibility

- Take responsibility for your own pattern of reaction, including the feelings, attitudes and behavior, blaming or withdrawing, and any controlling behaviors or threats. Whatever is owned can be renounced and repented, and finally forgiven. Forgiveness is a wonderful lubricant for relationships.

4. Find Common Ground

- Work on building communication and relational skills to promote understanding and find common ground on the issues that concern both of you, including the most common stress factors: finances, children, in-laws, and sex.
- As you understand your own and your partner's normal stress responses, you'll be able to talk more openly to negotiate sexual experiences that respect each other and provide pleasure and fulfillment.

6 : BIBLICAL INSIGHTS

Humble yourselves, therefore, under God's mighty hand, that he may lift you up in due time. Cast all your anxiety on him because he cares for you.

1 Peter 5:6–7

God certainly allows trouble to come into our lives, and sometimes He invites it to teach us to trust Him more deeply than ever before. In times of stress, we may be tempted to react in anger and try to control things ourselves, but the proper response is to bow to God, trust Him for wisdom and strength, and cast our cares on Him.

Rejoice in the Lord always. I will say it again: Rejoice! Let your gentleness be evident to all. The Lord is near. Do not be anxious about anything, but in everything, by prayer and petition, with thanksgiving, present your requests to God. And the peace of God, which transcends all understanding, will guard your hearts and your minds in Christ Jesus.

Philippians 4:4–7

> The conditions of modern-day living devour margin. If you are homeless, we send you to a shelter. If you are penniless, we offer you food stamps. If you are breathless, we connect you to oxygen. But if you are marginless, we give you yet one more thing to do.
>
> *Dr. Richard Swenson, Margin*

We can rejoice even in difficult times if we trust that God is good, powerful, and wise. Then we'll believe that He can produce something good even from a painful moment and He can teach us valuable lessons in the process. Our part is to choose to give thanks and to pray about every concern on our hearts. When we try to control everything, we remain anxious, but if we trust Him, His peace fills our hearts with confidence.

Therefore we do not lose heart. Though outwardly we are wasting away, yet inwardly we are being renewed day by day. For our light and momentary troubles are achieving for us an eternal glory that far outweighs them all. So we fix our eyes not on what is seen, but on what is unseen. For what is seen is temporary, but what is unseen is eternal.

2 Corinthians 4:16–18

Some stresses, like aging, aren't going to go away until we see Jesus face-to-face. But if we rivet our hearts to Him, we'll experience His wisdom and strength even as our bodies fail. We can trust Him that way, however, only if we learn to see eternal truths, not just the tangible, physical things around us.

Oh, the depth of the riches of the wisdom and knowledge of God! How unsearchable his judgments, and his paths beyond tracing out! "Who has known the mind of the Lord? Or who has been his counselor?" "Who has ever given to God that God should repay him?" For from him and through him and to him are all things. To him be the glory forever! Amen.

Romans 11:33–36

Our trust in God is directly tied to our grasp of His greatness and goodness, His wisdom and power. He knows everything about us, He cares deeply, and He is able to accomplish His purposes. He sometimes rescues us out of our problems, but more often He gives us wisdom and courage to take steps through them.

PRAYER STARTER 7

Father, my friends [friend] feel overwhelmed and worried about all the problems in their lives, and every aspect of their relationship is suffering. Give them hope, strength, and wisdom. Help them understand themselves and each other. Give them patience and kindness as they learn to support each other more than ever before. And give them a rich, satisfying sexual life in the middle of all of this . . .

RECOMMENDED RESOURCES 8

Dillow, Linda. *Calm My Anxious Heart*. NavPress, 2007.

_____. *A Deeper Kind of Calm*. NavPress, 2006.

Hart, Archibald. *Adrenaline and Stress*. Thomas Nelson, 1995.

_____. *The Anxiety Cure*. Thomas Nelson, 2001.

Minirth, Frank. *Happiness Is a Lifestyle*. Baker, 2005.

Swenson, Richard, MD. *Margin: Restoring Emotional, Physical, Financial and Time Reserves to Overloaded Lives*. NavPress, 2004.

_____. *The Overload Syndrome: Learning to Live within Your Limits*. NavPress, 1999.

Yancey, Phillip. *Reaching for the Invisible God*. Zondervan, 2002.

_____. *Where Is God When It Hurts?* Zondervan, 1997.

6 Birth Control and Reproduction

1 PORTRAITS

- Brian and Cindy feel they are not ready to have their first child and are looking for a safe and reliable contraceptive. Knowing there is some theological controversy about birth control, they seek counseling for accurate information and guidance.
- Dana and her husband have four kids and are expecting another one soon—and they could not be happier. They feel that God will give them as many kids as He wants, and they are not to tamper with God's plan for their family.
- Jenny had a little bit too much to drink but tells herself she had a good night last night, though she wonders if she allowed things to get out of control. Thinking she might become pregnant, she decides to find out about the Plan B method of birth control.

2 DEFINITIONS AND KEY THOUGHTS

- Birth control and family planning are *methods used to control pregnancy and birthing*—so that the process, timing, and number of children born are a matter of marital choice rather than random occurrences. These issues can involve a difficult set of decisions for couples. *The Bible does not address birth control specifically*, though many theologians and churches suggest that there are numerous biblical passages that provide some guidance for birth control–related decisions.
- Beliefs about contraception, even among Christians, vary greatly. *Some persons believe that any form of contraception—including abstinence from sex—is sinful.* These people tend to see the randomness of unplanned birthing as being in harmony with God's design and command to "be fruitful and multiply." *Other Christians feel all forms of birth control—including abortion—are acceptable.* Most Christians fall somewhere in between these two extremes.
- We believe *every child is a blessing from God and has incalculable worth.* While affirming that human life begins at conception with fertilization (the union of sperm and egg), we do not believe that the prevention of fertilization is morally wrong. However, we would oppose any method of birth control that acts after fertilization and terminates a conceived human life by preventing its implantation in the womb.

- In contrast to our position, some Christians do not see birth control that prevents implantation as a problem because many fertilized eggs, naturally, do not make it from the point of conception to the point of implantation in the woman's uterus. Also, some Christians contend that a fertilized egg is not a human, in the same way that a chicken egg is not a chicken—it is only potentially something more. *This position, however, is nearly impossible to reconcile with the biblical text.*

- The reality is that *many families are a combination of planned and unplanned children.* Many couples can point to one or more children who "just happened to come along" when they were wrestling with decisions of birth control and sterilization. Most families consider such children to be God's special gift—the one child whom God sends to remind us all that life is not something that can be wholly planned or humanly contained.

ASSESSMENT INTERVIEW : 3

When it comes down to it, no one can make the decision of family planning and birth control other than the married couple. Therefore, a primary approach to helping a couple is to educate them on the various methods of birth control and the theological issues that are present. From this, the couple can make a well-informed decision. The following questions will help guide such a conversation.

1. When do you believe life begins: at fertilization, at implantation, or some time later? Do you both agree?
2. Would you be satisfied using birth control that may prevent fertilization but will also prevent implantation if fertilization does take place?
3. How do you feel about abstaining from sex during certain times for the purposes of birth control?
4. How do you feel about using a condom?
5. How many (more) children do you want to have? When?
6. When you were pregnant with your last child, did you ever discuss permanent birth control options through surgery for either spouse? What was the outcome of that discussion?
7. What are your main concerns regarding birth control at this time? How is this affecting your marriage?

WISE COUNSEL : 4

A dramatic shift occurs when a couple is married. While before the wedding the church admonishes the couple to refrain from sexual contact, after the wedding the church admonishes the couple to refrain from abstaining from sexual contact!

A biblical basis for decisions regarding the timing of children and methods used to control pregnancy should flow out of a couple's love for God and their sexual expressiveness and love in marriage. *Couples should determine the number and timing of children* based, in part, on their financial position and the time they have to give to one another and to their children. Parents must have time to show children that they are deeply loved and to be their champions.

If a couple decides to utilize a method of birth control, *it should be one that values life*—one that does not kill or interfere with life once it has begun in the womb.

As the counselor, you should be aware that there seems to be some biblical evidence that *abstinence is not a theologically suitable method of birth control for husband and wife*. For many this is a minor or moot point because few spouses select this method. Still, it is important to be aware of this biblical interpretation and trend, which relies heavily on a passage from 1 Corinthians 7:5, where Paul writes, "Do not deprive each other [of sex] except by mutual consent and for a time, so that you may devote yourselves to prayer." For a larger relevant excerpt from that chapter, read verses 2–5.

Encourage your clients to *make prayer and even fasting a part of their decision-making process* regarding birth control and what is best for their marriage. Each spouse needs to spend time seeking God's will, and the couple needs to pray about it together. It is also important that the couple *research all of the options* that are available to make an informed decision.

Helping *facilitate healthy communication* between the husband and wife should be a primary intervention utilized in the counseling session. Encourage the use of "I" statements versus "you" statements when exploring thoughts and feelings regarding birth control and reproduction.

There are many methods of birth control that can be considered. The following is only a very brief overview. As a counselor, if you will be dealing with this issue regularly, you will need to keep abreast of relevant medical trends and advances as they appear (and in this field changes and advances do happen regularly).

Some basic advice to give to the couple is that *no contraceptive is 100 percent effective all the time* (except abstinence or surgery). However, many are quite good when used properly, and the greatest number of contraceptive failures occur when the methods are used carelessly or improperly. The following details some common contraception options for couples.

Timing Methods of Contraception: Natural Family Planning/Fertility Awareness Method

The idea behind natural family planning (NFP) and the fertility awareness method (FAM) is this: a woman is fertile during only a small window of time each month. This small window is believed to be between 100 and 120 hours. Hence, *if a couple abstains from sexual intimacy during this time, pregnancy can be avoided*. Conversely, NFP/FAM can be used to help achieve pregnancy by couples who are wishing to have a child.

The question most people ask concerning the various NFP/FAM methods is: "How can I determine exactly the time of the window of fertility?" If the time frame could be determined with 100 percent accuracy, NFP/FAM would be a perfect method of birth control. However, the window can only be estimated—though with high probability if done correctly. *Couples using NFP/FAM methods correctly have a much lower failure rate than condom users and close to that of users of birth control pills*.

To determine the window of fertility, NFP and FAM involve knowing when the woman is fertile by charting factors such as menstrual cycle length, morning body temperature, and cervical mucous. There are also numerous devices on the market to help determine when a woman is fertile.

NFP is the only birth control method approved by the Roman Catholic Church. However, some persons have theological problems with NFP because it violates the biblical command to abstain from sex only for the purpose of fasting and prayer (see 1 Cor. 7:1–5).

Barrier Methods of Contraception

Male Condoms

Male condoms are the most common type of barrier contraception. Most commonly, condoms are made of latex or polyurethane (though "natural" pigskin and new synthetic materials are used as well). *Latex condoms* are the most popular, being the most affordable and very effective. It should be noted that latex condoms can be used only with water-based lubricants—not oil-based lubricants, which harm the integrity of the latex. In addition, a small number of people have an allergic reaction to latex.

Polyurethane condoms are becoming widely available. These condoms are thinner and transmit heat more readily than do latex condoms, making intercourse feel more natural. It is not clear which are stronger—latex or polyurethane condoms—though some studies suggest neither is more likely to break. However, some say that since polyurethane condoms stretch less than latex condoms, there is an increased chance of breakage or slippage if a condom is too tight or too loose. Also, both oil- and water-based lubricants can be used with polyurethane condoms.

Condoms are probably the least enjoyable method of contraception for most men and many women. Condom size (width and length) affects both comfort and effectiveness. To be most effective, condoms should be put on before there is any genital contact. After ejaculation, during intercourse, the penis must be withdrawn before any loss of erection, and the base of the condom needs to be held in place during withdrawal.

Recent studies have found that *sexually active women who use condoms have a higher rate of depression* than sexually active women who do not use condoms.[1] There is a current theory that semen may function as an antidepressant when absorbed by a woman's vagina.[2]

> Sex is a powerful drive, and for most of human history it was firmly linked to marriage and childbearing. Only relatively recently has the act of sex commonly been divorced from marriage and procreation. Modern contraceptive inventions have given many an exaggerated sense of safety and prompted more people than ever before to move sexual expression outside the marriage boundary.
>
> *Focus on the Family, 2005*

Female Condoms

The female condom is a polyurethane sheath about 6.5 inches in length that is worn by a woman during sex. It lines the vagina and helps to prevent pregnancy and sexually transmitted diseases (STDs). *Female condoms have about twice the failure rate of male condoms, though they are thought to be better at protecting women from STDs.*

At each end of the condom is a flexible ring. The closed end of the sheath, which has a slightly smaller ring, is inserted into the vagina to hold the prophylactic in place. At the other (open) end of the condom, the ring stays outside the entrance to the vagina to act as a guide during penetration and to prevent the sheath from bunching up inside the vagina. Since the condom does not move with the penis, the sensation is more natural and enjoyable for the man than male condoms. However, some women find female condoms uncomfortable. *Note*: The female condom should not be used with a male condom because the friction between the two condoms may cause them to break.[3]

Diaphragms, Cervical Caps, and Shields

Diaphragms, cervical caps, and shields are all similar in that they are all inserted into the vagina before sex and cover a woman's cervix to prevent the union of sperm and egg.

- A *diaphragm* is a shallow, dome-shaped cup with a flexible rim.
- A *cervical cap* is a silicone cup shaped like a sailor's hat. It is smaller in diameter than a diaphragm though still fits securely to cover the cervix.
- A *shield* (for example, Lea's Shield) is a silicone cup similar to a cap, with an air valve and a tab to aid in removal.

Each method must be used with spermicidal cream or jelly. The spermicidal ingredient kills sperm, while the inserted device prevents sperm from entering the woman's cervix.

Diaphragms, caps, and shields are reusable items that *must be fitted to the woman's body by a doctor*. A new fitting is required if the woman gains or loses weight or has a vaginal birth. Caps are more difficult to fit in women who have given birth, and failure rates are higher. Accordingly, *sixteen out of one hundred* women who use a diaphragm will become pregnant during the first year of typical use. *Fourteen out of one hundred* women who have never been pregnant and use a cervical cap (FemCap brand) will become pregnant during the first year of typical use. *Twenty-nine out of one hundred* women who *have* given birth vaginally and use FemCap will become pregnant during the first year of typical use. *Fifteen out of one hundred* women who use the shield will become pregnant during the first year of typical use.[4]

Regarding user satisfaction, some people find using a diaphragm, cap, or shield to be a major interruption before sex, while others see it as a minor issue. Once in place, *these methods are very comfortable for both the man and the woman*, as neither should be aware of the product during intercourse.[5]

Sponges

The contraceptive sponge is a doughnut-shaped piece of polyurethane foam containing spermicide that is inserted into the vagina and placed over the cervix. Because of the spermicide, sponges work both to block and kill sperm. Similar to diaphragms and caps, a sponge can be left in place for twenty-four hours and is good for use during multiple acts of intercourse (though more spermicide may need to be applied). Also similar to caps, the sponge must be left in the vagina for six hours after the last act of intercourse. On the negative side, some men claim they can feel the sponge, or its removal tab, during intercourse. Also, the failure rate with sponges is high: 9 percent for women who have not had a child, and up to 20 percent for women who have.

Hormonal Methods of Contraception

Pills

Birth control pills, despite their widespread use, are quite controversial for some Christians. This is because, while some birth control pills (as well as the other hormonal contraceptives listed below) prevent fertilization of an egg, others prevent implantation of a fertilized egg (which to some is sacred life). To further complicate the topic, there is considerable debate about which hormonal methods prevent fertilization and which prevent implantation. Basically, *all hormonal methods of contraception contain a progestin, a synthetic form of progesterone (that prevents implantation), and some also contain a synthetic estrogen (that prevents ovulation and/or fertilization).* These two chemicals are present in different amounts and strengths depending on the contraceptive being used.

There are two common types of birth control pills, progestin-only pills (POPs) and combined oral contraceptives (COCs) that contain both progestin and estrogen. POPs allow ovulation at least some of the time. This means that *fertilization is possible,* while implantation is inhibited. Therefore, if a person understands life to begin at fertilization, POPs are the wrong choice. In contrast, COCs are *so effective at preventing ovulation that fertilization cannot occur.* Theoretically, the progestin in the pills could interfere with implantation, but if fertilization never occurs, this is irrelevant. Hence, COCs should be an acceptable form of contraception, even for couples who believe life begins at fertilization.

The Birth Control Shot

The birth control shot, also know as combined injectable contraceptives (CICs), are injections that are given monthly. This method is gaining popularity because of the *ease of use (one does not need to remember to take a daily pill), low side effects, and efficacy of the contraceptive.* CICs contain both estrogen and progestin, and it is likely that they are very effective at preventing ovulation, but because of the newness of CICs, *conclusive data is not available.*[6]

Implants

Implants consist of about six match-sized tubes containing progesterone that are surgically inserted, by a physician, under the skin in a woman's upper arm. The rods slowly release progesterone into the woman's bloodstream. Even though this method is progestin only, which thins the uterine lining making implantation impossible, because the delivery system provides a constant secretion of the progesterone hormone, ovulation is fully suppressed. Therefore, *fertilization cannot occur.* Implants, in general, *work for three to five years.* They are *99 percent effective* and are literally user-error free. Also, the cost of an implant is quite reasonable at 450 to 900 dollars for five years, as well as a removal charge of around 100 to

> Nothing in Scripture prohibits married couples from practicing birth control, either for a limited time to delay childbearing, or permanently when they have borne children and determine that their family is complete. . . . In our viewpoint, birth control is biblically permissible. At the same time, couples should not practice birth control if it violates their consciences (Romans 14:23)—not because birth control is inherently sinful, but because it is always wrong to violate the conscience.
>
> *John F. MacArthur, 2005*

300 dollars. Generally after implants are removed, women experience a fairly quick return of fertility.

The Ring

The ring method, the most popular being NuvaRing, is a flexible circle of about two inches in diameter that is worn in the vagina for three weeks each month, then removed for one week (during which menstruation usually takes place). Once inserted, the ring is not felt by the woman, and most men report they cannot feel the ring during intercourse. The hormones contained within the ring, which are a combination of estrogen and progestin, are *absorbed directly into the bloodstream through the vaginal wall*. This method is *very effective at preventing ovulation*. In addition, with the use of the NuvaRing, the uterine lining also becomes thinner than usual, which would inhibit implantation of a fertilized egg—if an egg were to become fertilized.

The Patch

Patches are becoming increasingly popular for many kinds of medication, from smoking cessation meds to antidepressants. Their popularity is rooted in the possibility of receiving medication in a convenient form, with less chance of missing a dose. For birth control, *a woman wears a small patch of approximately one inch for about three weeks a month*. From this patch the same hormones from traditional pill contraceptives are delivered into the woman's body.

Plan B

Plan B (levonorgestrel) *prevents pregnancy (by 89 percent) if taken within three days of intercourse*, and efficacy increases the sooner the pill is taken after intercourse. Though it is intended to be used after intercourse has occurred, Plan B is not RU-486 (the abortion pill)—*it will not work if the woman is already pregnant. Because the method destroys fertilized eggs, it has been widely condemned by Christians.* There is growing scientific evidence that Plan B stops ovulation but does not have any effect on a fertilized egg.[7] Plan B is considered an emergency contraceptive that can *prevent* a pregnancy after contraceptive failure (such as forgetting to take a pill or having a condom break), unprotected sex, or sexual assault.[8]

Intrauterine Device

An intrauterine device (IUD) is a small object that is placed in the uterus to prevent pregnancy. IUDs can last from one to ten years. The IUD is not noticeable during intercourse. While some claim that IUDs work by affecting the movements of eggs and sperm to prevent fertilization, generally they function by making the uterine lining unsuitable for implantation of a fertilized egg.

Sterilization Methods of Contraception

Spermicides

Spermicides have been around for a long time, perhaps, according to some, since 1850 BC. Today there are a number of spermicides available as *suppositories, gels, creams, foams, and even a plastic film.*[9] Many women and men like to use spermicides, either alone or in combination with some other form of birth control, because they are relatively inexpensive, are easy to use, and can be purchased without a prescription. Also spermicides have gained favor because *they do not require a physical separation of the male and female genital organs, as do condoms.*

However, spermicides do have disadvantages; the foremost is that they have *limited reliability* when used alone. Hence, many persons use spermicides in conjunction with condoms or a cervical cap–type device. Other downsides include timing issues. That is, spermicides are *effective for only a limited time*—typically an hour—and some need to be applied up to fifteen minutes before intercourse can occur. In addition, nonoxynol-9, a common active ingredient in spermicides available in the United States, causes irritation in some people. For women, frequency of use has been found to increase the chance of irritation significantly,[10] but when use is limited to no more than every other day, irritation is rare (only 3 percent more than with a placebo).

Vasectomy

The vasectomy has been described as the *most reliable form of birth control* available. For example, the U.K. national sterilization guidelines came to the conclusion that "the failure rate of vasectomy should be quoted as approximately 1 in 2,000 (0.05 percent)."[11] On rare occasions a vasectomy can reverse itself; however, it occurs in only .025 percent or 1 in 4,000 vasectomies.[12]

A vasectomy involves cutting (or, more recently, blocking) the vas deferens, a tube that transports sperm from the testicles. *Procedure failure is very rare, and complications are uncommon.* In addition, *no change in sex drive* is caused by vasectomy, although a few men seem to develop a psychosomatic response that interferes with normal sexual function. Also, since the testicles provide less than 5 percent of the seminal fluid that is ejaculated during orgasm, no difference in ejaculation is felt or noticed. Although vasectomies can sometimes be reversed, this is never assured, and the operation *should be considered a permanent fix.*

Female Tubal Ligation

A female tubal ligation can be done in the following ways:

Laparoscopy involves inserting a viewing instrument and surgical tools through small incisions made in the abdomen.

Open tubal ligation (laparotomy) is done through a larger incision in the abdomen. It may be recommended if the woman needs abdominal surgery for other reasons (such as a cesarean section) or has had pelvic inflammatory disease (PID), endometriosis, or previous abdominal or pelvic surgery. Often these conditions cause scarring or sticking together (adhesion) of tissue and organs in the abdomen. Scarring or adhesions can make one of the other types of tubal ligation more difficult and risky.

Mini-laparotomy ("mini-lap") is done through an incision that is less than two inches long.

> Evangelical couples may, at times, choose to use contraceptives in order to plan their families and enjoy the pleasures of the marital bed. The couple must consider all these issues with care, and must be truly open to the gift of children. The moral justification for using contraceptives must be clear in the couple's mind, and fully consistent with the couple's Christian commitments.
>
> *R. Albert Mohler, 2004*

Postpartum tubal ligation is usually done as a *mini-laparotomy* after childbirth. The fallopian tubes are higher in the abdomen right after pregnancy, so the incision is made below the belly button (navel). Often the procedure is done within twenty-four to thirty-six hours after the baby is delivered.

Laparoscopy is usually done with a general anesthetic. *Laparotomy* or *mini-laparotomy* can be done using general anesthesia or a regional anesthetic, also known as an epidural.

Reversing a tubal ligation is possible, but it is not highly successful. This is the reason tubal ligation is considered a permanent method of birth control.

Abortion

The last, and for Christians most objectionable, form of birth control is abortion. Various procedures, at various times of development of the fetus (including right up to the birth of the child), are used to *kill the fetus or child and extract it from the womb.*

In the United States, abortion has been legal since the U.S. Supreme Court declared it so in the infamous *Roe v. Wade* and related cases in 1973. For more than a decade now, the number of abortions in the United States has remained essentially stable at around *1.4 million each year.*

5 ACTION STEPS

1. Research

- Discover all of the options available for birth control to make an informed decision that is right for you as a couple.
- Look on the internet for information regarding birth control options. Websites that will provide helpful information are: www.WebMD.com, www.cmda.org, www.healthywomen.org. *Use the recommended resources in this section as a referral source for the couple.*
- Gather information from a trusted pastor at your church or another individual whom you see as a mature believer. It may help to know what God has revealed to this person regarding the issue of birth control.

2. Talk and Pray Together

- Set a time to sit down together and discuss the options and information you've found; then pray together about a decision.
- Schedule a day (after one or two weeks) on which the two of you will come back together for a decision. During the interval of one or two weeks, both of you should pray individually about this decision.

- Once you decide on the best option for you as a couple, pray and thank God for His guidance. From this time on, trust that God knows what is best for your marriage and that He will meet every need you may have for any planned or unplanned pregnancy that results from your union together.

- *Be sure to emphasize the importance of both individuals' seeking guidance from the Lord regarding this decision. You may want to suggest a time of fasting in addition to prayer.*

BIBLICAL INSIGHTS : 6

But if any of you lacks wisdom, let him ask of God, who gives to all generously and without reproach, and it will be given to him.

James 1:5 NASB

It is important to realize the need for God's direction and wisdom in choosing birth control. There are many different viewpoints regarding the use of contraception, but more important is God's plan and desire for this couple.

Then you will discern the fear of the LORD and discover the knowledge of God. For the LORD gives wisdom; from His mouth come knowledge and understanding. He stores up sound wisdom for the upright; He is a shield to those who walk in integrity.

Proverbs 2:5–7 NASB

God will bless the couple desiring wholeheartedly to do His will. By taking time to pray, and perhaps even fast, concerning their birth control decision, discernment and understanding will come. God will give both individuals peace regarding the method that is best for them.

This is what the LORD says—your Redeemer, who formed you in the womb: I am the LORD, who has made all things.

Isaiah 44:24

There are no 100-percent guarantees with any form of birth control, but we can trust God, who is the creator and sustainer of life. For Him, no pregnancy is unplanned. If God decides to create a child within a mother's womb, He has a beautiful plan and will give the parents what they need to raise this baby.

And again, "I will put My trust in Him." And again, "Behold, I and the children whom God has given me."

Hebrews 2:13 NASB

Couples must learn to trust in the Lord, pray, and ask for His wisdom—then, follow His lead. He will prove faithful!

7 PRAYER STARTER

Father in heaven, who knows all things perfectly, give this couple wisdom as they consider the issue of family planning and birth control. There are many strong opinions, God, and many complicated issues to consider. Provide this couple with clarity and divine guidance as they think about their family planning options . . .

8 RECOMMENDED RESOURCES

Billings, John. *The Ovulation Method: Natural Family Planning*. Liturgical Press, 1984.

Grenz, Stanley J. *Sexual Ethics: An Evangelical Perspective*. Westminster John Knox Press, 1999.

Nelson, Tommy. *The Book of Romance: What Solomon Says about Love, Sex, and Intimacy*. Thomas Nelson, 2007.

Paris, Jenell Williams. *Birth Control for Christians: Making Wise Choices*. Baker, 2003.

Weschler, Toni. *Taking Charge of Your Fertility*. HarperCollins, 2006.

Infertility   7

- Faith and her husband have been trying to have a child for years. The doctors say the only way for them to conceive is through in vitro fertilization. But because of their religious beliefs, they choose not to exercise that option. They ask their counselor, "Will we ever have the family we've dreamed of having?"
- After her third miscarriage in a row, Rhianna slipped into a deep depression and struggled with thoughts of suicide. She has been neglecting her two daughters and cannot escape her obsession with her failure to bear her husband, Jack, the son he always wanted.
- Two years after grieving the death of his family in a terrible auto accident, Brent began to contemplate what he had done in college—he had given his sperm to fertilize eggs that were frozen in some experimental reproduction project being run by the school's medical college. Though now in his early fifties, he wonders if he could parent a "test-tube" baby that might be waiting to be unfrozen.

DEFINITIONS AND KEY THOUGHTS : 2

- *Infertility is an inability to conceive or carry a child to delivery*. The term is usually limited to situations in which the couple has had intercourse regularly for one year without using birth control. The term *sterility* is restricted to lack of sperm production or the inability to ovulate.
- Approximately *40 percent of reported cases of infertility are due to problems in the male*; another *40 percent to problems in the female*; the remaining 20 percent are of unknown cause or due to problems in both the male and female.
- Infertility can be caused by *any interruption in the usual process of fertilization, pregnancy, and birth*. This usual process includes ejaculation of normal amounts of healthy sperm, passage of the sperm through the cervix and into the fallopian tube of the female, passage of an ovum (egg) down the fallopian tube from an ovary, fertilization in the fallopian tube, implantation of the fertilized egg in a receptive uterus, and the ability to carry the fetus to term. *In women, the most common problems are failure to ovulate and blockage of the fallopian tubes. In men, low sperm count is the most common problem.*
- Underlying problems with infertility include *disease*, such as diabetes or mumps in adult men, hormonal imbalances, endometriosis, pelvic inflammatory disease

(often caused by sexually transmitted diseases); the *abuse of alcohol and other drugs*; and *exposure to workplace hazards or environmental toxins. Uterine irritation* or infection that sometimes accompanies IUD use can also reduce fertility. Occasionally there is a chemical, hormonal, or immunological incompatibility between male and female. Psychological factors are difficult to evaluate because of the stressful nature of infertility itself.

3 : ASSESSMENT INTERVIEW

1. How long have you struggled with infertility? Have you seen a doctor about this? What did your doctor say and recommend as options for treatment? Are you currently receiving treatment for infertility?
2. Do you have any other children? If so, did you experience any complications during pregnancy and labor?
3. As a couple, have you been able to fully discuss the subject of infertility? How did the conversation go? Did you feel that your spouse heard and understood you?
4. Have you discussed together other alternatives, such as adoption? What was the outcome of these discussions?
5. How has infertility impacted your relationship as a couple? Do you feel connected to one another or distant?
6. If you are unable to conceive a child, how will this make you feel?
7. Have you felt any pressure from family or friends to conceive? Have you felt support from family and friends? What has been the overall response you have received from others?
8. What is the biggest issue you are struggling with right now in regard to infertility? Is it your marriage, your relationship with God, or something else?
9. Are you willing to commit to the counseling process to discuss these issues?

4 : WISE COUNSEL

Testing for Infertility

When a couple is struggling with infertility, the doctor may begin by *testing the husband's semen*. The doctor looks at the number, shape, and movement of the sperm. Sometimes doctors suggest testing *the level of a man's hormones*.

For a woman, the first step in testing is to find out if she is ovulating each month. There are several ways to do this. A woman can track her ovulation at home by:

- recording changes in her morning body temperature (basal body temperature) for several months
- recording the texture of her cervical mucus for several months
- using a home ovulation test kit (available at drug or grocery stores)

Doctors can also check if a woman is ovulating by doing *blood tests and an ultrasound of the ovaries*. If the woman is ovulating normally, more tests are needed. Some common tests of fertility in women include:

- *Hysterosalpingography.* In this test doctors use X-rays to check for physical problems of the uterus and fallopian tubes. They start by injecting a special dye through the vagina into the uterus. This dye shows up on the X-ray. This allows the doctor to see if the dye moves normally through the uterus into the fallopian tubes. With these X-rays doctors can find blockages that may be causing infertility. Blockages can prevent the egg from moving from the fallopian tube to the uterus and can also keep the sperm from reaching the egg.
- *Laparoscopy.* During this surgery the doctor makes a small cut in the lower abdomen and inserts a laparoscope to see inside the abdomen. With this instrument, the doctor can check the ovaries, fallopian tubes, and uterus for disease and physical problems. Doctors can usually find scarring and endometriosis with laparoscopy.

The number of couples seeking treatment for infertility has increased as more of them have postponed childbearing to a later age. *In women, fertility begins to decline in the mid-twenties* and continues, more and more sharply, until menopause. *Male fertility declines gradually until age forty, then declines more quickly.*

Treatment for infertility is geared to the specific problem. The first step may be treatment of underlying disease and, in men, avoidance of substances that might affect sperm count. Fertility drugs, some of which increase the likelihood of multiple births, are often prescribed. If necessary, surgical correction of blocked tubes can be attempted.

Assisted Reproductive Technology

Assisted Reproductive Technology (ART) is a modern treatment term that describes several methods used to help infertile couples. ART involves removing eggs from a woman's body, combining them with sperm in the laboratory, and putting the embryos back into a woman's body. Success rates vary and depend on many factors. Some things that affect the success rate of ART include:

- age of the partners
- reason for infertility
- policies of the clinic
- type of ART
- if the egg is fresh or frozen
- if the embryo is fresh or frozen

The U.S. Centers for Disease Control and Prevention (CDC) collects success rates on ART for some fertility clinics. According to the 2003 CDC report on ART, the average percentage of ART cycles that led to a healthy baby were as follows:

63

- 37.3 percent in women under the age of 35
- 30.2 percent in women ages 35–37
- 20.2 percent in women ages 38–40
- 11.0 percent in women ages 41–42

ART can be expensive and time-consuming. But it has allowed many couples to have children, who otherwise would not have been conceived. Common methods of ART include:

- *In vitro fertilization (IVF)* means fertilization outside of the body. IVF is the most effective ART. Often it is used when a woman's fallopian tubes are blocked or when a man produces too few sperm. Doctors treat the woman with a drug that causes the ovaries to produce multiple eggs. Once mature, the eggs are removed from the woman. They are put in a dish in the lab along with the man's sperm for fertilization. After three to five days, healthy embryos are implanted in the woman's uterus.

- *Zygote intrafallopian transfer (ZIFT)* or tubal embryo transfer is similar to IVF. Fertilization occurs in the laboratory. Then the very young embryo is transferred to the fallopian tube instead of the uterus.

- *Gamete intrafallopian transfer (GIFT)* involves transferring eggs and sperm into the woman's fallopian tube, so fertilization occurs in the woman's body. Few medical practices offer GIFT as an option.

- *Intracytoplasmic sperm injection (ICSI)* is often used for couples in which there are serious problems with the sperm. Sometimes it is also used for older couples or for those with failed IVF attempts. In ICSI, a single sperm is injected into a mature egg. Then the embryo is transferred to the uterus or fallopian tube.

ART procedures sometimes involve the use of *donor eggs (eggs from another woman), donor sperm, or previously frozen embryos.* Donor eggs are sometimes used for women who cannot produce eggs. Also donor eggs or donor sperm is sometimes used when the woman or man has a genetic disease that can be passed on to the baby.

About *12 percent of women* (7.3 million) in the United States aged 15–44 had difficulty getting pregnant or carrying a baby to term in 2002.

National Center for Health Statistics of the Centers for Disease Control and Prevention

If the couple is seeking counsel because they want to find out the cause of the infertility or know if they will ever have children, you should provide a referral to a primary care physician. Be sure to continue follow-up sessions as they progress through this process.

Doctors search for the causes of a couple's infertility by doing a complete fertility evaluation. This process usually begins with physical exams and by taking health and sexual histories. If there are no obvious problems, like poorly timed intercourse or absence of ovulation, tests will be needed. Finding the cause of infertility is often a long, complex, and emotional process. It can take months for the doctor to complete all the needed exams and tests. The couple may need ongoing encouragement and guidance from a counselor to get through this difficult time.

ACTION STEPS : 5

1. Get a Thorough Checkup from an Infertility Specialist

- Begin the process by getting a medical evaluation, as well as addressing any emotional experiences or relationship problems that may be occurring between you and your spouse.
- *Provide the client with a referral list of reputable doctors in your area who specialize in infertility.*

2. Talk Together and Consider the Options

- Research every option that a doctor may suggest. It is important to become students of infertility, knowing its causes and treatment options rather than just taking the word of your doctor.
- Whatever is at the root of the problem, good communication and genuine expressions of empathy and support will strengthen the bond between you and your spouse.

3. Pray Together

- Once a medical cause is ruled out or discovered, spend time in prayer together as a couple and individually. Ask for God's peace and wisdom that only He can give.
- You may also want to consider a time of fasting before making a decision regarding how you will deal with the issues that have been discovered.

4. Face Any Emotional Roadblocks

- Many emotions will surface during this time. Anger, confusion, stress, frustration, sadness, grief, and loss are just a few common and normal responses. Unless these emotions are expressed, they will begin to form a root of bitterness in the heart that will destroy your relationship.
- Be honest about the emotional damage and destructive reactions that may be present in your response to infertility.
- *Help the couple express their inmost feelings and learn how to communicate them to one another in a positive manner.*

5. Consider Attending a Support Group

- Attending a group for couples with infertility issues can be a healing next step. Getting to know others who have also struggled with infertility will allow you to learn from their experience, feel less alone in your pain, and give you a chance to encourage those in the group.
- *Provide the couple with a list of groups that meet in your area.*

6. Consider Adoption

- Adoption is an extremely viable option for an infertile couple. Spend time in prayer about the possibility of adopting and begin looking into and meeting with adoption agencies in your local area.
- *Help the couple compile a list of adoption options and the issues involved, for example, the financial requirement and the challenges adoption can pose.*

7. Get involved

- Getting involved with and serving children can help fill your need to nurture and care for little ones, especially if adoption is found not to be a viable option. You could serve in a Sunday school class, nursery, or mentoring program. In this way you will be passing a legacy of faith and strength on to the next generation.

6 : BIBLICAL INSIGHTS

Now when Rachel saw that she bore Jacob no children, Rachel envied her sister, and said to Jacob, "Give me children, or else I die!" And Jacob's anger was aroused against Rachel, and he said, "Am I in the place of God, who has withheld from you the fruit of the womb?"

Genesis 30:1–2

Infertility causes many emotions to surface, including anger, grief, loss, sadness, guilt, and shame. These feelings can add further stress and strain to the marital relationship. As they try to handle the stress, spouses may lash out in anger at each other, which can result in multiple problems in their future relationship. Husbands and wives must remember that God is the creator and sustainer of life and He is in control no matter what. By surrendering to His plan and will, couples will be blessed for their faithfulness.

And he had two wives: the name of one was Hannah, and the name of the other Peninnah. Peninnah had children, but Hannah had no children. This man went up from his city yearly to worship and sacrifice to the LORD of hosts in Shiloh. Also the two sons of Eli, Hophni and Phinehas, the priests of the LORD, were there. And whenever the time came for Elkanah to make an offering, he would give portions to Peninnah his wife and to all her sons and daughters. But to Hannah he would give a double portion, for he loved Hannah, although the LORD had closed her womb.

1 Samuel 1:2–5

God loves His children. He sees the pain that couples experience when infertility strikes their marriage, and He is still in control and a very present help in the time of need. Husbands and wives need to learn the importance of leaning on God for strength and focus on supporting one another through the pain of infertility.

Trust in the LORD with all your heart, and lean not on your own understanding; in all your ways acknowledge Him, and He shall direct your paths.

Proverbs 3:5–6

Husbands and wives would be wise to commit these verses to memory and trust that God is in control. He sees their pain and knows what they are going through. He loves them very much. Even though His hand may not be evident at this time in their life, they can still trust that He sees the bigger picture.

PRAYER STARTER 7

Lord, thank You for Your goodness and Your love for this couple. We pray to You today because this couple wants to begin a family and is having trouble conceiving a child. We ask, God, for Your will to be done in this situation and for Your comfort during this time. We thank You for the love of this couple and ask that You bring children into their lives to raise up in the days ahead . . .

RECOMMENDED RESOURCES 8

Glahn, Sandra. *The Infertility Companion: Hope and Help for Couples Facing Infertility.* Zondervan, 2004.

Saake, Jennifer. *Hannah's Hope: Seeking God's Heart in the Midst of Infertility, Miscarriage, and Adoption Loss.* NavPress, 2005.

Schalesky, Marlo. *Empty Womb, Aching Heart: Hope and Help for Those Struggling with Infertility.* Baker, 2001.

Vredevelt, Pam. *Empty Arms: For Those Who Suffered a Miscarriage, Stillbirth, or Tubal Pregnancy.* Multnomah, 2001.

Weschler, Toni. *Taking Charge of Your Fertility.* HarperCollins, 2006.

Woodward, Shannon. *Inconceivable: Finding Peace in the Midst of Infertility.* David C. Cook, 2006.

PART 2

Sexual Problems and Relationship Challenges

8   Low Sexual Desire

1 PORTRAITS

- Virginia's mother taught her about sex at a young age. She told Virginia that sex is dirty but is an obligation women have. Today she is married and avoids sex with her husband when she can.
- Rob admits, "I've never had much of a libido." He can perform sexually, but he just isn't very interested in sex.
- Suzanne has been on the Pill for twelve years. She has seldom had an orgasm and, to be honest, doesn't seem to have many sexual desires. Her husband feels increasingly frustrated, but she doesn't have any answers for him.

2 DEFINITIONS AND KEY THOUGHTS

- *Low or inhibited sexual desire is characterized by a very limited or suppressed desire for sexual contact* that may result in either limited or infrequent sex with one's partner or in no sexual interest whatsoever.
- *The Diagnostic and Statistical Manual for Mental Disorders IV, Text Revision* (DSM-IV-TR) provides this definition and offers two separate diagnoses of low sexual desire disorder: "hypoactive sexual desire disorder" and "sexual aversion disorder."

  — *Hypoactive sexual desire disorder* refers to a person who *experiences a persistent lack of sexual desire.* Once sexual behavior is initiated, however, sexual performance may be adequate. Hypoactive sexual desire disorder occurs in approximately 20 percent of adults.
  — *Sexual aversion disorder* is apparent when a person feels *repulsed by sexual contact.* Sexual activity is minimized or avoided.

- A study of 1,250 women between twenty and seventy years old, conducted by Dr. S. R. Leiblum, a researcher for the Robert Wood Johnson Medical School, found:

  — *One in four premenopausal women and one in three menopausal women* have low sexual desire.

— The women *participated in sexual activity*—initiating sexual activity, having intercourse, and experiencing orgasm (sexual climax) and sexual pleasure—*far less frequently* than other women.

— They *felt less sexually desirable* and less satisfied with their sex life, which contributed to a less-than-satisfactory relationship.

— Younger women who were menopausal because their ovaries had been surgically removed were significantly more distressed than older women about their low sexual desire.

- Typically, before menopause, women maintain their level of sexual desire because *testosterone-producing cells live longer than estrogen-producing cells*. Testosterone is a male sex hormone, but women also produce it in small amounts. Women require a small amount to maintain a healthy sex drive. Dr. Diana Dell of Duke Medical Center was cited on WebMd as observing: "Women's sexual desire is not as simple as testosterone. There are a whole lot of issues—her health, her partner's health, her partner's dysfunction problems. Testosterone only addresses the hormonal part of her problem. We've become very mechanical with lots of human functions. Testosterone may improve sexual function, but it might not. I have patients with lifelong low testosterone and have given them testosterone supplements. They have noticed some improvement, but it isn't magic."

- *Men tend to report low sexual desire*—and even impotence (see chapter 11)—*as a result of heart disease, obesity, diabetes, cancer, and chronic degenerative disorders* that adversely impact libido and sexual desire. Also, many of the *medications* for these chronic conditions—and for depression—*have an adverse impact on male sexual performance and desire*. Many men cannot take the medications that have come onto the market in recent years for erectile dysfunction because they take medicines for heart, cholesterol, diabetes, and high lipid medical conditions.

- *Causes of low sexual desire disorders* include but are not limited to:

  — emotional problems in a relationship

  — lack of affection in a relationship

  — lack of trust in a relationship

  — personal stress

  — past sexual abuse

  — side effects of medication and drug interactions

  — physical and chronic illness

  — negative, internalized messages about sex being dirty or immoral

  — negative sexual experiences

  — side effects of birth control pills

- While hormonal and physical issues can and do affect sexual desire and impotence, *in some cases the origin of hypoactive sexual desire and sexual aversion is psychological, not physical.*

3 ASSESSMENT INTERVIEW

The following interview questions assume that the data will not be used in court for any reason. If this is not true, delete question 4 from this list.

1. What makes you think your desire for sex is abnormally low?
2. How long have you experienced less desire than you think is normal?
3. What are your goals for counseling?
4. Have you had a bad sexual experience?
5. Are you able to perform sexually?
6. Are there any problems in your marriage that may be affecting your sexual desire?
7. Are there extenuating circumstances (such as health problems, stress, past sexual abuse, and so on) that might be affecting your sex drive?

4 WISE COUNSEL

Early in counseling someone for low sexual desire, *consider the possibility of any health-related complications.* If any question about health exists, it is necessary to refer the person to a physician for a thorough medical checkup to rule out the many physical issues that can and do affect sexual desire.

The biggest misconception is that low sexual desire [in women] is all hormonal, but libido is a lot more complex than that, and overlaps with every sphere of human experience, including vascular health, mental health, nutrition, body image, stress level, and the quality of your relationship generally.

Dr. Juan J. Remos, Miami Institute for Age Management and Intervention

Sexual fulfillment has been closely linked to marital satisfaction and strong religious commitment. *When couples affirm the Bible's teaching about sex in marriage and adopt positive sexual attitudes,* it can help them experience their full sexual potential.

The counseling process may *focus primarily on stress-related issues,* especially any chronic conditions, including current problems, past abuse, and negative messages that may have been internalized. In most cases, these will be the primary cause of the problem.

The marriage partners need to learn to *communicate clearly and effectively* about their sexual desires. It's not a workable situation for one to have low sexual desire and the other to accept passively the absence of sex in the relationship. Michelle Weiner-Davis, author of *The Sex-Starved Marriage: A Couple's Guide to Boosting Their Marriage Libido,* says a situation like this is not fair and can easily lead to adultery. She explains that marriage necessitates compromises in many areas of life—where to live, how much to spend, time with in-laws, whether to have kids, whose career to focus on, and when to have sex. *Too often couples neglect to talk about their sexual needs and expectations:* how often they're going to have sex and what the quality of their sex will be. These are decisions spouses need to make together.[1]

God has provided us with at least four *natural aphrodisiacs*: time, talk, touch, and tenderness.

- *Time.* Love takes time. *A couple must commit time to each other.* African writer Ernestine Banyolak illustrates beautifully the need for time in lovemaking.

A man's experience is like a fire of dry leaves. It is easily kindled, flaring up suddenly and dying down just as quickly. A woman's experience, on the other hand, is like glowing charcoal. Her husband has to tend to these coals with loving patience. Once the blaze is burning brightly, it will keep on glowing and radiating warmth for a long time.[2]

- *Talk.* Great lovers are able to share meaningful parts of their life with the one they love. *Good sex is the fruit of caring for, accepting, and valuing your love before, during, and after lovemaking.* Most couples who come for counseling have lost their "pillow talk."

- *Touch.* We have lost the art of touch. Secure lovers are able to participate in meaningful nonsexual touch. Back rubs, holding hands, a gentle kiss, holding each other, a stroke of the hair, *such meaningful touch is a gateway to bonding emotionally, relationally, and physically.* These acts, if repeated often, will serve to draw a couple closer and enhance their intimacy. A client recently said, "He doesn't even know what I like—how I like to be touched anymore." Most sex therapy programs stop the sex and teach couples to start with nonsexual touch all over again.

- *Tenderness.* Noted author Ingrid Trobisch says, "The greatest erogenous zone in a woman's body is her heart."[3] Sex was never meant to be a single act of expression or feeling. On the contrary, gentleness, acts of kindness, and self-sacrifice are all part of lovemaking. Seemingly small acts fit into the word *love*, combining to become the building blocks of sexual satisfaction. Sex is about joining with one's partner as God designed, for warmth, intimacy, and bonding. (See Proverbs 5:15–19; Song of Solomon 7:10–13; 1 Corinthians 7:3–5; Hebrews 13:4.)

> Depressed libido is a recognized side effect of birth control pills.
> The secret is to forget about doing what you think is normal, and instead embrace whatever it is that makes you feel fun and young and sexy. Feeling desired is a prelude to feeling desire.
>
> *Kathryn Hall,*
> *Reclaiming Your*
> *Sexual Self*

ACTION STEPS 5

1. Get a Thorough Checkup

- Problems with a decreased interest in sexual activity can be a response to emotional, relational, or physiological factors. A positive first step includes getting a medical evaluation, as well as addressing any emotional experiences or relationship problems that may be occurring.
- *Since the client may not feel comfortable confiding in his family physician, provide a referral list of reputable doctors in the area.*

2. Consider Medical Treatment

- If it is considered likely that your decreased sexual desire has a physiological cause, there are several treatments you may want to try that have been found effective. Hormone therapy for women, including low doses of testosterone, has been found effective in treating female hypoactive sexual desire disorder, while

Viagra and other erectile dysfunction treatments have been found effective in helping many men. Discuss possible options with your doctor.

3. Focus on the Relationship

- If a medical cause is ruled out, spend time talking to your spouse about how to work together in improving your relationship. Whatever is at the root of the problem, better communication and genuine expressions of empathy and support will strengthen the bond between you.

4. Face Emotional Roadblocks

- Some of the stresses in a relationship can be managed or eliminated, but some are quite persistent. Denying the impact of stress doesn't solve the problem.
- Consider that stresses at work, money problems, and any current fears or anger either of you is harboring can negatively affect sexual desire. Other common problems couples face that affect sexual desire include destructive arguments, current or past affairs, financial and career stressors, and a lack of quality time together.
- Emotional issues from one's past—such as pain from past sexual abuse or feelings of betrayal—can affect sexual desire.
- Be honest about the emotional damage and destructive reactions either of you has to these stresses.

5. Continue with Counseling and Psychotherapy

- Counseling can be effective in the treatment of sexual desire disorder by addressing any emotional issues behind the problem.

  When couples are counseled together, their relationship often improves and symptoms of sexual aversion and low sexual desire dissipate.

6 BIBLICAL INSIGHTS

Do not be anxious about anything, but in everything, by prayer and petition, with thanksgiving, present your requests to God. And the peace of God, which transcends all understanding, will guard your hearts and your minds in Christ Jesus.
Philippians 4:6–7

Low sexual desire frustrates individuals and causes strain in relationships because one spouse, and perhaps both, has unrealized expectations. The first step is to turn to God, the source of wisdom, love, and strength. He can give peace that is the platform for rich communication.

Nothing is off-limits for prayer, including sexual desires and expectations. This passage in Philippians invites us to ask God for direction and assistance as we navigate all of life's challenges, including sexual desires and experiences.

Husbands, love your wives, just as Christ loved the church and gave himself up for her. . . . However, each one of you also must love his wife as he loves himself, and the wife must respect her husband.

Ephesians 5:25, 33

Do not deprive one another except with consent for a time, that you may give yourselves to fasting and prayer; and come together again so that Satan does not tempt you because of your lack of self-control.

1 Corinthians 7:5 NKJV

Frustration may cause people to become passive or aggressive, and neither of these responses builds relationships. The husband's God-given role is to love his wife unconditionally, with tenderness and understanding, patiently listening and caring for her. The wife should respect her husband and respond to him with love and emotional support.

May your fountain be blessed, and may you rejoice in the wife of your youth. A loving doe, a graceful deer—may her breasts satisfy you always, may you ever be captivated by her love.

Proverbs 5:18–19

> Hypoactive sexual desire is the most common sexual complaint among women, affecting all ages and stemming from a range of causes, including depression and the treatments for depression, health issues, marital stress, and waning hormones.

Low sexual desire doesn't have to ruin a marriage. Sex is a wonderful gift for couples to enjoy, but like all human endeavors, it has been affected by the fall and it fails to work perfectly. If a couple is having trouble with low levels of desire, they shouldn't give up. They should keep pursuing the wonderful gift of sex.

PRAYER STARTER 7

Father, You've given sex to this dear couple as a gift of love to them, but they're having trouble enjoying it. Help us discern the cause of the problem, and give them the courage to take the necessary steps to move forward in their sexual lives, as well as in their love and understanding of one another . . .

RECOMMENDED RESOURCES 8

Chapman, Gary. *Making Love: The Chapman Guide to Making Sex an Act of Love.* Tyndale, 2008.

Dillow, Linda, and Lorraine Pintus. *Intimate Issues: 21 Questions Christian Women Ask about Sex.* Random House, 1999.

LaHaye, Tim, and Beverly LaHaye. *The Act of Marriage.* Zondervan, 1998.

_____. *The Act of Marriage after 40.* Zondervan, 2000.

Leman, Kevin. *Sheet Music: Uncovering the Secrets of Sexual Intimacy in Marriage.* Tyndale, 2003.

Penner, Clifford L., and Joyce J. Penner. *The Gift of Sex: A Guide to Sexual Fulfillment.* Thomas Nelson, 2003.

Rosenau, Douglas E. *A Celebration of Sex: A Guide to Enjoying God's Gift of Sexual Intimacy.* Thomas Nelson, 2002.

Wheat, Ed, and Gaye Wheat. *Intended for Pleasure: Sex Technique and Sexual Fulfillment in Christian Marriage.* 4th ed. Revell, 2010.

Orgasmic Disorders   9

PORTRAITS 1

- Her whole life, Kimberly had never experienced a sexual problem—until now. Since menopause started, her sex drive has taken a nosedive. Worse yet, when she is in the mood, her clitoris feels completely numb and unresponsive.
- Rob has been battling depression for a few months. Lately his mood has improved, but his sex life is still in the dumps. He says, "I can become aroused but I can't reach orgasm. Could this be because of the antidepressants?"
- Beth is a newlywed, exploring her sexuality for the first time. She knows this should be the most exciting time of her life, but it has become a frustrating experience for her to become so sexually aroused and not experience a release. She wants to know what she and her husband can do to help her "finish."

DEFINITIONS AND KEY THOUGHTS 2

- *Orgasmic disorder* is a condition in which an individual is *unable to reach sexual climax* (have an orgasm) or when climax is severely delayed to the point that it causes psychological distress for one or both sexual partners. With male and female orgasmic disorder, the absence or delay of orgasm occurs even after long and intense sexual stimulation.
- With female orgasmic disorder, a woman may report that when orgasms occur, *the climax is of a lesser quality* than was previously experienced—being less intense and feeling more localized. Some women with female orgasmic disorder have described that their clitoris "feels dead."
- About *10 to 15 percent of women* appear to suffer from primary orgasmic dysfunction. Surveys generally suggest that 33 to 50 percent of women experience orgasm infrequently and are dissatisfied. According to the *Psychology Today* website, performance anxiety is believed to be the most common cause of orgasm issues, and *90 percent of orgasm problems appear to be psychogenic or nonorganic.*
- Some women experience a delayed or absent orgasm because *their mate does not sufficiently stimulate their clitoris.* The amount and type of physical stimulation necessary for orgasm varies widely between women. For instance, only about one-half of women reach orgasm during sexual intercourse, and *many women require oral or manual (hand) stimulation of the clitoris to reach orgasm during sex.*

- *Educating the woman and her sexual partner* about sexual stimulation and female sexual anatomy often solves the problem and completely resolves the issue of female orgasmic disorder.
- *Success rates in sex therapy tend to range from 65 to 85 percent.* In primary orgasmic dysfunction, treatment is usually successful in 75 to 90 percent of cases. A positive prognosis is usually associated with being younger, being emotionally healthy, and having a loving, affectionate relationship with a partner.
- Male orgasmic disorder is *not to be confused with premature ejaculation*, which is an orgasm that occurs too early during sexual intercourse (see chapter 10). *The inability to climax in men is a problem of impotence, the inability to maintain an erection, or the inability to ejaculate,* which are based on various and chronic medical disorders. There are also various medical treatments for these conditions.
- *Male orgasmic disorder is fairly rare as a lifelong condition.* However, in its acquired form this dysfunction is not uncommon. The cause of this dysfunction is sometimes physical and medical, although it is sometimes confused with retrograde ejaculation. Retrograde ejaculation is when the man ejaculates into his bladder instead of out the urethra. More often than not, the cause of male orgasmic disorder is a *past traumatic sexual experience, strict religious upbringing, hostility, over-control, or lack of trust.*

3 ASSESSMENT INTERVIEW

1. How long have you been sexually active?
2. Are you able to achieve climax using manual stimulation?
3. Have you been able to have orgasms in the past? When did the problem begin?
4. Are there any relationship problems that could affect your ability to climax?
5. Are you on any medications that can cause sexual side effects?
6. (*For women*) Have you begun menopause? Have you had any type of sexual surgery?
7. Does anything ever improve your ability to experience orgasm?
8. Could past trauma or sexual abuse be affecting your sex life?
9. What is your faith view about being sexually active?
10. Have you consulted with a medical doctor about this problem?

4 WISE COUNSEL

Orgasmic disorder is a problem that *interferes with the beauty and joy* of something God has made sacred—the "act of marriage." As you begin to address the problem of orgasmic disorder, be assured that God gives wisdom, direction, and progress.

Consider the *different possible causes* of the problem. Some common causes of orgasmic disorder include:

- *Medication or drug side effects.* A number of medications can cause delayed or absent climax, especially in men. Drugs that affect orgasm include:

  — alcohol
  — high blood pressure medications
  — antidepressants (MAOIs or SSRIs)
  — antianxiety medications (such as benzodiazepines)
  — narcotics or amphetamines

- *Trauma from sexual abuse.* People who have had a traumatic sexual experience, such as sexual abuse, are more susceptible to having sexual disorders, including orgasmic disorder.[1]
- *Menopause.* Sex hormones, such as *estrogen and testosterone, are particularly affected during menopause.* The physical changes during menopause can also cause decreased clitoral sensitivity, which can delay climax during sex and necessitate increased clitoral stimulation.
- *Sex change operation or organ surgery.* Female surgeries *involving the pelvic region,* a hysterectomy, or the removal of ovaries can cause female orgasmic disorder due to the possible damage or severing of nerves (which decreases the feeling of sexual stimulation) or to hormonal changes that often take place after the surgery.

About 10% of women never attain an orgasm, regardless of stimulation or situation.
National Women's Health Resource Center, 2007.

ACTION STEPS 5

1. Gain Understanding

- Understanding a woman's anatomy and physiology is especially important when addressing female orgasmic disorder. While male sexual stimulation is generally straightforward, female sexual stimulation involves finding and stimulating a small area of the vagina known as the clitoris.
- Men are not necessarily the only ones who don't understand female anatomy. A woman may need to become more familiar with her anatomy and sexual sensations as well. Understanding what is sexually pleasing (and what is not sexually pleasing) will help a woman communicate to her partner what will lead her toward orgasm.

2. Consider Drug and Hormone Therapy

- Consulting with a medical doctor can be helpful in the treatment of orgasmic disorder. Sexual hormones, such as estrogen and testosterone, have been found to help with orgasmic function.

- Also, since a number of medications have sexual side effects, check with your doctor about altering the dosage of or changing a medication, which may improve orgasm function.
- *Be prepared to offer your client a referral to reputable doctors in your local area, as they may not feel comfortable seeing their primary care physician.*

3. Experiment

- Often orgasmic disorder can be eased with additional sexual foreplay. Experiment with additional and prolonged stimulation. Nonintercourse stimulation (oral or manual) that is directly applied to the clitoris can be effective in producing an orgasm.

4. Consider Counseling and Psychotherapy

- Counseling can be effective in the treatment of orgasmic disorder by addressing any emotional issues related to the inability to achieve an orgasm. Common emotional issues that interfere with orgasm include depression, stress and anxiety, and past sexual trauma.
- In addition, couples with relationship problems often experience sexual difficulties. Try improving your relationship through receiving counseling as a couple, and you may find that symptoms of orgasmic disorder dissipate.

6 BIBLICAL INSIGHTS

Let the husband render to his wife the affection due her, and likewise also the wife to her husband.

1 Corinthians 7:3 NKJV

Be kind and compassionate to one another.
Ephesians 4:32

The inability to achieve orgasm or the lack of regular, satisfying orgasms can cause friction and distress in a relationship. Partners need to be kind and compassionate with each other, recognizing that God has given each to the other, with authority over each other's body. A husband and wife must learn to listen carefully, touch tenderly, and be very patient.

My lover is mine and I am his; he browses among the lilies. Until the day breaks and the shadows flee, turn, my lover, and be like a gazelle or like a young stag on the rugged hills.

Song of Songs 2:16–17

Solomon's reference to browsing "among the lilies" is about the husband caressing and stimulating his wife's most sensitive sexual areas. God gave women these wonderfully sensitive places as gifts to be explored and enjoyed within the intimacy of a marriage relationship.

Similarly, God gave men accessible and easily stimulated sex organs to enjoy in a committed marriage relationship.

His left arm is under my head and his right arm embraces me. Daughters of Jerusalem, I charge you: Do not arouse or awaken love until it so desires. . . . You who dwell in the gardens with friends in attendance, let me hear your voice! Come away, my lover, and be like a gazelle or like a young stag on the spice-laden mountains.

Song of Songs 8:3–4, 13–14

> Only 30–44% of women experience orgasm during intercourse without direct clitoral stimulation.
>
> *J. S. Greenberg et al., Exploring the Dimension of Human Sexuality*

In this passage, Solomon may be referring to a particular sexual position in which the husband manually stimulates his wife's most sensitive sexual place. The couple is described as active, and even athletic, in their enjoyment of sex together. This kind of love, value of one another, and knowledge of sexual pleasures are essential if both partners are to have a rich sexual experience.

PRAYER STARTER 7

Lord, thank You for sex in marriage. It is a beautiful gift. Help this couple honor You with their sexuality. Help them build emotional, spiritual, and sexual closeness. They want Your help in finding the fullest expression of sexual love. Give wisdom and patience, Father, and grant success in the pursuit of Your gift of wonderful sex . . .

RECOMMENDED RESOURCES 8

Dillow, Linda, and Lorraine Pintus. *Intimate Issues: 21 Questions Christian Women Ask about Sex.* Random House, 1999.

Ethridge, Shannon. *The Sexually Confident Wife.* Broadway, 2008.

Leman, Kevin. *Sheet Music: Uncovering the Secrets of Sexual Intimacy in Marriage.* Tyndale, 2003.

Penner, Clifford L., and Joyce J. Penner. *52 Ways to Have Fun, Fantastic Sex.* Thomas Nelson, 1994.

_____. *The Gift of Sex: A Guide to Sexual Fulfillment.* Thomas Nelson, 2003.

Rosenau, Douglas E. *A Celebration of Sex: A Guide to Enjoying God's Gift of Sexual Intimacy.* Thomas Nelson, 2002.

Wheat, Ed, and Gaye Wheat. *Intended for Pleasure: Sex Technique and Sexual Fulfillment in Christian Marriage.* 4th ed. Revell, 2010.

10 Premature Ejaculation

1 PORTRAITS

- As a teenager, Herb had little privacy. To avoid getting caught when he masturbated, he rushed through it as quickly as possible. Now as an adult, he finds that rushing through sexual activity is the norm, not the exception.

- Brian is nervous about sexual performance. For several years he suffered from erectile dysfunction (ED). Now with the help of "the little blue pill," he becomes erect without a problem, but he's so worried about the ED he can't seem to keep ejaculation under control.

- Will has had emotional struggles all his life. He grew up in an alcoholic home, and he developed some mild symptoms of obsessive-compulsive disorder when he was just a boy. Since he became sexually active in college, he has struggled with premature ejaculations. Since he married, the problem has never been resolved—or even addressed. His embarrassment created a world of silence. Because he manually manipulates his wife to orgasm (sexual climax) every time they have sex, she doesn't seem to worry about his problem. Now, though, he wants to do something about it.

2 DEFINITIONS AND KEY THOUGHTS

- Premature ejaculation—sometimes known as *rapid ejaculation*—refers to the problem of *ejaculating before one is ready or wants to experience an orgasm*. It is *the most common sexual problem among men* and is said to affect between 25 and 40 percent of men at any given time. The Mayo Clinic estimates that premature ejaculation affects one out of every three men.[1]

- Masters and Johnson defined premature ejaculation on the basis of gender.[2] It is the condition of a man ejaculating before his sex partner achieves orgasm *in more than 50 percent of sexual encounters*. However, there is no medical standard for how long it should take a male to ejaculate during sex. A common rule of thumb is four minutes, but that is an arbitrary figure.

- The American Psychiatric Association, in the DSM-IV-TR, lists the *diagnostic criteria* for premature ejaculation as follows:

    A. Persistent or recurrent ejaculation with minimal sexual stimulation before, on, or shortly after penetration and before the person wishes it. The clinician must take into account factors that affect duration of the excitement phase, such as age, novelty of the sexual partner or situation, and recent frequency of sexual activity.

B. The disturbance causes marked distress or interpersonal difficulty.

C. The premature ejaculation is not due exclusively to the direct effects of a substance (e.g., withdrawal from opioids).[3]

- Even though premature ejaculation is a common problem and very often treatable, many men are *embarrassed to seek treatment* for it.
- Premature ejaculation was once thought to be a purely psychological issue. However, the sexual problem is now considered both *psychological and biological.*[4]
- Premature ejaculation is classified as either primary or secondary:

  — *Primary premature ejaculation* refers to having the sexual problem *from the time of becoming sexually active.*

  — *Secondary premature ejaculation* refers to the onset of the sexual problem *after a previous sexual relationship without ejaculation problems.*

ASSESSMENT INTERVIEW 3

1. How long have you been suffering from premature ejaculation?
2. Are there ever times when you are not experiencing premature ejaculation? Are you aware of what may be different about these other situations?
3. What have you done to try to overcome the problem?
4. Have you consulted with a medical doctor? If so, what were the results?
5. Have you tried controlling your breathing during sex? (*See information about controlled breathing under Action Steps.*)
6. Have you tried stress management techniques before sex?
7. Have you tried the squeeze technique? (*See a description of this technique under Action Steps.*) Did it work? Has your wife learned how to properly squeeze the head and shaft of your penis until the ejaculation passes? Did she agree to do it with you?
8. Have you experienced long-term emotional difficulties (such as abuse or abandonment by your family of origin) that might contribute to the problem?

WISE COUNSEL 4

When a man suffers from premature ejaculation, he can experience a great deal of *embarrassment, shame, and self-blame.* God wants His people to enjoy the gift of sex, and He will give wisdom and direction as men take steps to overcome this very treatable and common sexual problem. Because of the fallen world we live in, sometimes our bodies do not work in the way God created them to work. Sexual difficulties are a part of living in an imperfect world; however, we can be sure that God's love will never change. And while we're not perfect, we are fearfully and wonderfully made.

Help the client *understand the causes* of premature ejaculation, including:

- *Psychological causes.* Some experts believe that early sexual experiences may lead to premature ejaculation. Such experiences include:

  — situations in which a man may have been hurried to reach climax, such as to avoid being discovered having sex or masturbating
  — being made to feel guilty about sex, causing a man to rush through sexual experiences
  — concerns about erectile dysfunction or sexual performance producing anxiety during sexual intercourse

- *Biological causes.* In addition to psychological causes, there may be biological causes for premature ejaculation. These include:

  — abnormal hormone levels
  — abnormal levels of brain chemicals or neurotransmitters
  — abnormal reflex activity of the ejaculatory system
  — specific thyroid problems
  — inflammation or infection of the prostate or urethra
  — genetic factors

5 ACTION STEPS

For many men, treatment for premature ejaculation includes a combination of medication and sexual therapy.

1. Have a Thorough Medical Evaluation

- Since there are now so many proven medical reasons for a wide range of sexual disorders, it is always prudent to see a physician first and review any possible medical or drug conditions that may be affecting sexual performance.

2. Try Sexual Therapy

- Sexual therapy can be an effective tool for overcoming premature ejaculation. Two sexual therapy techniques include the following:

  — Focusing on foreplay and the experience of sex, instead of sexual intercourse and orgasm, can help you overcome anxiety that can contribute to premature ejaculation.
  — Stimulation of your wife will facilitate her orgasm, which will take the pressure off you and your concerns about ejaculating before she reaches orgasm.

— In *The Act of Marriage after 40*, Tim and Beverly LaHaye state, "Men should keep in mind that lovemaking is an experience where you want your wife to cross the finish line of orgasm before you do. With a little experience, you can be right behind her!"[5]

3. Use the Squeeze Technique

- A four-step method known as the squeeze technique can help you delay ejaculation.

  — Step 1. Begin sexual activity as normal, until you feel that you are about to ejaculate.
  — Step 2. Before ejaculation occurs, squeeze the end of the penis at the point where the head (glans) joins the shaft. Hold the squeeze for several seconds—until the urge to ejaculate passes.
  — Step 3. Once the penis is released, wait thirty seconds before commencing sexual activity. Squeezing the penis may cause it to become less erect. However, when sexual contact is resumed, a full erection will return.
  — Step 4. Repeat the process when approaching ejaculation.

- After using the squeeze technique over a period of time, you will learn how to control ejaculation without using this technique.

4. Control Your Breathing and Your Thoughts

- Controlling your breathing can help delay ejaculation during sex. By consciously slowing your breath rate and taking longer and deeper breaths, ejaculation can be delayed.
- The same principle applies to simple imaginal control of your mind. Before you are ready for ejaculation, think of being in other pleasurable but nonsexual situations—like golfing or hunting or fixing the car. Then when your wife is near climax, return to your sexual focus.

5. Control Anxiety and Stress

- Since premature ejaculation often occurs in moments of high anxiety, using techniques that lower anxiety (or decrease stress) will help control ejaculation. In some cases, long-term emotional and psychological problems contribute to premature ejaculation. Addressing these issues in counseling may affect every area of your life and relationships, not only your problem with premature ejaculation.

> Only 44% of people say that they are fully satisfied with their sex lives. Drivers in sexual satisfaction are not only physical; emotional factors also play an essential role. Of individuals who are sexually satisfied, 82% report feeling respected and cherished during sex.
>
> *Durex Sexual Wellbeing Global Survey: 2007–2008*

6. Use Anesthetic Creams

- Some topical anesthetic creams are used to treat premature ejaculation. Usually these creams contain either lidocaine or prilocaine, which dull the sensitivity of the penis. A potential negative side effect is that these creams may also dull the nerves of the woman's vagina, lowering her level of pleasure.

7. Use Medications

- Certain medications, such as some antidepressants, have a side effect of delayed ejaculation. You may want to try such a medication to overcome premature ejaculation. Talk to your doctor about the possible use of a selective seratonin reuptake inhibitor (SSRI) antidepressant medication to overcome premature ejaculation.

6 : BIBLICAL INSIGHTS

May your fountain be blessed, and may you rejoice in the wife of your youth. A loving doe, a graceful deer—may her breasts satisfy you always, may you ever be captivated by her love.

Proverbs 5:18–19

What creates sexual satisfaction?

- 37% of couples want to feel less stressed out and tired.
- 36% of couples want more quality time alone with their partner.
- 31% of couples want more fun, better communication, and intimacy.
- 29% of couples want a higher sex drive.

Durex Sexual Wellbeing Global Survey: 2007–2008

Sex is a gift from God to be thoroughly enjoyed by both married partners. Premature ejaculation interferes with the man's (and likely, his wife's) fullest pleasure, but embarrassment shouldn't prevent them from overcoming this problem.

But if we hope for what we do not yet have, we wait for it patiently.
Romans 8:25

In this passage Paul is referring to our ultimate hope of waiting for full redemption, but we can apply the principle of hopeful waiting to every aspect of our lives, including progress in our sex lives. Our hope is in God to lead us, provide for us, and take us through a process toward success.

Be joyful in hope, patient in affliction, faithful in prayer.
Romans 12:12

A man and his wife can pray about everything, including their sexual experience. As they turn to God, they can be joyful that God knows, He cares, and He wants them to enjoy His gift of great sex. The process of learning and growing can be a time of rich communication, understanding, and love between them as they trust God together.

PRAYER STARTER : 7

Lord, thank You for sex in marriage. It is a beautiful gift. Help us to honor You with our sexuality. Help this dear couple communicate clearly and lovingly as they deal with this problem together. Give them spiritual and sexual closeness, and help them learn to enjoy sex to the fullest . . .

RECOMMENDED RESOURCES : 8

The Mayo Clinic online resources: www.mayoclinic.com/health/premature-ejaculation/DS00578.

Medical News Today online: www.medicalnewstoday.com/sections/erectile_dysfunction.

Penner, Clifford L., and Joyce J. Penner. *The Gift of Sex: A Guide to Sexual Fulfillment*. Thomas Nelson, 2003.

Wheat, Ed, and Gaye Wheat. *Intended for Pleasure: Sex Technique and Sexual Fulfillment in Christian Marriage*. 4th ed. Revell, 2010.

11 Sexual Arousal Disorder

1 PORTRAITS

- Randy and Colleen are newlyweds, but things aren't going very well for them. They can't seem to get things working in or out of the bedroom. Randy complains about Colleen's unresponsiveness: "This is so frustrating. You would think at least this would be easy and natural."

- Tammy and her husband just moved so he could pursue his career. They have a new house, a new job, and new everything. "It's good but it's stressful," she explains. They feel as if they left their sex life back where they used to live. Sometimes he's excited about sex, but she isn't, and at other times, she's interested, but he's too exhausted. Seldom are they on the same page.

- Brenda is in her fifties. She has been content in her marriage for many years, and everything seems to be fine—except in the bedroom. "I just don't seem to turn on anymore," she sighs. "Some friends tell me this is simply what happens when women grow older."

2 DEFINITIONS AND KEY THOUGHTS

- Sexual arousal disorder is the inability to attain or maintain a sexual response. In men this involves an inability to maintain erection, while in women it can involve an inadequately lubricated vaginal area, as well as lack of vaginal dilation and decreased sensation.

- Sexual arousal disorder *occurs in both women and men*. With men, the problem is usually called *erectile dysfunction*. Female sexual arousal disorder is often referred to as *frigidity*. The symptoms of sexual arousal disorder include:

  — lack of vaginal lubrication or dilation
  — decreased genital tumescence
  — decreased genital or nipple sensation

- *Occasional impotence may occur in nearly 50 percent of American adult men*, and chronic impotence affects about one in eight American men, with the chances increasing as a person ages.

- For both men and women, *these conditions may appear as an aversion to, and avoidance of, sexual contact with a partner*. In men there may be partial or complete failure to attain or maintain an erection or a lack of sexual excitement and pleasure in sexual activity. In women there may be an inability to lubricate enough to complete the sex act.[1]

- The DSM-IV-TR diagnostic criteria for *female sexual arousal disorders* include:

  — Persistent or recurrent inability to attain, or to maintain until completion of the sexual activity, an adequate lubrication-swelling response of sexual excitement.
  — The disturbance causes marked distress or interpersonal difficulty.
  — The sexual dysfunction is not better accounted for by another Axis I disorder (except another sexual dysfunction) and is not due exclusively to the direct physiological effects of a substance (e.g., a drug of abuse, a medication) or a general medical condition.[2]

- Sexual arousal disorder is *sometimes psychological.* Present issues such as depression, anxiety, stress, anger, relationship conflict, or a lack of trust in a relationship can lead to a variety of sexual arousal and performance problems. The major pharmaceutical company Merck provides the following information regarding female sexual arousal disorder:

  > If the disorder has been present since puberty, the woman may not know how the genital organs (particularly the clitoris) function or what arousal techniques are effective. The lack of knowledge leads to anxiety, which worsens the problem. Many women who have sexual arousal disorder associate sex with sinfulness and sexual pleasure with guilt. Fear of intimacy and a negative self-image may also contribute.[3]

- *The issue is usually biological before it is psychological.* Changes in hormones, reduced blood flow in particular regions of the body, diabetes, drug or alcohol use, and nerve damage can affect sexual arousal. In addition, a decreased interest in sex has been found to occur in women as they approach menopause.

- It is wise for people suffering with problems of sexual arousal to receive both *a medical and a psychological evaluation.* A medical cause can often be ruled out if one presents sexual arousal problems along with a strong correlation of anxiety or relationship problems.

- Both *hormone therapy and blood-flow enhancing medications* (such as Viagra, for men) have been found to be useful for improving sexual arousal.

ASSESSMENT INTERVIEW 3

1. How long have you (or your partner) experienced sexual arousal problems?
2. How often do the problems occur? Are they constant or intermittent? If the sexual arousal problems are intermittent, is there anything you have identified as helpful in overcoming the sexual arousal problem?
3. Do you have any medical conditions that could account for problems in sexual performance?

4. Have you had a medical checkup to rule out any medical issues? Are you (or your partner) taking any medications that could cause erectile dysfunction or female sexual arousal disorder?

5. Has there been a recent negative sexual experience in the relationship?

6. Are there issues in the relationship that are eroding your emotional intimacy?

7. Has there been broken trust in the relationship? If so, explain the situation.

8. Are there any issues from your past (or your partner's past) that could be affecting sexual arousal (such as past abuse, betrayal, or embarrassment about sexual performance)?

9. What has been previously tried to overcome the sexual arousal challenges? Has it helped at all? Have you had any success that we can return to and build on?

10. (*For the man*) Do you ever awaken in the morning or during the night with an erection?

11. Are both of you willing to explore a solution and work together in overcoming this challenge?

4 : WISE COUNSEL

Even though sexual fulfillment has been highly linked to marital satisfaction and strong religious commitment, some Christians—especially those who were raised to believe that sex is somehow dirty or a taboo subject—do not connect their faith with their sex lives. *Affirming the Bible's teaching about the goodness of sex in marriage* and adopting helpful sexual attitudes can help couples experience their full sexual potential.

Whether the couple's sexuality has brought intimacy to their relationship or led them to pain and despair, *it is important to remember that we are created as sexual beings in God's image.* Genesis 2:24–25 shows God's design for a man and a woman to be united as one flesh. This sexual union occurred before mankind fell into sin. Thus *people were created to be free to share their bodies openly with their spouse, delight in each other sexually, and honor God with their pleasure.*

Invite the client to *share her feelings about the problem of sexual arousal.* Your understanding and empathy will help lower the anxiety level. In many cases, medical attention resolves the problem, and your direction to seek medical help will offer hope of a solution. Be aware, however, that emotional damage (fear, anxiety, depression, and anger) may linger and need attention so that the marriage grows stronger as the sex drive returns.

5 : ACTION STEPS

1. Get a Thorough Medical and Psychological Checkup

- Problems with sexual arousal or a decreased interest in sexual activity can be a response to emotional, relational, or physiological factors.

- A positive first step includes getting a medical evaluation, as well as addressing any emotional experiences or relationship problems that may be occurring.

2. Consider Medical Treatment

- If it is considered likely that decreased sexual arousal has a physiological cause, there are several treatments that have been found to be effective.
- Hormone therapy for women, including low doses of testosterone, has been found effective in treating female sexual arousal disorder.
- For men, medications that increase blood flow to help maintain the erection— including the name-brand medications Viagra, Levitra, and Cialis—are often effective in overcoming erectile dysfunction.
- *Be prepared to provide the client with a list of reputable doctors in your local area, as they may not feel comfortable seeing their primary care physician.*

3. Work on Improving the Relationship

- Talk with your spouse about how each of you can work together to improve your relationship as God intends.
- Common problems that affect sexual arousal and desire include destructive arguments, unresolved anger, current or past affairs, and a lack of quality time together.

4. Face Any Emotional Roadblocks

- Consider that stress at work, money problems, and any current fears or anger can negatively affect sexual arousal. If either of you is feeling one of these stressors, intimacy will never be achieved. Also, emotional issues from the past—such as pain from sexual abuse or feelings of betrayal— can affect sexual arousal.

5. Try the Sensate Focus Technique

- The sensate focus technique is a type of sex therapy that can help couples who are having sexual difficulties due to psychological factors. The goal of the technique is to reduce the anxiety associated with sexual behavior and sexual performance, while simultaneously teaching the partners what each finds pleasurable. This technique is used to treat sexual arousal disorder symptoms as well as orgasmic disorder issues.

    The sensate focus technique is a three-step process. Both partners must become comfortable with each step before moving to the next step.

    1. The first step is about touching sensations. It is not about sexual arousal or sexual intercourse. Each partner takes turns touching the

> Between 20 and 30 million men in the United States are said to be affected by impotence problems, according to recent estimates. About 52 percent of men between 40 and 70 years old have some degree of erectile dysfunction.

other partner. These are sensual but not sexual touches, so genitals and breasts are off-limits in step one.

2. Next, the partners take turns touching any part of the other's body, including the breasts and genitals. However, the focus is still on the touching sensations, not on sexual arousal. Sexual intercourse is not allowed in step two.

3. In the final step, the partners no longer need to take turns; mutual touching is allowed. Once the couple is comfortable with the process of touching and being touched, this third step also allows sexual intercourse. Still, the focus during sexual intercourse is to be on mutual enjoyment of sex rather than orgasm.

6 : BIBLICAL INSIGHTS

I am my beloved's, and his desire is toward me.
Song of Solomon 7:10 NKJV

Throughout the Song of Solomon, the husband and wife delight in each other's physical attractiveness. Explicit descriptions of their love underscore the importance of the soul relationship and deep commitment of the couple to one another.

When a man and a woman become one in marriage, the bond of sexual intimacy strengthens their relationship. Within the bonds of marriage, God approves of and encourages sexual pleasure.

The husband should fulfill his marital duty to his wife, and likewise the wife to her husband. The wife's body does not belong to her alone but also to her husband. In the same way, the husband's body does not belong to him alone but also to his wife. Do not deprive each other except by mutual consent and for a time, so that you may devote yourselves to prayer. Then come together again so that Satan will not tempt you because of your lack of self-control.

1 Corinthians 7:3–5

Arousal disorders can be a frustrating problem in marriage, but the couple shouldn't give up and settle for a nonsexual friendship. They need to be committed to finding a solution, which requires good communication, creativity, and patience.

But the fruit of the Spirit is love, joy, peace, patience, kindness, goodness, faithfulness.

Galatians 5:22

The individual or couple struggling with arousal disorder needs to turn to the Lord. Trusting in Him unleashes the Spirit's work to transform hearts, give wisdom and patience, and change the direction of a relationship.

PRAYER STARTER :7

Lord, thank You for sex in marriage. It is a beautiful gift. Help this couple honor You with their sexuality. Help them build emotional, spiritual, and sexual closeness, and restore passion to their sexual relationship. Father, You want them to experience life to the fullest, and this is part of Your plan for them. Give them patience with themselves, with each other, and with the process of change . . .

RECOMMENDED RESOURCES :8

Dillow, Linda, and Lorraine Pintus. *Intimate Issues: 21 Questions Christian Women Ask about Sex.* Random House, 1999.

Ethridge, Shannon. *The Sexually Confident Wife.* Broadway, 2008.

Leman, Kevin. *Sheet Music: Uncovering the Secrets of Sexual Intimacy in Marriage.* Tyndale, 2003.

Penner, Clifford L., and Joyce J. Penner. *The Gift of Sex: A Guide to Sexual Fulfillment.* Thomas Nelson, 2003.

Psychology Today online: www.psychologytoday.com/conditions/sexual-arousal-disorder.

Rosenau, Douglas E. *A Celebration of Sex: A Guide to Enjoying God's Gift of Sexual Intimacy.* Thomas Nelson, 2002.

Wheat, Ed, and Gaye Wheat. *Intended for Pleasure: Sex Technique and Sexual Fulfillment in Christian Marriage.* 4th ed. Revell, 2010.

12 Sexual Pain Disorder

1 PORTRAITS

- Blair has had a great sex life with her husband. She hadn't experienced painful sex since her first sexual experience about thirty years ago in high school—until now. "I don't want the sex life between my husband and me to be over, but I am experiencing intense pain and burning sensations during intercourse," she explains sadly, "and it's getting worse each time."
- Mary and Joel have been married for almost two years. Mary was a virgin at the time of their marriage; however, prior to meeting Mary, Joel engaged in casual sex with several women. Recently Joel has struggled with pain during sexual intercourse. "It burns like crazy when we have sex," says Joel. "Do you think this may be related to an STD?" he asks anxiously, as if expecting to have contracted something.
- High school sweethearts Jim and Nancy have been together for more than twenty years. Nancy confided, "My husband and I like having rough sex, but sometimes it hurts pretty bad afterward. What can I do to help the problem?"

2 DEFINITIONS AND KEY THOUGHTS

- *Sexual pain disorder* is defined through two major classifications: *dyspareunia* and *vaginismus*.

  — *Dyspareunia* can occur in both men and women and refers to *pain in the pelvic area* during or after sexual intercourse.
  — *Vaginismus* occurs in women only and involves *an involuntary muscular spasm* of the tissue surrounding the vagina. This causes the vagina to close, which makes penetration painful or impossible. Vaginismus occurs in fewer than 2 percent of women.

- According to the American Psychological Association, dyspareunia is *due to physiological factors* at least 75 to 80 percent of the time.[1] When psychological and emotional factors are involved, feelings of guilt or shame about sexual contact or memories of past sexual abuse are often seen.
- Vaginal pain during sexual intercourse can be *due to a variety of causes* including:

— an aggressive or impatient sexual partner
— premature lovemaking following surgery or childbirth, which involved an episiotomy
— decreased levels of female hormones during or after menopause (vaginal lining loses its normal moisture)
— inflamed hemorrhoids
— genitourinary tract infections (such as a bladder infection)
— vulvar vestibulitis (inflammation of the vestibule of the vagina—the area of the perineum between the labia minora, including the opening of the vagina and the urethra) is among the most common causes of dyspareunia in women, and is commonly overlooked
— herpes sores[2]

Note: Vaginal pain that occurs when the penis enters the vagina and decreases during intercourse is commonly caused by inadequate lubrication. Often this is due to lack of sufficient sexual arousal and stimulation.

- *Male dyspareunia* also has common causes. *Pain occurring while obtaining an erection* may be associated with inflammation of the foreskin, physical trauma to the penis, infections, genital allergies, or Peyronie's disease. The most common causes of pain during male ejaculation are prostatitis and urethritis.

ASSESSMENT INTERVIEW 3

1. When did the sexual pain begin? Has the pain increased in its intensity over time or remained the same?
2. Is there any time when it is not painful to have sexual intercourse? On a scale of 1 to 10, how intense is the pain during, before, and after intercourse?
3. Has anything helped decrease the amount of sexual pain you've experienced?
4. Is your spouse aware of the pain you feel during sex?
5. Does your spouse also experience pain during sexual intercourse?
6. Where specifically does the pain occur, for example, in the labia, vagina, glans penis?
7. Do you have any history of sexual brokenness—forced, negative, or hurtful sexual experiences in the past?
8. Do you believe that your sexual activity is in any way embarrassing, shameful, or immoral?

WISE COUNSEL 4

If a client is experiencing sexual pain, *a physical exam* should be performed by a licensed physician. Be prepared to offer a referral list of primary care doctors and gynecologists in your area.

If no diagnosis of a physical problem is made, the couple may be discouraged. If so, *help reframe this discouragement* by reminding them both that a "clean bill of health" is a major blessing. Then begin the process of uncovering possible psychological or emotional factors contributing to the sexual pain.

If emotions or psychological issues are a factor, *addressing thoughts and feelings about sexual intercourse* can be helpful. Explore with your clients their view of sexuality. Complete a thorough evaluation that assesses functioning in these areas: family of origin relationships, presenting problems, medical history, educational background, abuse or legal issues/involvement, and prior treatment history. A complete assessment will help to determine any underlying issue that may be a contributing factor to or root cause of sexual pain.

The American Psychological Association has given the following *advice on treating vaginismus*:

> The treatment of choice with vaginismus is an extensive therapy program combining education and counseling with behavioral exercises. Exercises include pelvic floor muscle contraction and relaxation (Kegel exercises) to improve voluntary control. Treatment should then include gradually more intimate contact culminating in intercourse.[3]

Key areas to begin examining with the couple are their communication, their dependence on prayer, and how supportive they are of each other. Rate their *current level of communication*. Ask about their *prayer life* and whether they pray together regularly regarding the pain they are experiencing. Have them talk about whether they feel supported in this marriage. If the couple does not see any problems in any of these areas, discuss how they can increase their current functioning at an even higher and more positive level. For example, if the couple is currently praying about their problem but are not praying together, encourage them to pray as a couple at least once a day and perhaps also undertake a period of fasting before the Lord.

5 ACTION STEPS

1. Be Patient

- Being less aggressive and more gentle during the act of sex will allow a woman more time to become vaginally lubricated. In addition, if you both agree, include sexual foreplay prior to intercourse to decrease sexual pain.
- After a pregnancy or a surgery in the pelvic area, always follow the advice of your doctor regarding the right time to reengage in the practice of sexual intercourse.

2. Use Lubricants

- If the problem is associated with vaginal dryness, a lubrication fluid, cream, or gel can be applied to the wife's vagina or the husband's penis to ease insertion of the penis during sex.

3. Use Medications

- Certain medications can help relax the vagina during intercourse; can increase sexual hormones, such as estrogen or testosterone; and can help change the physical sensation of sexual intercourse. Be sure to discuss this option with your primary care physician or gynecologist.

- In some instances, surgery can be an effective treatment for sexual pain disorder in women. If the husband is experiencing painful intercourse due to a penile skin infection or an infection of the urethra, a physician can prescribe antibiotics.

- If painful intercourse is caused by herpes sores, the best treatment is to allow time for the sores to heal. A physician may be able to prescribe a medication to promote healing and delay future outbreaks.

4. Use the Sensate Focus Technique

- The sensate focus technique is a type of sex therapy that can help couples who are having sexual difficulties due to psychological factors. The goal of the technique is to reduce the anxiety associated with sexual behavior and sexual performance, while simultaneously teaching the partners what each finds pleasurable. This technique may be useful in slowly guiding your sexual experience.

   The sensate focus technique is a three-step process. Both partners must become comfortable with each step before moving to the next step.

   1. The first step is about touching sensations. It is not about sexual arousal or sexual intercourse. Each partner takes turns touching the other partner. These are sensual but not sexual touches, so genitals and breasts are off-limits in step one.

   2. Next, the partners take turns touching any part of the other's body, including the breasts and genitals. However, the focus is still on the touching sensations, not on sexual arousal. Sexual intercourse is not allowed in step two.

   3. In the final step the partners no longer need to take turns; mutual touching is allowed. Once the couple is comfortable with the process of touching and being touched, this third step also allows sexual intercourse. Still, the focus during sexual intercourse is to be on mutual enjoyment of sex rather than orgasm.

5. Be Supportive of Each Other and Pray for God's Intervention

- Lay your concerns before the Lord in prayer together as a couple. Ask for healing and restoration according to His will and plan for your marriage. Support one another through this process in any way possible and openly communicate feelings that are present.

6 BIBLICAL INSIGHTS

Therefore, as God's chosen people, holy and dearly loved, clothe yourselves with compassion, kindness, humility, gentleness and patience.

Colossians 3:12

Compassion is a choice, not just a warm feeling that comes naturally. Frustrations can mount in any marriage, and especially when the couple experiences sexual difficulties. Both husband and wife can choose to "clothe" themselves with the character of Christ and show His love to each other in a time of heartache and discouragement. This love will affect every part of their relationship.

This is what the LORD says: "Let not the wise man boast of his wisdom or the strong man boast of his strength or the rich man boast of his riches, but let him who boasts boast about this: that he understands and knows me, that I am the LORD, who exercises kindness, justice and righteousness on earth, for in these I delight," declares the LORD.

Jeremiah 9:23–24

Sexual pain is an important issue in a marriage, one that can drive partners apart in frustration, or perhaps draw them closer together. Christian couples can begin by focusing on the kindness of God. He delights in showing His grace and mercy toward us, and as we experience His love, we'll be able to let that kindness overflow toward one another. We begin, then, with a richer, deeper experience of God's grace as the foundation for communication with each other.

Peace I leave with you; My peace I give to you; not as the world gives do I give to you. Do not let your heart be troubled, nor let it be fearful.

John 14:27 NASB

Many times when a person experiences pain, especially sexual pain, it can cause fear. Anxiety concerning whether or not one will fully recover or if this pain will be lifelong can further complicate the issue of sexual pain. It is important to lean on God for the peace that only He can give. We must trust Him to be faithful and believe in His strength to overcome this challenge.

Threats to Sexual Intimacy

- 44% of women experience vaginal dryness.
- 42% of men struggle with maintaining an erection.
- One-third of couples have experienced painful sex.
- Couples spend an average of 18 minutes for lovemaking sessions.
- 43% of couples emphasized the role of experimentation in increasing satisfaction.
- More than 80% of people correlate mutual respect with long-term relationship satisfaction.

Durex Sexual Wellbeing Global Survey, 2006–2007

7 PRAYER STARTER

Dear Lord, thank You for the act of marriage. Today my friend is suffering with a sexual problem. He is experiencing pain during sex, which You have given to a husband and wife as a gift to enjoy. Help him heal from sexual pain so that the act of marriage can be fully enjoyed . . .

RECOMMENDED RESOURCES 8

Berkowitz, R., and R. Barbieri. *Kistner's Gynecology and Women's Health.* New York: CV Mosby, 1999.

Dillow, Linda, and Lorraine Pintus. *Intimate Issues: 21 Questions Christian Women Ask about Sex.* Random House, 1999.

Ethridge, Shannon. *The Sexually Confident Wife.* Broadway, 2008.

Heim, L. "Evaluation and Differential Diagnosis of Dyspareunia." *American Family Physician* 63 (2001): 1535–44.

Leman, Kevin. *Sheet Music: Uncovering the Secrets of Sexual Intimacy in Marriage.* Tyndale, 2003.

Mahutte, N. "Medical Management of Endometriosis and Associated Pain." *Obstetrics and Gynecology Clinics of North America* 30, no. 1 (2003): 133–50.

Penner, Clifford L., and Joyce J. Penner. *The Gift of Sex: A Guide to Sexual Fulfillment.* Thomas Nelson, 2003.

Rosenau, Douglas E. *A Celebration of Sex: A Guide to Enjoying God's Gift of Sexual Intimacy.* Thomas Nelson, 2002.

Wheat, Ed, and Gaye Wheat. *Intended for Pleasure: Sex Technique and Sexual Fulfillment in Christian Marriage.* 4th ed. Revell, 2010.

13 Masturbation and Self-Sex

1 PORTRAITS

- Pat has been masturbating since he was in junior high school. Now in his mid-forties, he still enjoys it occasionally. His wife, though, thinks his behavior is immature and inappropriate but says nothing to him about it.

- Carla enjoys sex with her husband, Ray, but she really enjoys using a vibrator. She sometimes feels guilty for getting so much pleasure out of a sex toy, but she can't wait to use it again.

- Jacob is in high school. Like most adolescent males, his thoughts drift often to sex, but unlike most of them, he masturbates as many as ten times a day. He thinks he's no different from other boys his age, but others don't agree. One of his coaches caught him masturbating in the locker room before practice and told his mother. She's not surprised, having seen or heard him do it many times at home.

- Janice's husband, Robert, travels on business for several days at a time, and he's gone at least two weeks each month. When he's home, they enjoy great sex together, and when he's away, Janice regularly pleasures herself. He thinks it's kinky for her to enjoy sex without him.

2 DEFINITIONS AND KEY THOUGHTS

- Masturbation is *self-stimulation of the genitals* to achieve sexual arousal and pleasure, usually to the point of orgasm (sexual climax). It is commonly done by touching, stroking, or massaging the penis or clitoris until an orgasm is achieved. Some women also use stimulation of the vagina to masturbate or use sex toys, such as a vibrator.

- People masturbate for *a variety of reasons*:

  — It feels good.
  — A partner isn't available for intercourse.
  — It relieves sexual tension.
  — It avoids the risk of pregnancy and sexually transmitted diseases.

- Years ago many in authority taught that teenaged masturbation was a form of sexual perversion and that it led to blindness or paralysis or other terrible outcomes. Today many people view it as *a developmental behavior* that in and of itself isn't wrong.

- The heart of the debate on masturbation, however, comes down to two primary issues: *fantasy* and *self-control*.

In *The Act of Marriage after 40*, Tim and Beverly LaHaye observe:

> All forms of masturbation have to be evaluated, not in the light of the physical experience, but in the mental attitude at the time. Usually, male masturbation is associated with pornography or fantasies that are pornographic, and that's when it's detrimental. Masturbation can also become self-addicting. . . . I think *masturbation is a matter between the individual and God.* If you can do it without feeling the need to confess it as sin, the physical function of bringing oneself to orgasm is not in itself a sinful act.[1]

We agree that the act of self-sex in and of itself is not wrong. But when people masturbate *in conjunction with pornography or sexual fantasies,* which is often the self-absorbing case for maturing teens and adults, it is. In addition, masturbation usually leads to a chronic behavior, and Paul challenged each of us to let nothing master or control us (1 Cor. 6:12; 1 Thess. 4:3–5).

- The essential nature of sex is the union of two people physically and emotionally, so masturbation *shouldn't be used as a substitute* for healthy, normal sexual activity in marriage. *When it becomes a distraction or a substitute* for sexual and emotional interaction in marriage, it is a problem that needs to be addressed and can be a sign that the relationship is not healthy.

- Some sex therapists suggest that masturbation *can serve to improve a couple's sexual experiences* because each person learns what pleases him or her and can communicate this information to the other.

- Often individuals and couples use *sex toys,* such as vibrators, to enhance sexual stimulation. For those struggling sexually, sex therapists may recommend them. However, some partners feel threatened because they can't compete with the sensation provided by the toy. In addition, it is possible to get addicted to the use of toys and other substitutes so that sex becomes primarily or exclusively a self-absorbed means to orgasmic pleasure. The key question is whether a relational and loving tipping point has been reached and sex is being used for selfish purposes rather than for pleasing one's spouse. In 1 Corinthians 7:3 Paul reminds us that in marriage our body is not our own but the other spouse's.

- Should we have pleasure and enjoyment in our sexual practices? Absolutely, but *no man or woman is going to die because he or she didn't have sex.*

> The husband should fulfill his marital duty to his wife, and likewise the wife to her husband. The wife's body does not belong to her alone but also to her husband. In the same way, the husband's body does not belong to him alone but also to the wife.
> *1 Corinthians 7:3–4*

ASSESSMENT INTERVIEW 3

1. What is your concern about masturbation? Are you concerned about your own behavior or the behavior of your child or partner?
2. When did you first masturbate?
3. Why is there the need to masturbate? Can you stop?

4. How has frequency changed since you started?
5. How often do you (or this person) masturbate?
6. Is masturbation (or the preoccupation with it) interfering with healthy communication and relationships? If so, explain how.
7. What would you describe as a healthy and appropriate use of masturbation (for yourself or the person in question)?
8. What is your attitude toward the use of vibrators and other sex toys?

4 : WISE COUNSEL

A wise counselor needs to assess the person's inherent view of the subject of masturbation to determine if her behavior is one of *defiance or resistance* to even communicating about the subject.

In the case of Jacob in one of this chapter's opening portraits, masturbation had become an unhealthy obsession. In such a case, the path to freedom can be a very difficult road. See part 3, "Sexual Addiction and Deviance."

The Bible has *very little, if anything, to say about masturbation*, but it has a lot to say about God's gift of sex and marriage and the sinful abuse of God's good sexual gift. If self-sex is enjoyed as a gift from God and is an adjunct to a rich, healthy sexual relationship in marriage, it may not be a problem. If, however, someone has passed the tipping point—and this is quickly and easily done in our sex-obsessed culture—and *masturbation is coupled with lustful fantasies or has become a substitute for relational intimacy, it is wrong and must be addressed.*

A significant issue in counseling is when someone reveals their *level of preoccupation* with masturbation and its prominence in their life. Those who can't stop thinking about masturbation and schedule their day around this behavior need help to manage their habitual behavior and face what it has become. Those whose relationships are affected need counseling as a couple to resolve the violation of their love vows and any underlying communication problems and expectations.

Sex therapists may advise clients to experiment with masturbation to *explore ways they can enjoy their bodies to the fullest.* We suggest that couples discuss this and participate in it together if this is the goal. Then they can communicate the information about their pleasures to their spouse so they both enjoy richer sexual experiences.

5 : ACTION STEPS

1. Talk about and Explore Perceptions of Self-Sex

- What were you taught in your past to believe about masturbation? By talking about and exploring your perceptions and belief system regarding masturbation, you will be able to identify any underlying issues that may be present and causing distress or confusion.

- *When clients bring up the topic of masturbation, ask questions about their background and their understanding of the practice, including their own experiences with self-sex and their feelings about them.*

2. Become Educated and Informed

- Seek guidance and education from your counselor. Become a good student and explore God's vision for healthy sexuality.
- *Gently correct any misinformation the client may have about masturbation.*
- *Explain the nature, beauty, joy, and purpose of sex in marriage, and encourage the individual or couple to pursue the best possible sexual relationship.*
- *Get to the heart of the motivation behind the behavior.*

3. Focus on the Primary Relationship

- Discuss and explore any fears or mistrust that has developed in your marriage or in the primary relationship affected by masturbation.
- Your concern about self-sex (your own, your partner's, or your child's) may have caused a strain in the relationship. Distrust may have been caused by the exposure of self-sex, or you may realize that masturbation is used as a substitute for healthy sex with your partner. Talk about your fears and mistrust, which are usually a far bigger issue than the specific acts of self-sex.

BIBLICAL INSIGHTS 6

But the fruit of the Spirit is love, joy, peace, patience, kindness, goodness, faithfulness, gentleness and self-control. Against such things there is no law.
Galatians 5:22–23

A primary concern with masturbation is self-control. When a man or woman masturbates, the behavior usually becomes all consuming and often includes lust and fantasies about other people. Obviously this falls short of the fruit of the Spirit, which is something we should pray for regularly.

"Everything is permissible"—but not everything is beneficial. "Everything is permissible"—but not everything is constructive. Nobody should seek his own good, but the good of others.
1 Corinthians 10:23–24

Self-sex is, by its nature, self-focused. A developmental challenge and intimacy issue for teens and lonely adults respectively, it is not the pinnacle of God's design for a husband and wife. If it becomes the primary source of sexual satisfaction and begins to interfere with sexual intimacies in marriage, then it has become a problem that must be addressed.

And whatever you do, whether in word or deed, do it all in the name of the Lord Jesus, giving thanks to God the Father through him.

Colossians 3:17

Couples may engage in masturbation and enjoy it as part of their God-given sexuality if it is performed with gratitude—not to escape a relationship or as an obsession. Usually this is the case for couples who, due to their work or other duties, are frequently separated from one another or dealing with some physical challenge or disease, yet focused on each other.

7 PRAYER STARTER

Father, thank You for this person's concern about her sexuality. You have given sex as a wonderful gift for us to enjoy, and we want to enjoy it to the fullest. We understand how fragile this gift truly is and how easily it can be abused and misused by anyone. We ask for Your wisdom about the role self-sex might play in this enjoyment. Show this person how this might serve her marriage, if at all, when she is apart from her husband . . .

8 RECOMMENDED RESOURCES

Ethridge, Shannon. *The Sexually Confident Wife*. Broadway, 2008.

LaHaye, Tim, and Beverly LaHaye. *The Act of Marriage*. Zondervan, 1998.

_____. *The Act of Marriage after 40*. Zondervan, 2000.

Leman, Kevin. *Sheet Music: Uncovering the Secrets of Sexual Intimacy in Marriage*. Tyndale, 2003.

Penner, Clifford L., and Joyce J. Penner. *The Gift of Sex: A Guide to Sexual Fulfillment*. Thomas Nelson, 2003.

Rosenau, Douglas E. *A Celebration of Sex: A Guide to Enjoying God's Gift of Sexual Intimacy*. Thomas Nelson, 2002.

Wheat, Ed, and Gaye Wheat. *Intended for Pleasure: Sex Technique and Sexual Fulfillment in Christian Marriage*. 4th ed. Revell, 2010.

Oral Sex 14

PORTRAITS 1

- Sara feels most sexually alive when she and Jim stimulate each other orally. "There's nothing like it," she explains. "It brings me to orgasm almost every time." Then she heard from a Sunday school teacher in their church that such an act was a sinful and disgusting practice. Now she is confused and frightened, wondering if God condemns her for doing something she thought was okay and enjoys so much.

- Colleen and Phil are juniors in high school, and both are involved in their church youth group. Their relationship has been getting more physical. She wants to preserve her virginity, but he wants sex. A friend tells Colleen that there's a way both can get what they want, describing to her how to do oral sex.

- Bert and Beverly consider themselves to be "friends with benefits." Bev broke off their steamy relationship because Bert kept pushing for intercourse and Bev had vowed to remain a virgin until marriage. But since they both liked performing oral sex on and with one another, enjoying the orgasms without intercourse per se, they decided to continue giving each other this pleasure. Bev had to redefine her definition of virginity so that her performing oral sex did not violate her vow.

DEFINITIONS AND KEY THOUGHTS 2

- Oral sex is the *oral and manual stimulation of a partner's sex organs*. Oral sex performed on a man is called *fellatio*, and oral sex performed on a woman is called *cunnilingus*.

- A study by the National Center for Health Statistics shows that slightly *more than half of American teenagers fifteen to nineteen have participated in oral sex*, and for eighteen- and nineteen-year-olds, the figure is 70 percent.

- *The Act of Marriage after 40* survey reports that in *44 percent* of the couples surveyed, *the husband "sometimes" orally stimulates his wife's clitoris*. Similarly, in *41 percent* of couples, wives *"sometimes" orally stimulate their husband*.[1] A wider survey of sexual practices found that about three out of four men and two out of three women enjoy oral sex, and a significant number (10 percent of men and 18 percent of women) prefer oral sex over intercourse to achieve orgasm.[2]

- Oral sex is sometimes practiced *to avoid an unwanted pregnancy* or to engage in sexual activity that does not break the woman's hymen—preserving a woman's virginity.
- Due to the intimate nature of oral sex, the *subjective, emotional, and spiritual ramifications go beyond an objective semantic definition of sex.* Married couples who have engaged in oral sex with somebody other than their spouse have claimed that they aren't cheating. Also, many singles who engage in oral sex believe they are still virgins, technically speaking. *We believe that oral sex crosses over God's purity standard when it is practiced before or outside the marital bond.*
- Often singles and those practicing oral sex outside a covenant marriage believe the myth that oral sex is not as dangerous as sexual intercourse. However, medically speaking oral sex is the same as and often more dangerous than sexual intercourse. *STDs can be transmitted by participating in oral sex.* For example, recent research has shown that oral sex can be the cause of a form of throat cancer called oropharyngeal cancer. The prevalence of this cancer has doubled in the past thirty years and is believed to be linked to HPV-infected fluids in the throat. Herpes, gonorrhea, chlamydia, and HPV can also all be contracted through the oral cavity.[3]

3 : ASSESSMENT INTERVIEW

1. Are you looking for more excitement in your sex life? Explain what you are hoping for.
2. What are the reasons you are considering having oral sex?
3. Are you using oral sex for birth control reasons?
4. Do you want to have oral sex to avoid vaginal intercourse?
5. Have you ever experienced oral sex in the past?
6. Has your partner ever had oral sex? Does he talk about it in a way that turns you off or makes you feel inadequate?
7. What are your fears about oral sex? Have you openly discussed these fears with you partner? How did he respond? Do you feel pressured to have this kind of sex?
8. Do you know the physical risks of oral sex?

4 : WISE COUNSEL

Oral sex appears to be widely and increasingly practiced. As the data seems to indicate, a significant number of married couples participate in oral sex, and some prefer this sexual activity, as intercourse alone may not stimulate them to orgasm.

On the other hand, there are people who engage in oral sex because their partner pressures them to do so. One wife, while she engaged in oral sex, felt very disappointed and disconnected from her husband sexually and relationally because oral sex was the only kind he wanted. She didn't understand why he didn't want to make love (have vaginal intercourse) to her, which we believe is violating a higher standard—the call to love and intimacy.

So experiences and opinions about oral sex and its practice vary widely, including and especially in the church. While many consider it to be a normal and permissible practice, if performed between husband and wife, others consider it unnatural and outside of God's design for sexual activity. Most experts refer to Hebrews 13:4, which says the marriage bed is "undefiled" (KJV) before God. The decision to engage in oral sex (or any sexual practice not directly noted and condemned in the Scriptures) is ultimately a matter of discussion and agreement between husband and wife.

ACTION STEPS 5

If a couple decides to explore or engage in oral sex, have them follow these informed rules.

1. Talk Honestly and Openly with One Another

- As a couple, sit down and discuss your opinions and viewpoints regarding the practice of oral sex. Be prepared to express how you feel in a positive way and be open to hear your spouse's feelings as well.
- As always, good communication between a husband and wife is essential. Discuss your desires and fears about sex and specifically about oral sex. The more you understand each other, the more you can help each other find maximum pleasure in your sexual experiences.

2. Show Love and Respect

- Don't let your spouse pressure you into oral sex. Pray together and individually, asking for God's peace and direction as to whether this practice is right for your marriage.
- Set boundaries and show respect for each other's wishes. Mutual love and respect is the best foundation for a gratifying sexual relationship, and it sets the stage for gradual experimentation, even for a typically fearful partner.

3. Consider Experimentation

- Consider experimenting with different forms of oral sex, always mindful of where the boundaries of morality and comfort exist for each of you.
- Any practice can become routine, leaving a couple feeling stuck in the same cycle. Try to find new and exciting ways to stimulate and enjoy each other.
- If oral sex or any other kind of sexual practice becomes a consuming drive for either of you, especially to the exclusion of the other person's desires, further

In a sample of college students, 61% did not consider performing oral sex to be having sex, and 60% did not consider receiving oral sex to be having sex.

The Journal of Sex Research, *2008*

discussion and exploration is needed—perhaps with a professional counselor—as to the nature of the drive and what might be done to increase intimacy.

6 BIBLICAL INSIGHTS

May your fountain be blessed, and may you rejoice in the wife of your youth. A loving doe, a graceful deer—may her breasts satisfy you always, may you ever be captivated by her love.

Proverbs 5:18–19

God's gift of sex can be a great delight and the source of wonder and bonding for the loving couple. Any skill needs to be developed, and sex is no different. Creativity, trial and error, and good communication are essential for a rich, rewarding sexual life. Oral sex should be an expression of the deepest love for one another. If not, it can be manipulative and destructive.

Like an apple tree among the trees of the forest, so is my beloved among the young men. In his shade I took great delight and sat down, and his fruit was sweet to my taste.

Song of Solomon 2:3 NASB

> 10% of men and 18% of women reported a preference for oral sex to achieve orgasm.
>
> The Janus Report on Sexual Behavior

In many cultures, including Solomon's, the apple tree has been used as a symbol for sexual love and expression. Because of the poetic phrase "sweet to my taste," numerous theologians have hypothesized that this passage in Song of Solomon could be referencing an oral sexual act to express love between a man and wife.

"For this reason a man will leave his father and mother and be united to his wife, and the two will become one flesh." This is a profound mystery—but I am talking about Christ and the church. However, each one of you also must love his wife as he loves himself, and the wife must respect her husband.

Ephesians 5:31–33

This classic passage on marriage tells us that women thrive on a husband's unconditional love, and men bask in the respectful love of their wife. Both look to Christ as their example, and both delight in giving themselves to the other. Love and respect can be expressed in many ways and in all times, even in the bedroom when the couple is experimenting with sexual techniques. They should never lose track of the essence of marriage—each person selflessly giving to the other for the other's pleasure.

7 PRAYER STARTER

Father, thank You for this couple. They want to delight in each other and experience sex as the gift You've given them. Lord, give them wisdom and creativity. Help them talk openly and honestly about their desires and fears and guide them to a decision about sexual practices on which they both can fully agree. Lord, help make sex even richer and more meaningful for them . . .

RECOMMENDED RESOURCES : 8

Cutrer, William, and Sandra Glahn. *Sexual Intimacy in Marriage.* Kregel, 2007.

Dillow, Linda, and Lorraine Pintus. *Intimate Issues: 21 Questions Christian Women Ask about Sex.* Random House, 1999.

LaHaye, Tim, and Beverly LaHaye. *The Act of Marriage.* Zondervan, 1998.

_____. *The Act of Marriage after 40.* Zondervan, 2000.

Leman, Kevin. *Sheet Music: Uncovering the Secrets of Sexual Intimacy in Marriage.* Tyndale, 2003.

Penner, Clifford L., and Joyce J. Penner. *52 Ways to Have Fun, Fantastic Sex.* Thomas Nelson, 1994.

_____. *The Gift of Sex: A Guide to Sexual Fulfillment.* Thomas Nelson, 2003.

Rosenau, Douglas E. *A Celebration of Sex: A Guide to Enjoying God's Gift of Sexual Intimacy.* Thomas Nelson, 2002.

Wheat, Ed, and Gaye Wheat. *Intended for Pleasure: Sex Technique and Sexual Fulfillment in Christian Marriage.* 4th ed. Revell, 2010.

15 Anal Sex

1 PORTRAITS

- Diane and her husband, Dan, have been trying new things to spice up their sex life. After reading an article about anal sex, Dan tells Diane, "Here's something we haven't tried—anal sex." Diane grimaces and recoils when she hears of it, exclaiming, "That's something I will never do!"

- Bill is very confused—anger and fear are coursing through him after his wife left him. He had been watching porn movies that praised the joys of anal sex. While he and his wife were having sex, he pulled out and inserted himself into his wife's anus. She screamed in pain and fought him, but he had a strong grip on her and continued until he was done. They had a big fight afterward, and she packed up and left, telling him she was going to her doctor for a checkup after the "rape" he had committed on her.

- Tom and Tammi were rethinking their decision to join the "swinger's club"[1] that they hoped would enliven their sex lives. Tammi had reluctantly allowed a strange man to enter her anally, and he was very rough. Now two days later she could not even sit down because the pain was so great, and she was still seeping blood from the swollen orifice.

2 DEFINITIONS AND KEY THOUGHTS

- Anal sex generally refers to the act of *inserting one's penis into another person's rectum*. However, the term *anal sex* is also used to refer to the act of inserting one's fingers or other object into a person's rectum for the purpose of sexual pleasure. Anilingus, the act of orally stimulating another person's rectum, is also sometimes referred to as anal sex.

- The most recent U.S. data from a national representative sample comes from the 2002 National Survey of Family Growth (NSFG), which surveyed more than 12,000 men and women aged 15–44. Results show that *34 percent of men and 30 percent of women reported engaging in anal sex at least once.*[2]

- In 2002, *11 percent of males and females aged 15–19* had engaged in anal sex with someone of the opposite sex; 3 percent of males aged 15–19 had had anal sex with a male.[3]

- Anal sex is a sexual practice *considered to be somewhat high risk* due to the potential for physical damage that can occur during the act, infections that can occur due to the septic nature of the rectum, and the increased potential for catching sexually transmitted diseases.

- You can get a *sexually transmitted disease* from sexual activity that involves the mouth, anus, vagina, or penis. *STDs are serious illnesses* that require treatment. Some STDs, like AIDS, cannot be cured and are deadly.[4]

- If the couple is determined to practice or explore anal sex, they must be in agreement and very clear in advance about what they are doing and what to do if and when any limits of pain or moral disgust are reached. *Some of the risks of anal sex can be managed by wearing a condom, using a personal lubricant, and full and direct communication between partners during the anal sex act.* (*Note*: lubrication is important with anal sex because the natural rectal mucosa does not provide much lubrication.)

- Anal sex is practiced *for sexual pleasure*. The anus is generally known to be tighter than the vagina, which may yield more physical pleasure, or a different physical sensation during sex, for both men and women. The anus also contains a cluster of nerves that can create sexual pleasure for the receptive person.

- On a relational level, *anal sex is often seen as a cold and distant way to experience sexual pleasure*.

- Anal sex can have *symbolic* value and may represent the male partner controlling or dominating the female.

ASSESSMENT INTERVIEW 3

1. How would you describe your sex life?
2. What are the reasons you are considering having anal sex?
3. Are you using anal sex for birth control reasons?
4. Do you want anal sex to avoid vaginal intercourse?
5. Have you ever experienced anal sex in the past?
6. Has your spouse ever had anal sex? Does she talk about it in a way that turns you off or makes you feel inadequate?
7. What are your fears about anal sex? Have you openly discussed these fears with your spouse? How did she respond?
8. Do you feel pressure to have this kind of sex?
9. Do you know the physical risks of anal sex?
10. Do you have any spiritual concerns regarding the practice of anal sex?

WISE COUNSEL 4

In their book *Getting Your Sex Life Off to a Great Start*, Clifford and Joyce Penner write:

Anal intercourse should be avoided for physical reasons. It's just not wise! If the man enters the woman's anus and then her vagina, he then contaminates her reproductive tracts and sometimes her urinary tract since it is so close to her vagina. When the man's penis enters the woman's anus, the stretching often causes the blood vessels in her rectum to burst, which makes both her and her husband vulnerable to infection.[5]

We agree with the Penners that anal sex is a dangerous practice. Even more, we feel the behavior diminishes any type of relational intimacy and degrades the sexual expression of love.

5 ACTION STEPS

If after having considered all the possible results, a couple decides to go ahead and explore or engage in anal sex, have them follow these informed rules.

1. Communicate

- Talking with one another about personal beliefs and feelings associated with anal sex is vital. The more you understand each other, the more you can help each other find maximum pleasure in the sexual experience.
- Discuss your desires and fears about sex and specifically about anal sex.

2. Be Considerate

- Mutual love and respect create the best foundation for a gratifying sexual relationship.
- With your counselor, learn the importance of establishing healthy boundaries and showing respect for each other. Consider how to compromise, which you both may need to practice.

3. Prepare and Protect

- The rectal mucosa does not lubricate the way a vagina lubricates during sexual intercourse. Using a lubricant will make the act of anal sex more enjoyable for both of you and reduce the risk of physical injury.
- Communication is important during, as well as before, anal sex. Talking to your spouse about what feels good and what is painful will reduce the risk of physical injury.

4. Guard Your Heart and Mind from Obsession

- If anal sex or any other kind of sexual practice becomes an obsessive and exclusive desire for either partner, apart from the intimacy of vaginal sex, discuss with each other—and perhaps with a counselor—why you feel this way and what might be done to build intimacy.

BIBLICAL INSIGHTS 6

Love suffers long and is kind; love does not envy; love does not parade itself, is not puffed up; does not behave rudely, does not seek its own, is not provoked, thinks no evil.

1 Corinthians 13:4–5 NKJV

This passage reminds us that love—and not one's selfish interests—should always prevail in marriage, including and especially in the bedroom. When one partner is not interested in pushing sexual boundaries, the other should honor that in love and learn to be content and grateful for the love and intimacy the couple already share and the relationship that is still being developed. God will enlarge and honor such love and contentment and will assist in making sex very pleasurable and satisfying for both.

May your fountain be blessed, and may you rejoice in the wife of your youth. A loving doe, a graceful deer—may her breasts satisfy you always, may you ever be captivated by her love.

Proverbs 5:18–19

God's gift of sex can be a great delight and the source of wonder and bonding for the loving couple. Any skill needs to be developed, and sex is no different. Creativity, trial and error, and good communication are essential for a rich, rewarding sexual life. Anal sex, if practiced, should be an expression of the deepest love for one another. If not, it can be manipulative and destructive.

Husbands, love your wives, just as Christ loved the church and gave himself up for her to make her holy, cleansing her by the washing with water through the word, and to present her to himself as a radiant church, without stain or wrinkle or any other blemish, but holy and blameless. In this same way, husbands ought to love their wives as their own bodies. He who loves his wife loves himself. After all, no one ever hated his own body, but he feeds and cares for it, just as Christ does the church—for we are members of his body. "For this reason a man will leave his father and mother and be united to his wife, and the two will become one flesh." This is a profound mystery—but I am talking about Christ and the church. However, each one of you also must love his wife as he loves himself, and the wife must respect her husband.

Ephesians 5:25–33

- 37% of college students believe that oral sex is sexual abstinence.
- 24% of college students believe that anal sex is sexual abstinence.
- 61% of college students feel that mutual masturbation is sexual abstinence.

P. F. Horan, J. Phillips, and N. E. Hagan, "The Meaning of Abstinence for College Students"

This classic passage on marriage tells us that women thrive on a husband's unconditional love, and men bask in the respectful love of their wife. Both look to Christ as their example, and both delight in giving themselves to the other. Love and respect can be expressed in many ways and in all times, even in the bedroom when the couple is experimenting with sexual techniques. They should never lose track of the essence of marriage—each person selflessly giving to the other for the other's pleasure.

113

7 : PRAYER STARTER

Father, thank You for this couple. They want to delight in each other and experience sex as the gift You've given them. Lord, give them wisdom and creativity. Help them talk openly and honestly about their desires and fears, and guide them to a decision about sexual practices on which they both can fully agree. Lord, help make sex even richer and more meaningful for them . . .

8 : RECOMMENDED RESOURCES

Dillow, Linda, and Lorraine Pintus. *Intimate Issues: 21 Questions Christian Women Ask about Sex.* Random House, 1999.

Ethridge, Shannon. *The Sexually Confident Wife.* Broadway, 2008.

LaHaye, Tim, and Beverly LaHaye. *The Act of Marriage.* Zondervan, 1998.

_____. *The Act of Marriage after 40.* Zondervan, 2000.

Leman, Kevin. *Sheet Music: Uncovering the Secrets of Sexual Intimacy in Marriage.* Tyndale, 2003.

Penner, Clifford L., and Joyce J. Penner. *52 Ways to Have Fun, Fantastic Sex.* Thomas Nelson, 1994.

_____. *The Gift of Sex: A Guide to Sexual Fulfillment.* Thomas Nelson, 2003.

Rosenau, Douglas E. *A Celebration of Sex: A Guide to Enjoying God's Gift of Sexual Intimacy.* Thomas Nelson, 2002.

Wheat, Ed, and Gaye Wheat. *Intended for Pleasure: Sex Technique and Sexual Fulfillment in Christian Marriage.* 4th ed. Revell, 2010.

Sexually Transmitted Diseases 16

PORTRAITS : 1

- Mary hasn't been feeling well. She thought she had a virus, but it hasn't gone away in more than two months. She feels feverish, has a headache, feels pain when she urinates, and has a vaginal discharge. She can't bring herself to think she might have contracted a sexually transmitted disease. A friend told her it might be genital herpes.

- Bob has had several sex partners, but he considers himself lucky because he's never gotten any STDs. After he got married, though, his wife contracted gonorrhea. He was furious and accused her of sleeping around. She insisted that she hadn't been unfaithful. Both were tested, and they found that he had infected her.

- James tried to tell himself that it was "jock itch," but the condition gradually got worse. He had some bumps on his penis, and no matter how much over-the-counter medicine he put on it, the bumps seemed to be getting larger.

- Allen had been faithful to his wife for twenty years, but he had secretly longed for sex with another man. Brent was a new hire in Allen's division at the company, and soon Allen learned that Brent was gay. They had unprotected sex several times, and nearly a year later, Allen began to feel really sick. His doctor tested him and told him the bad news. It was HIV/AIDS, and the virus was growing aggressively.

DEFINITIONS AND KEY THOUGHTS : 2

- *Sexually transmitted diseases* (STDs, sometimes called sexually transmitted infections or STIs) have become *increasingly common in our society*. They require *medical diagnosis and treatment*, and often the complications to a person's life necessitate emotional, relational, and *spiritual intervention by a counselor*.

- The United States has an epidemic of sexually transmitted diseases (STDs). *More than seventy million Americans currently have an STD.*

- STDs can be *caused by bacteria* (for example, chlamydia, gonorrhea, syphilis), *viruses* (for example, HIV/AIDS, hepatitis, herpes, HPV), *or parasites* (trichomoniasis). Chlamydia is the most common bacterial STD. Human papillomavirus (HPV) infection is the most common viral STD. *People contract STDs during sexual activity.* This includes vaginal sex, oral sex, and anal sex. A few infections—

HPV and herpes—can even be spread by contact with infected skin. Others, such as HIV and hepatitis, can be spread through needle sharing. You can get STDs from someone who has no symptoms.

- The Medical Institute for Sexual Health reports that most people with STDs will not immediately develop symptoms; however, they can still transmit the infection to sexual partners. The most common symptoms include an abnormal discharge from the penis or vagina, a burning sensation when urinating, and abdominal pain. Rashes, ulcers, and warts on the skin can also signal a sexually transmitted disease.[1]

- Most bacterial STDs can be *treated with antibiotics*, and the symptoms of other STDs (such as HIV/AIDS) can be treated but not cured. A vaccine has recently been developed for all eleven- and twelve-year-old girls to prevent human papillomavirus (HPV). The Centers for Disease Control recommendation allows for vaccination to begin at age nine. Vaccination also is recommended for females aged thirteen through twenty-six who have not been previously vaccinated, who have not completed the full series of shots, and who have not yet had sexual intercourse.

- Condom use for vaginal sex *reduces the risk of infection* for:

  — HIV by 85 percent
  — gonorrhea by about 50 percent
  — chlamydia by about 50 percent
  — herpes by about 50 percent
  — syphilis by about 50 percent
  — HPV by 50 percent or less[2]

- STDs can *cause serious and permanent health problems*. They can cause premature births, stillbirths, and spontaneous abortions. In women complications from infection include pelvic inflammatory disease (PID), tubal pregnancy, infertility, and cervical cancer. In pregnant women STDs can lead to miscarriage, stillbirths, preterm delivery, and birth defects. In men HPV infection can cause penile cancer. Some STDs, such as HIV, can be life threatening.

3 ASSESSMENT INTERVIEW

1. Why do you think you might have a sexually transmitted disease?
2. What are your symptoms? How long have you experienced them?
3. Have you seen a doctor for diagnosis and treatment?
4. Are you being treated for the problem? Is it working?
5. How is the problem affecting you emotionally?
6. How is it affecting your relationships?
7. Does your spouse know? Has she been tested and diagnosed?
8. What are your goals for counseling?

WISE COUNSEL :4

STDs are *serious medical problems* and need to be addressed in counseling with a combination of grace and gravity.

Counselors need to refer clients who have or are suspected of having STDs to a competent physician who can *accurately diagnose and treat the infection.* The counselor's role is to help the client process and resolve the emotional, relational, and spiritual implications of the disease.

Become a partner with the doctor. When the client comes back to see you, *support the doctor's assessment and treatment plan and offer encouragement* about the benefits of addressing the problem. If it is appropriate and if you have a relationship with the doctor, ask for input about how you can further support the medical treatment plan. (Remember to obtain a letter of written consent from your client to speak with any third party.)

Many people experience shame because they contracted an STD from illicit sexual contact, but *others innocently and unknowingly contracted the infection* from a spouse who had been previously infected. Treatment, then, must be tailored to the specifics of each person's case, *addressing the issues of grace, forgiveness, forgiving others, and restoring broken trust.*

If the client is single, make recommendations about *abstinence.* If the client is married, he and his partner will benefit from being counseled together to *resolve difficult relational issues* brought on by the infection and its treatment.

ACTION STEPS :5

1. Have a Medical Evaluation

- Make an appointment to see a doctor to be tested for STDs. Early diagnosis and intervention are the best method of treatment.
- STDs are health problems that must be addressed as quickly as possible by a physician.
- *Help the client overcome any stigma of shame at the prospect of getting medical treatment. Stress the benefits of early diagnosis and treatment so he will be motivated to take the necessary steps. Provide the names of doctors or clinics you trust.*
- Return for counseling to learn how to deal with the complications of the STD.

2. Address Your Feelings

- Be open to discussing any feelings of guilt, shame, or anger that may be in your heart. Talk honestly and openly regarding perceptions you have of STDs. Stay consistent in attending counseling to fully address your emotions regarding this diagnosis.
- If you contracted the infection from illicit sexual behavior, you will need to experience God's forgiveness. Remember that no sin is beyond God's grace.

- If you were unknowingly and innocently infected by your spouse, you will need help in being honest about the hurt and anger you feel, as well as in choosing to forgive her.
- Remember that the process of healing, for both you and the one who infected you, will take time and courage.

3. Take Responsibility

- If you have been diagnosed with an STD, take the proper steps to ensure that you will not infect your spouse. Also, if you have concern that anyone other than your spouse may also be infected, be sure to act responsibly and notify that person. Even though this will be very difficult to do, it is the respectful thing to do.

6 : BIBLICAL INSIGHTS

This is how God showed his love among us: He sent his one and only Son into the world that we might live through him. This is love: not that we loved God, but that he loved us and sent his Son as an atoning sacrifice for our sins.

1 John 4:9–10

No matter what we've done, God hasn't forgotten us and He hasn't stopped loving us. Whether a sexually transmitted disease is our fault or someone else's, God still has a gracious plan for our lives.

The measure of God's love is the sacrifice of Jesus to pay for our sins. His death on the cross forgives every sin and communicates the wealth of His love and grace to us.

We also rejoice in our sufferings, because we know that suffering produces persever- ance; perseverance, character; and character, hope. And hope does not disappoint us, because God has poured out his love into our hearts by the Holy Spirit, whom he has given us.

Romans 5:3–5

God wants to use everything in our lives—difficulties as well as blessings—to shape us and draw us closer to Him. Even when we are the victims of another's irresponsible behavior, we can trust that God will somehow use it for good in our lives. We may not see it soon, but we can trust God will eventually produce fruit in our lives.

Get rid of all bitterness, rage and anger, brawling and slander, along with every form of malice. Be kind and compassionate to one another, forgiving each other, just as in Christ God forgave you.

Ephesians 4:31–32

In a marriage, sexually transmitted diseases can cause tremendous heartache and anger. First, we need to remember that Christ paid for our sins. Then, when our hearts are overwhelmed with God's grace toward us, we can choose to forgive those who have hurt us. We may not feel loving and warm toward them for a while, but forgiveness is a choice we can make as soon as we're ready.

PRAYER STARTER 7

Father, nothing is beyond Your sight, and nothing is beyond Your grace. This man is hurting today because of a disease, and he needs Your care to overcome fear, doubts, hurt, and anger. Thank You, Lord, that You are near, that You are patient, and that You help us take one step at a time toward hope and healing . . .

RECOMMENDED RESOURCES 8

The Centers for Disease Control and Prevention: www.cdc.gov/std.
The Medical Institute for Sexual Health: www.medinstitute.org.
WebMD: www.webmd.com/sexual-conditions.

17 HIV Transmission and AIDS

1 PORTRAITS

- Clara was devastated as she sat in her internist's office and heard that she had contracted HIV/AIDS. Her physician's upbeat assertion that this was no longer a death sentence hardly penetrated the cold horror that was overtaking her soul. As a nurse, she knew that effective treatment meant a cocktail of toxic drugs. Her thoughts immediately flew to her vacation lover, a middle-aged divorcé like herself who lived in England and promised up and down on that idyllic vacation island that he was clean—free of any sexual diseases.

- Ben was sick and tired of being sick and tired—and he so missed the freewheeling days of uninhibited gay sex that he enjoyed a decade earlier. He decided to come out about being HIV positive and return to some gay bars where he knew he could hook up with others who were also HIV positive. *So what if I hook up with other gays again,* he thought, *at least we'll be honest.*

- Jeannie was horrified when her ob-gyn revealed she was carrying the AIDS virus. *I'm six months pregnant,* she thought and then went to the bathroom at her physician's office and vomited. She realized that she must have contracted it from her husband, whom she suspected was being sexual with someone else while she was pregnant.

2 DEFINITIONS AND KEY THOUGHTS

- Being *HIV positive means one has contracted the virus that leads to AIDS* and certain death if it is not treated, as is so often the case in poorer countries around the world. *When AIDS progresses to an advanced disease state, it leads to the destruction of the body's immunosuppressant system*, leading to death by certain cancers or pneumonia, TB, or other opportunistic diseases that lay waste to the body—diseases that would otherwise normally be killed by the body's immune system.

- *Acquired immunodeficiency syndrome (AIDS) is caused by the human immunodeficiency virus (HIV).* The term *AIDS* applies to the most advanced stages of HIV infection.

- In 2008, the Centers for Disease Control estimated that in the United States *approximately 56,300 people were newly infected with HIV in 2006.* More than half (53 percent) of these new infections occurred in gay and bisexual men. Black men and women are estimated to have an incidence rate that is seven times higher than the incidence rate among whites.[1]

- *The cumulative estimated number of diagnoses of AIDS through 2007 in the United States and dependent areas was 1,051,875.*[2]

- Because early HIV infection often causes no symptoms, a doctor or other health-care worker can *usually diagnose it only by testing a person's blood for the presence of antibodies (disease-fighting proteins) to HIV.* Generally these antibodies do not reach levels in the blood that can be measured until one to three months following infection, and it may take the antibodies as long as six months to be produced in quantities large enough to show up in standard blood tests. Therefore, people exposed to the virus should get an HIV test within this time period.

- *Today contracting the HIV/AIDS virus is not an automatic death sentence if one is diagnosed early and begins a complex regimen of drug treatments that can suppress the growth of the virus and control its lethality for many years.* Consider the dramatic revelation of former basketball star Magic Johnson nearly twenty years ago that he was HIV positive and had to retire early from a great pro ball career. Today he remains active in business and as a sports commentator because he faithfully maintains an expensive drug regimen that keeps him alive.

- *HIV is spread most commonly by having sex with an infected partner. HIV also is spread through contact with infected blood,* which frequently occurs among injection drug users who share needles or syringes contaminated with blood from someone infected with the virus. Women with HIV can transmit the virus to their babies during pregnancy, birth, or breast-feeding. However, if the mother takes the drug AZT during pregnancy, she can significantly reduce the chances that her baby will be infected with HIV.

- *Many people do not develop any symptoms when they first become infected with HIV. Some people, however, have a flulike illness within a month or two after exposure to the virus.* More persistent or severe symptoms may not surface for a decade or more after HIV first enters the body in adults or within two years in children born with HIV infection. This period of asymptomatic infection is highly individual. *During the asymptomatic period, however, the virus is actively multiplying, infecting, and killing cells of the immune system, and people are highly infectious.*

- As the immune system deteriorates, a variety of complications start to take over. *For many people, their first sign of infection is large lymph nodes or swollen glands that may be enlarged for more than three months. Other symptoms may be experienced months to years before the onset of AIDS.*

ASSESSMENT INTERVIEW 3

Oftentimes clients will come to a counselor first to discuss fears they have about possible exposure to and/or potential symptoms of HIV. If this is the case, the questions to consider would include physical symptoms as well as mental and emotional struggles.

1. Do you notice or struggle with a lack of energy?
2. What about weight loss or reduced appetite?
3. Are you having increasingly frequent fevers and sweats?
4. Do you experience persistent or frequent yeast infections (oral or vaginal)? How about any persistent skin rashes or flaky skin?
5. (*For women*) Are you having any pelvic inflammatory disease that does not seem to be responding well to treatment?
6. Do you notice any short-term memory loss or any problems concentrating or staying on task or any cognitive declines that you have become aware of?
7. Do you have symptoms of depression or mood swings—irritability, weight loss, lack of enjoyment or pleasure in things, excess crying or feeling numb, sleep disturbance of any kind?
8. Do you notice an increase in your use of alcohol or drugs, whether prescribed or not?
9. Have you spoken with a doctor? If not, do you have any fears about seeing a doctor for a medical evaluation?

For the Client Already Diagnosed with HIV/AIDS

1. When did you find out you were HIV positive? How did you feel? What prognosis did you receive from your doctor?
2. Does anyone know about the diagnosis?
3. Do you know how you may have contracted HIV? Do you fear you may have infected others?
4. What do you know about HIV/AIDS? What kind of treatment did your doctor suggest?
5. How have you adjusted since hearing of your diagnosis? How have you been feeling? Have any of your behaviors changed, such as eating habits, sleeping patterns, social life? Have you withdrawn from others or are you seeking out relationships?
6. What is the worst thought you have had about your diagnosis?
7. What are you doing with these thoughts? Are you talking to anybody about your fears?
8. What physical symptoms are bothering you the most? Are you on any particular medications to help you?

4 WISE COUNSEL

HIV/AIDS is a *serious medical problem* and needs to be *addressed cooperatively by physicians, mental health professionals, and pastors. Counseling must be done with a combination of grace and gravity*, with both seriousness and solace. Counselors need to refer clients who have, or are suspected of having, HIV/AIDS to a competent physician who can *accurately diagnose and treat the infection*. The counselor's role is to help the client process and resolve the emotional, relational, and spiritual implications of the disease.

After the client has seen a doctor, *support the doctor's assessment and treatment plan and offer encouragement* about following the doctor's plan. As much as possible, *become a partner with the doctor.* If it is appropriate and if you have a relationship with the doctor, ask for input about how you can further support the medical treatment plan. (Remember to obtain a letter of written consent from your client to consult with any third party.)

Many people experience horror and shame because they have contracted HIV/AIDS from illicit sexual contact or drug abuse, but *others innocently and unknowingly contracted the infection* from a spouse who had been previously infected or a tainted blood transfusion. Treatment, then, must be tailored to the specifics of each person's case, *addressing the issues of grace, forgiveness, forgiving others, and restoring broken trust.*

If the client is single, make recommendations about *abstinence*. If the client is married, both parties will benefit from being counseled together to *resolve difficult relational issues* brought on by the infection and its treatment.

For emotional disorders, especially depression in the context of HIV or AIDS, treatment should be managed by a mental health professional—for example, a psychiatrist, psychologist, professional counselor, or clinical social worker—who is in close communication with the physician providing the HIV/AIDS treatment. This is especially important when antidepressant medication is prescribed so that potentially harmful drug interactions can be avoided. In some cases, a mental health professional who specializes in treating individuals with depression and co-occurring physical illnesses such as HIV/AIDS may be available. People with HIV/AIDS who develop depression, as well as people in treatment for depression who subsequently contract HIV, should make sure to tell any physician they visit about the full range of medications they are taking. Often recovery from depression takes time. Medications for depression may take several weeks to work and may need to be combined with ongoing psychotherapy.

Another member of the treatment team, if possible, should *be a pastor or spiritual advisor who can work closely with both the physician and mental health professional treating the HIV/AIDS sufferer.* A counselor and/or pastor should be prepared to address such issues as relationship with God, life and death, meaning and purpose, and relations with family and friends.

ACTION STEPS 5

1. See a Physician

- HIV/AIDS is a health problem that must be addressed as quickly as possible by a physician. Early diagnosis and treatment are essential.

- Do not let any stigma of shame at the prospect of getting medical treatment keep you from seeing a doctor. Early diagnosis and treatment are essential to successfully fighting the disease.
- Do not neglect your emotions and spiritual needs while being treated for HIV/AIDS. Continue to see your counselor for help and support. You cannot cope with HIV/AIDS alone, and the support of a counselor who understands the nature of the virus is especially important because your friends and family may not have a good understanding.
- *Provide the client with the names of doctors or clinics you trust.*

2. Identify Feelings and Emotions

- Uncover and address any feelings and thoughts you have regarding your diagnosis or the possibility of receiving an HIV diagnosis. Emotions that may exist are fear, guilt, shame, and anger. By opening up with your counselor, you will be able to identify strategies that will help you cope more effectively as God gives you courage and strength. This is not as likely to happen, though, if you're not honest about how you feel.
- Many people fear death and debilitation and feel intense shame and even self-loathing when they find they have HIV/AIDS. Talk honestly with your counselor about these feelings and perceptions and allow her to offer you hope for the future.

3. Ask for Forgiveness and Forgive

- If you contracted the infection from illicit sexual behavior, you will need to experience God's forgiveness, you will need to contact your sex partner to inform her, and if married you will have to face honestly the major repentance/forgiveness issues in your relationship with your spouse. No sin is beyond God's grace and forgiveness, but there are consequences for our decisions.
- If you were unknowingly and innocently infected by someone else, you will need help in being honest about the hurt and anger you feel, as well as in choosing to forgive the one who infected you.
- The process of healing, for both the victim and the victimizer, is a journey. Be patient with the process and take responsibility for your behavior now, no matter who caused your illness.
- God can use every event in our lives for good if we let Him. No matter how the disease was contracted, God will use this to teach you valuable lessons and draw you closer to Him.

BIBLICAL INSIGHTS : 6

This is how God showed his love among us: He sent his one and only Son into the world that we might live through him. This is love: not that we loved God, but that he loved us and sent his Son as an atoning sacrifice for our sins.

1 John 4:9–10

We serve an amazingly merciful God. He gave His only Son as a sacrifice for any sin we will ever commit. As Christians we have been forgiven and set free—no matter what! However, this does not give us permission to live life with no boundaries and solely for self-fulfillment. There are consequences to every choice we make. True and abundant life is found only in living for Christ and His glory.

We also rejoice in our sufferings, because we know that suffering produces perseverance; perseverance, character; and character, hope. And hope does not disappoint us, because God has poured out his love into our hearts by the Holy Spirit, whom he has given us.

Romans 5:3–5

God wants to use everything in our lives—difficulties as well as blessings—to shape us and draw us closer to Him. Even when we are the victims of another's irresponsible behavior, we can trust that God will somehow use it for good in our lives. As we learn to persevere through the trial and continue to live for Him, He will develop strength in our heart and spiritual maturity in our walk through life's journey.

Each heart knows its own bitterness, and no one else can share its joy.

Proverbs 14:10

With such a painful diagnosis as HIV/AIDS, anger can be an easy and sometimes immediate reaction, especially if one innocently contracted the virus from a spouse or another infected person.

Anger that is not expressed leads to bitterness. To battle the feelings of anger, a person must first remember that Christ paid the price for her sin. Then the heart will be overwhelmed with God's grace, and the person can't help but choose to forgive the one who has caused hurt. However, this may take time, and she may not feel loving and warm toward the other person for a while, but forgiveness is a choice she can make even before she is ready to renew a relationship with the person.

AIDS was first reported in the United States in 1981 and has since become a major worldwide epidemic.

In 2007 the estimated number of persons diagnosed with AIDS in the United States and dependent areas was 37,041.

At the end of 2007 the estimated number of persons living with AIDS in the United States and dependent areas was 468,578.

PRAYER STARTER : 7

Father, thank You for Your grace, mercy, and forgiveness. This woman in front of me is in pain today, and I ask that You intervene in the ways You see fit and provide her with peace that only You can give. Help her feel Your presence in the midst of this storm, and may she know that You still love her and have a plan for her life from this day on . . .

8 RECOMMENDED RESOURCES

The Centers for Disease Control and Prevention: www.cdc.gov/std.

The Medical Institute for Sexual Health: www.medinstitute.org.

Stanford, Shane. *When God Disappears: Finding Hope When Your Circumstances Seem Impossible*. Regal, 2008.

HIV/AIDS Treatment Information Service: 800-HIV-0440

National Institute of Allergy and Infectious Diseases (NIAID): 301-496-5717, www .niaid.nih.gov

WebMD: www.webmd.com/sexual-conditions.

Adult Survivors of Sexual Abuse 18

PORTRAITS 1

- Madeline entered college as a dedicated feminist, choosing to go to a women's college in the South. Early on she was attracted to Chloe, and they became lesbian lovers midway through the first semester. When her parents wrote asking about visiting, she wrote back and said she would not see her stepfather, who she claimed had sexually abused her from age twelve to fifteen.

- Brenda had been a dutiful wife and mother for ten years and had borne two children: eight-year-old Tina and five-year-old Tim. Yet when her children began visiting their grandparents, Brenda started having nightmares that would not stop. Her physician sent her to a therapist, and he uncovered the meaning of the nightmares. She was having flashbacks of sexual abuse by her father that she had suppressed completely for all these years. He had started to abuse her when she was eight years old, the same age as Tina.

- Rick looked forward to his marriage with great anticipation, but he could not perform sexually on his wedding night or any night thereafter. He talked to his pastor and unloaded the horrid story of sexual abuse by his uncle that went on for nearly five years. His pastor referred him to a professional Christian counselor after Rick talked about sex as something dirty and unholy.

DEFINITIONS AND KEY THOUGHTS 2

- Fairy tales, ice cream, candy, bike rides, going to the beach, pajama parties—childhood should be filled with such joys. *For those abused as a child, just the mention of childhood days can trigger a host of flashbacks and feelings of disgust.*

- In her book *Counseling Survivors of Sexual Abuse,* Dr. Diane Langberg writes:

  Sexual abuse of a child occurs whenever a child is sexually exploited by an older person for the satisfaction of the abuser's needs. It consists of any sexual activity—verbal, visual, or physical—engaged in without consent. The child is considered unable to consent due to the developmental immaturity and an inability to understand sexual behavior.[1]

- Child sexual abuse became a public issue in the 1970s and 1980s. Prior to this time sexual abuse remained rather secretive, not spoken about in public. *Stud-*

ies on child molestation were nonexistent until the 1920s, and the first national estimate of the number of child sexual abuse cases was published in 1948.[2]

- *No child is psychologically prepared to cope with repeated sexual stimulation.* Even a two- or three-year-old, who cannot know that the sexual activity is wrong, can develop problems resulting from the inability to cope with the overstimulation.[3]

- *The child of five or older who knows and cares for the abuser becomes trapped between affection or loyalty for the person and the sense that the sexual activities are terribly wrong.* If the child tries to break away from the sexual relationship, the abuser may threaten the child with violence or loss of love. When sexual abuse occurs within the family, the child may fear the anger, jealousy, or shame of other family members, or he may be afraid the family will break up if the secret is told.[4]

- The *perpetrator profile*:

    — The perpetrator is the person who *coerces and initiates sexual abuse* on a child.

    — There are *two types of perpetrators*: one type experiences the child whom he abuses as an adult; the other thinks of himself as a child.[5]

    — The first type of perpetrator struggles in maintaining healthy relationships with his peers. He doesn't fit in, feels inadequate, behaves awkwardly. He desires to relate with adults but doesn't know how. As a result, *the child he abuses becomes the pseudo-adult.*

    — The second type of perpetrator *believes that he is still a child* and will therefore engage sexually with someone he perceives to be at the same mental and emotional level.

- Often sexual abuse takes the form of incest. An older family member—father, stepparent, uncle, or older brother—is sexually abusing a minor.[6]

- The *Child Maltreatment Report* in 2002 reported that less than 3 percent of parents committed sexual abuse; however, 28.9 percent was committed by *other relatives*, and 11.2 percent was committed by the *unmarried partner of a parent*. More than one-third of perpetrators were adults in *other types of relationships* to the child victims, including camp counselors, school employees, and hospital staff.[7]

- *Incest survivors tend to be very reluctant to reveal what has occurred.* Many young incest victims are told by the perpetrator that what is happening is a "learning experience" and an older family member does it in every family. *Incest victims may fear they will be disbelieved, blamed, or punished if they tell what has occurred.*

- There is evidence emerging that as many as *one in three incidents of child sexual abuse are not remembered by adults* who experienced them, and that the younger the child was at the time of the abuse, and the closer the relationship to the abuser, the more likely he is not to remember.[8]

ASSESSMENT INTERVIEW 3

Cases of child sexual abuse often end up in court, and many therapists have been attacked legally in recent years for conducting interviews with children that have been judged to be overly directive or suggestive of the defendant's guilt. Therefore, prosecutors have added trained interviewers to their staff who use anatomically correct dolls and conduct indirect interviews with children with mostly open questions.

If there is a chance that your client's case will end up in court, please make a referral for such legally sensitive interviewing to be done elsewhere and inform the courts, lawyers, and anyone else that you intend to interview and work only for therapeutic goals and purposes. Indicate your intention to assert privilege with all your therapeutic communications and case notes.

Interviewing abused children is a unique and legally sensitive art that requires special training and experience. All such cases should be referred to an expert in this area of counseling.

The following assessment is done for therapeutic purposes only and assumes that the interviewee is at least twelve years of age or older.

1. What has happened that has brought you here today?
2. Is this the first time you or your family has sought help?
3. Tell me about your family. How are things going at home?
4. Tell me about your past. Have you had any painful or unusual things happen—even a long time ago? How long did this go on?
5. Can you tell me who was doing this to you? (*If the person is reticent, explain that you need to know if you are to help him, others who might be abused, and the abuser. In addition, if your client is a minor and still in contact with the abuser, immediate reporting action may need to be taken.*)
6. Do you know if others in your home are being abused?
7. What problems are you currently having as a result of what happened? (*Listen to how the abuse has affected the person. No two people are alike in the story or the consequences of sexual abuse. Be aware that sexual abuse victims tend to minimize the impact of the abuse.*)
8. Tell me how you feel about what has happened to you. (*The client needs to have permission to feel his true emotions.*)
9. Do you feel responsible for the abuse? Do you feel responsible for keeping it a secret?
10. What was told to you about what might happen if this secret ever came out? (*Reassure the client that he is not alone and that he is not responsible for the abuse.*)
11. What do you believe about yourself? Are you a mostly good or mostly bad person? (*Uncover unhealthy beliefs that have developed as a result of abuse.*)
12. What do you believe about the person who did these things to you? (*Listen for rationalizations, such as, "He couldn't help it; he was drunk." These defenses have helped the client cope but have also made him less capable of seeing himself as a true victim of abuse.*)

> Incidence of incest between siblings has been reported as 74% of cases being opposite-sex siblings; 26% same sex, with 16% between brothers and 10% between sisters.
>
> *Christine A. Courtois*, Healing the Incest Wound

13. What would you like to have happen as a result of our meeting today? What will help you heal from this?
14. Whom have you told about this? How did that person respond?
15. Where do you think God has been in all of this?

4 WISE COUNSEL

Studies have shown that *one in three girls* is sexually abused before the age of eighteen, and *one in six boys* is sexually abused before the age of eighteen.[9]

The internet has also become an easy and accessible avenue to abuse. Research findings suggest that *one in five children is solicited sexually while on the internet.*[10]

The most important step for every counselor to take in working with clients who have been sexually abused is to *create an environment of safety and trust.* Victims of sexual abuse have been violated in the most demeaning and demoralizing way and thus find it difficult to fully trust anyone. A safe place in which a client can express his innermost pain, shame, and guilt is vital to his ultimate healing.

Therapists who are safe will always

- *speak the truth*—name the abuse as evil and as a manifestation of the heart of the perpetrator, not the victim.
- *be governed by love and patience*, exemplifying the attitude and personhood of Jesus Christ.
- *do safe things*—follow ethical guidelines, maintain appropriate boundaries, adhere to confidentiality.
- *be governed by the needs of the client*, not their own.

> In the United States, 1 in 6 women and 1 in 33 men *reported experiencing an attempted or completed* rape at some time in their lives.
>
> *Centers for Disease Control*

Victims of sexual abuse are vulnerable and deeply wounded. Their abuse has shaped the way they view themselves and their world. It is the responsibility of the counselor to *identify any underlying beliefs that are false and contribute to the client's current emotions and behaviors.*

Feeling understood and believed will be a catalyst to the client's recovery. Often a client presents with feelings of shame and guilt—believing that in some way he is responsible for or deserves the abuse he has suffered. It is likely that this belief system formed when the client disclosed the abuse to others and they reacted in ways that caused the client to feel at fault.

Therapy with survivors of sexual abuse means *working with their vivid and intrusive memories of shaming and often violent acts against them.* Images of a perpetrator can be so frightening and real that the victim cannot sleep. Lies that the perpetrator has told the client and that have been reinforced by the forces of evil are deeply embedded and must be confronted.

Take hope in this—as a Christian counselor, *you have the privilege of accessing the throne of God on behalf of your client to defeat the evil* that was done so that all things might be made new and healed![11]

ACTION STEPS : 5

1. Talk about the Abuse

- The first step to healing is to talk it out. Find someone you trust—a pastor, teacher, or counselor—who is not part of the problem and tell him honestly what has happened. Getting out of an abusive situation requires getting help, and you have taken the first step. You have come to talk.

  — Abuse is treatable and you will be a survivor.
  — You are not responsible for the abuse, only for your recovery.
  — Express, accept, and be prepared to deal with your thoughts, behavior, and feelings (even the irrational ones!).

- *Be careful not to retraumatize the person with your questions about the abuse. Trust and safety are of vital importance. Rule out any suicidal risk, depression, or medical concerns—especially if the abuse was recent. Assess also the nature of and length of the abuse—its degree of severity and its history. Sometimes the person comes seeking help for other problems that actually stem from sexual abuse.*

2. Give Yourself Time to Heal

- Healing from sexual abuse is a long, difficult process, and people vary in the amount of time they require for healing. Don't put yourself on a time line or tell yourself you should "be over this by now."
- *Be sensitive and assess your client's current emotional state and his ability to go further or do more. Praise your client for the courage it takes to seek help, tell his story, and bring what was once in darkness into the light.*

3. Grieve

- You have been violated, and emotive rage and tears are normal and need to be expressed. Allow yourself to experience and process emotion, rather than holding it in.
- *Some clients may go to the opposite, compensatory extreme and be numb, seemingly without any effect at all in the face of their loss. In such cases, don't force clients to cry or feel sad before they are ready. Let yourself feel the necessary pain with them and walk with them to grieve the loss experienced.*

4. Learn to Regain Power

- Begin to learn how to stand up for the abused child within you. Recapture your power, voice, and control that the perpetrator took from you unjustly. Use the power of Jesus, who understands completely your pain as He too suffered unimaginably in His shameful trial and death on the cross.

- Being believed and being able to tell your story of abuse are important first steps. Allow your counselor to help you stand strong, have a voice, and be empowered over the one who has exerted power over you.
- *Some people may want to confront their abuser. Others will not or will be unable to do so until they are stronger. Be sensitive to where your client is in the healing process.*

5. Attend a Support Group

- Healing is a journey. Experts who work with survivors of sexual abuse know the power of empathy and sympathy in the healing process. You do not have to go through this alone. Utilize the expertise and willingness of others to walk with you prayerfully, offering the support you deserve.
- Attending a group for survivors of sexual violence can be a positive healing step. By sharing your story with others who have experienced a similar kind of pain, you can grow as well as help others grow—simultaneously.
- *Be ready to provide a list of referrals to local Christian professionals who have experience in counseling survivors of sexual abuse and incest as well as support groups that meet in your area.*

6. Set Healthy Boundaries

- As an abuse survivor, your personal boundaries were severely violated, which most likely left you with confusion and a lack of knowledge regarding what is healthy and normal. An important step is to establish healthy boundaries and be able to communicate these boundaries in an assertive and positive manner.
- Learn to differentiate between safe and unsafe people and what is appropriate and what is not appropriate regarding physical and verbal interactions with others.

7. Two Advanced Steps

- Try to find meaning in the pain.
- Commit to the process of forgiveness. Forgiveness is a multilayered journey— you will have to make daily decisions to continue to forgive.

Additional notes to the counselor:

- *Continue reassuring your client that healing will take place. Sessions may get tougher as you delve into his past, but encourage him throughout the process to persevere and be strong. Provide praise and encouragement to your client throughout this learning process.*
- *You may need some professional guidance to truly deal with the depth of pain that sexual abuse has caused your client. It is not wrong or a sign of weakness to consult with a counselor who has some expertise in counseling sexual abuse survivors. Be sure to obtain written consent from your client when speaking to third parties.*

BIBLICAL INSIGHTS :6

You intended to harm me, but God intended it for good to accomplish what is now being done, the saving of many lives.

Genesis 50:20

If anyone had good reason for revenge, it was Joseph. His brothers' jealousy provoked them to horrible abuse—selling him as a common slave to be taken away forever (Gen. 37:11–28). Before being raised to power in Egypt, Joseph had lost thirteen years of personal freedom.

Joseph wisely understood that God had overruled his brothers' abuse, making their evil turn out for good. This response of strength and faith can come only from those who trust God to rule—and overrule evil—in their lives.

Do not take revenge, my friends, but leave room for God's wrath, for it is written: "It is mine to avenge; I will repay," says the Lord. . . . Do not be overcome by evil, but overcome evil with good.

Romans 12:19, 21

> Sexual violence is perhaps the most terrifying way one human can harm another, and this is especially tragic when incest occurs.

God knows all that has occurred in our lives, including and especially the pain, the betrayal, and the brokenness. He was present in the darkness and continues to walk with us. The offenses done to us were done to Him as well—including the shame of being disrobed at the cross.

He promises to repay—vengeance is His and His alone. Our job is to heal and to forgive.

Do not let the evil overcome you; do not give the abuser that much power in your life. Overcome the evil by doing good to others and to yourself.

Nothing in all creation is hidden from God's sight. Everything is uncovered and laid bare before the eyes of him to whom we must give account.

Hebrews 4:13

Sometimes people think they can hide portions of their life from everyone. They try to hide angry tempers, deep jealousies, or sexual sin.

Sexual violence hasn't escaped God's notice. The abuser may have thought he got away with it, but God knows. And God promises to judge appropriately.

PRAYER STARTER :7

Oh, God, Your heart breaks when people are hurt so terribly. Thank You for this person who has come for help and healing from You. And thank You, Lord, for Your kindness and strength. Give wisdom and courage as he takes the next steps to be honest about the pain. You never abandon us, and You will help this dear person experience Your love and peace . . .

8 RECOMMENDED RESOURCES

Allender, Dan. *The Wounded Heart Workbook: A Companion Guide for Personal or Group Use.* NavPress, 2008.

Heitritter, Lynn, and Jeanette Vought. *Helping Victims of Sexual Abuse: A Sensitive Biblical Guide for Counselors, Victims, and Families.* Bethany House, 2006.

Langberg, Diane. *Counseling Survivors of Sexual Abuse.* Xulon Press, 2003.

_____. *On the Threshold of Hope.* Tyndale, 1999.

Infidelity and Affairs 19

- Joanne had never had a doubt in her mind about Tom's commitment to their marriage. He held a good job and stayed involved in the kids' lives, coaching soccer on the weekends and doing repairs around the house. With Tom's job change, Joanne began to feel more distance between them. She didn't like where their relationship was headed but couldn't quite put her finger on what was wrong. Tom traveled nearly every week, and when he was at home, he was often tired and disengaged from the family. Joanne tried to write it off as Tom's stressful job, but then she found a credit card statement that detailed hotels and restaurant charges in New York. Those were the dates he had said he was in Detroit on business.

- Amy often struck up small talk while working out at the gym, so when she met Bob, she didn't think twice about their conversation. Over the next few months, Bob and Amy saw each other quite often, and soon they were scheduling their days around working out together at the gym. Amy never mentioned Bob to her husband. She just didn't think he would understand.

- Ever since his high school days, Justin had turned girls' heads with his athletic appearance and sandy brown curls. Justin dated around some, but when he and Dianne got married, he knew he had found his true love. Three years later, with a baby on the way, Justin and Dianne began to experience an emotional disconnect. Often Dianne was tired after a long day at work, and many nights she collapsed into bed directly after dinner. Though Justin tried to understand, he became increasingly frustrated because of Dianne's disinterest in the sexual aspect of their relationship. All he and Dianne talked about was getting ready for the baby, so when a high school friend added him on Facebook, Justin was excited to catch up with her and have someone to talk to. What started as innocent chatting online eventually led to secret calls and emails every day. They both knew their friendship was headed in the wrong direction but tried to tell themselves it must be God's will if it felt so right.

DEFINITIONS AND KEY THOUGHTS 2

- *Adultery* occurs when someone has a *sexual relationship with someone other than his or her spouse.* This relationship may or may not include an emotional connection. *Adultery-of-the-mind*, which Jesus tagged as being just as sinful as behavioral adultery, involves fantasizing about sex with others who aren't your spouse. Often this is the result of involvement with pornography and is usually done as an aid to masturbation, leading to sexual addiction and often raising up a serious emotional and sexual barrier in one's marriage.

- How common is adultery? There are widely contrasting statistics: some say *two out of three married men and 50 percent of married women* have cheated on their spouse. Others believe that only 10 percent of couples experience the betrayal of adultery.[1]

- The influential *Chicago Sex Survey*, which changed the perspective of the prevalence of sexual activity in America, indicated that during the past year, 93.7% of all married partners maintained just one sexual partner (presumably their spouse), while 2.3% had no sex, 3.4% had 2–4 sex partners, and 0.7% had 5 or more partners. Over a 5-year period, 78.6% remained faithful (had one partner), 14.8% had 2–4 partners, 2.6% had 5–10 partners, and 1.6% had 20 or more partners. Across the entire adult life span (from age 18), married people had one partner just 37.1% of the time, 2–4 partners 28% of the time, 5–10 partners 19.4% of the time, 11–20 partners 8.7% of the time, and 21 or more partners 6.8% of the time.[2]

- *Often an affair begins as an emotional relationship, nurtured by emotional strands of connectedness.* This occurs when husband or wife turns to someone outside the marriage for primary emotional support. For example, when a couple is experiencing conflict, hostility, or distancing, and the husband or wife turns to an opposite-sex friend for companionship, support, and sharing of personal matters, an emotional affair has begun. *Very few affairs start sexually.*

- *Why people cheat on their spouse:*

  — Spouses may become involved in affairs because they are exposed to situations for which they are *unprepared* or *have not set wise boundaries.*

  — Many affairs begin gradually as *well-meaning friendships.* The people involved are unaware of how the relationship is changing until significant sexual behavior occurs.

  — Infidelity can also be traced to emotional deprivation in childhood, in which a person has a *constant hunger for approval and attention.* For example, if the wife cannot fulfill her husband's need for approval, he will feel cheated and let down and may seek the attention of another woman.

  — Many adulterers think they are looking for love when in fact they are seeking to *feel better about themselves.*

  — A person may be unfaithful as an act of *retaliation and anger* against her spouse (whether consciously or unconsciously).

  — As money and positions of power increase, people may experience a *sense of entitlement* to life's pleasures, including the expectation of fulfilling all their sexual desires.

— *Poor communication, unresolved conflict, and/or unrealistic expectations* leading to marital dissatisfaction are also reasons for extramarital affairs. A perceived need that goes unfulfilled in marriage may be sought elsewhere. Yet it is also true that very few affairs begin because one is desperate for sex.

— Ultimately, adultery is a *self-centered choice.* A person intentionally ignores the needs of her spouse and family and the commandments of God to satisfy her selfish desires. At its root, adultery is a *lifestyle of deception.*

ASSESSMENT INTERVIEW :3

For the Faithful Spouse

1. How did you find out about the infidelity?
2. How long have you known? What have you done about it so far?
3. In light of this information, what do you feel you need to know and do right now?
4. What feelings has this stirred up for you? (*It is not uncommon for the person to feel a variety of emotions from resentment to sadness.*)
5. What do you want to do about your relationship with your spouse?
6. Is she still seeing the other person?

For the Unfaithful Spouse

1. Have you told your spouse?
2. What prompts you to want to discuss this now?
3. Do you want to restore your marriage? (*It is not uncommon for the offending spouse to feel confused as to what she wants to do, especially if the affair was long-standing and/or involved a deep emotional commitment.*)

If the Unfaithful Spouse Wants to Restore the Marriage

1. Are you willing to completely cut off all ties to the third party? (*This is the most significant question. You will be able to tell a lot by how the person replies. Is there hesitation? Does she avoid eye contact?*)
2. Do you desire to explore the reasons that perpetuated the affair?
3. Are you aware of the needs you have that you were seeking to meet through this relationship?
4. What do you see are the effects of your affair on your spouse?
5. Are you willing to take full responsibility for your actions without placing any blame on your spouse?
6. Are you committed to being accountable for your time and relationships on a daily basis?
7. Are you willing to pursue professional counseling?

4 : WISE COUNSEL

Forgiveness, rebuilding trust, and restoration are possible after infidelity. Increasing numbers of couples are braving the path of *healing and restoration* of their marriages. To begin the healing process, both spouses will need to do the following:

- *Stabilize the marital crisis and set appropriate boundaries* for the marriage and against any further involvement with the third party. Chaos may be the norm after the revelation of any affair, and chaos can easily lead to hasty and foolish decision making by either or both spouses. It is essential to help them stabilize their current relationship (whether together or separated) and set clear boundaries for time together as a couple and for ending the illicit affair.
- *Understand what caused the infidelity in the marriage.* This will require a long, thoughtful look at the marital pattern that has developed, as well as what each person has contributed to the marital breakdown. Difficult though it is, each spouse *should focus on his or her own issues as opposed to criticizing and blaming* the other person for the problem of infidelity.
- *Rebuild trust in each other* by telling each other the truth and by being accountable to each other. It is vital for each person to keep his or her word. If one spouse promises to do something, she needs to follow through and do it. Finally, trust can be rebuilt by using gestures of affection and nonsexual touch to express caring and affirmation.
- *Take time for restoring and enriching the marriage.* The restoration process *involves identifying and reestablishing what was healthy* about the marriage before the adultery. The enriching process involves learning and implementing new skills and behaviors to strengthen the relationship.

Counseling the Faithful Spouse

Dr. Elisabeth Kübler-Ross has outlined a *normal process of grieving* that occurs when someone has been deeply wounded. Normally grief involves several stages, which operate more or less cyclically.[3] They include:

- *Shock and denial.* "No, not me!" In the initial stage, the wounded spouse is unwilling to accept the reality of her spouse's unfaithfulness. She may blatantly deny facts presented about her spouse's activities.
- *Anger.* "Why me?" In this stage, the person is aware of being violated and hurt and may express deep resentment and/or rage toward the unfaithful spouse.
- *Bargaining.* "If I do this, you'll do that." The person wants to see changes in behavior as an avenue for avoiding further pain. For example, she says, "If you stay, I'll change," rather than addressing the deeper implications of the infidelity.
- *Depression.* "It really happened." During this stage the person realizes the full impact of infidelity on the marriage and mourns the loss of what the relationship once was. The wounded spouse realizes she will need to make a decision about the future of the relationship.

• *Acceptance.* "This is what happened." The wounded spouse has come to terms with all of the implications of the unfaithful spouse's actions and is willing to move forward. In this stage, valuable lessons are recognized, learned, and internalized.

These stages *can be experienced rapidly* within a few hours, or more normally, *in days or months*, depending on the individual. You need to *evaluate which stage the person is currently experiencing* and be sensitive so that you can gently encourage her to work through that stage. *Note*: The stages of grieving may be experienced out of order or several at once, and a person may repeat these stages many times.

Encourage the person to *avoid making any immediate, long-term decisions.* It is not uncommon for a hurt spouse to have feelings of wanting to end the marriage because the task of rebuilding the relationship may seem to take too much energy. *Separation*, especially if the affair has been going on for a long time, *may allow both parties time and emotional space* to process feelings and clarify the situation. The goal of separation is to have the couple *begin to build a friendship* and reestablish trust.

Counseling the Unfaithful Spouse

Require disclosure of the steps leading up to the affair, including the major aspects of the relationship and any information that was kept hidden. Be careful in the disclosure process, however. Too much information—revealing the graphic details of the affair, which either one or both parties may secretly wish to do for various illicit reasons—may do more harm than good.

Remind the person that *there will be a "withdrawal" factor* as she breaks off any connection with the third party. She will need to *begin a lifestyle of accounting for all of her time* to begin to rebuild trust.

She needs to *reengage emotionally with her spouse* by spending as much time as possible with him. Healing and restoration *will take time*. Developing new patterns and a commitment to learn about oneself and one's spouse on a deeper level will be involved in the healing process.

Seeking forgiveness also involves restoration and a deeper commitment to love and honor her spouse than has been previously given.

The couple will need to work with their pastor and/or a professional counselor who can help them *evaluate the communication and relational patterns* that may have contributed to the affair.

ACTION STEPS 5

1. Pray

Seek daily time before God in prayer, reading the Scriptures, and asking Him for the ability to grow in Christlike attitudes and actions. Only He can give you the grace to forgive and the power to say no to sin.

2. Have No Contact

The unfaithful spouse must agree to have no contact whatsoever with the third party. Like any addiction, the only way out is to immediately end the behavior and begin the detoxification process.

3. Make a Commitment

The unfaithful spouse must be willing to make a radical commitment to regain the trust that has been broken.

4. Begin a New Lifestyle

The unfaithful spouse must commit to a lifestyle of transparency and honesty, with no area off-limits for inquiry. Seek the support of a friend or pastor to hold you accountable.

5. Forgive

The faithful spouse must commit to the process of forgiveness. Forgiveness is an act and a process—you will have to make daily decisions to continue to forgive.

6. Work on Reconciliation

Forgiveness is required, but reconciliation is conditional. Reconciliation is based on true remorse and repentance. While the Bible never commands divorce because of unfaithfulness and many couples do stay together and eventually grow a stronger marriage, some couples may never be able to work through the brokenness if the unfaithful spouse is not repentant.

6 BIBLICAL INSIGHTS

Drink water from your own cistern, running water from your own well.
Proverbs 5:15

This beautiful metaphor describes the joy of marital fidelity. To "drink water from your own cistern" pictures the marriage partners belonging only to each other, enraptured with each other's love.

By contrast, to become enraptured by another, to turn to adultery, may feel exciting at first but will end up being "bitter as wormwood, sharp as a two-edged sword" (Prov. 5:4 NKJV).

God's Word clearly teaches that married people should keep their vows and remain committed to each other.

May your fountain be blessed, and may you rejoice in the wife of your youth. A loving doe, a graceful deer—may her breasts satisfy you always, may you ever be captivated by her love. Why be captivated, my son, by an adulteress? Why embrace the bosom of another man's wife? For a man's ways are in full view of the LORD, and he examines all his paths. The evil deeds of a wicked man ensnare him; the cords of his sin hold him fast.

Proverbs 5:18–22

The Bible does not speak against sexual fulfillment—in fact, sexual delight and marital love are exalted in the Song of Solomon. Sexual fulfillment is always depicted in the Bible as within the boundaries of marriage.

Sexual sin can be very appealing, almost an overwhelming temptation, but adultery is a great tragedy, for it has severe consequences. People risk everything they have built over a lifetime—marriage, family, ministry, respect, and honor—when they commit adultery.

Married couples can rejoice in their marriage and be satisfied with one another's love (Prov. 5:18–19). To violate that commitment will lead to pain, grief, and self-destruction.

Later I passed by, and when I looked at you and saw that you were old enough for love, I spread the corner of my garment over you and covered your nakedness. I gave you my solemn oath and entered into a covenant with you, declares the Sovereign LORD, and you became mine.

Ezekiel 16:8

We can find great comfort in the fact that our heavenly Father can empathize with the pain of someone who has been betrayed by a loved one. Knowing that He understands can help us trust Him in our own hurt and pain.

You have heard that it was said, "Do not commit adultery."
Matthew 5:27

Quoting from Exodus 20:14, Jesus reminded His listeners of the commandment against adultery. Then He said that looking at another person lustfully is committing adultery in one's heart. Jesus explained that thinking about an act is the same as doing it, because actions begin with thoughts and desires.

Since lust and adultery are first embraced in the mind and heart, believers should try to avoid situations that cause temptation.

[Solomon] had seven hundred wives, princesses, and three hundred concubines, and his wives turned his heart away.

1 Kings 11:3 NASB

Though he was considered the wisest man to ever live, even Solomon could not keep his heart focused on what mattered most, his relationship with God. As was the case with Solomon, our affections will never stay focused on one relationship when others are competing for it.

Jesus used the analogy of marriage to describe His relationship with the church for a reason. When we turn our hearts to idols, we commit adultery in our relationship with Him. Even when our relationships are at their worst, we need to start by turning our affections back to the relationship rather than to someone else, because no man or woman will ever meet our heart's deepest longing for intimacy and connection.

7 PRAYER STARTER

Dear Lord, there is much pain here today. Hurt and betrayal are affecting this marriage. You have promised, Lord, that You are close to the brokenhearted and will bind up their wounds. You are the Healer, the Restorer. We ask for Your guidance in this painful situation . . .

8 RECOMMENDED RESOURCES

Arterburn, Stephen, Fred Stoeker, and Mike Yorkey. *Every Heart Restored: A Wife's Guide to Healing in the Wake of a Husband's Sexual Sin.* WaterBrook, 2004.

Carder, Dave. *Torn Asunder: Recovering from Extramarital Affairs.* Moody, 2008.

Dobson, James. *Love Must Be Tough.* Tyndale, 2007.

Harvey, Donald R. *Surviving Betrayal: Counseling an Adulterous Marriage.* Baker, 1995.

Laaser, Debra. *Shattered Vows: Hope and Healing for Women Who Have Been Sexually Betrayed.* Zondervan, 2008.

Laaser, Mark. *Healing the Wounds of Sexual Addiction.* Zondervan, 2004.

Spring, Janis Abrahms, and Michael Spring. *After the Affair: Healing the Pain and Rebuilding the Trust When a Partner Has Been Unfaithful.* Harper Paperbacks, 2007; not written from a Christian perspective.

Vernick, Leslie. *How to Act Right When Your Spouse Acts Wrong.* WaterBrook, 2009.

Forgiveness and **20**
Rebuilding Trust

PORTRAITS **1**

- When Rachel and Dan got married, neither of them had any idea how Rachel's experiences in a broken home would affect their marriage. Dan is certainly not perfect, but he's a man of kindness and integrity—the kind of man most women dream of marrying. But Rachel never seemed to be able to truly trust him. She harbored doubts about his intentions, his past relationships, and many of his current choices. Her suspicion was usually hidden just under the surface, but it surfaced often enough to drive Dan crazy.

- Marsha had been sexually abused by her father and her uncle for several years. When she went to high school, they finally stopped, and she never told anyone about it. Then she and Bart married, and their sex life was "bipolar"—sometimes hot and passionate but sometimes ice cold. Bart knew something was wrong, and he asked Marsha a few questions when she cried uncontrollably for no apparent reason. Finally, she broke down and told him the truth about her past and her difficulty in trusting men.

- Both Mandy and Jeremy had experienced many sexual partners before they were married, but they were sure they'd found their true love in each other. For a while things seemed to go very well in their relationship, but they both realized they could never talk about anyone of the opposite sex without getting reactions of anger, jealousy, and suspicion. Their fears dominated their relationship, and joyful, uninhibited sex was replaced by destructive imagination during sex with each other.

DEFINITIONS AND KEY THOUGHTS **2**

- *Trust is the most important ingredient in any relationship*, but it can be very fragile. It takes time to build yet can be destroyed in an instant. It is, however, the glue of any meaningful connection with another person. *Trust is always a two-way street*: it involves being vulnerable to another person yet also being trustworthy so that the other person has good reason to extend his trust.

- Forgiveness is the foundation for rebuilding trust in a relationship that's been broken. The Oxford English dictionary *defines forgiveness as granting free pardon and giving up all claim on account of an offense or debt*. Keep in mind, when a person chooses to forgive, it doesn't mean he is letting the offender "off the hook."

To forgive in no way means that the hurtful behavior is accepted and feelings of pain no longer exist. *Forgiveness means that the victim is choosing not to allow the hurt and pain to control or dominate his life.*

- People who have experienced trauma, abuse, and infidelity will need *time to work through their pain* and come to a place where they are ready to forgive. This is a journey one must take to be free. *God's Word teaches us how to forgive* through example and describes the *ultimate act of unconditional forgiveness* when Christ died on the cross for our sins. It is an example that we can follow in our own day-to-day relationships.

- Though secrecy prevents accurate statistics, it is estimated that:

  — *22 percent of married men have strayed* at least once during their married lives.

  — *14 percent of married women have had affairs* at least once during their married lives.

  — *Younger people are more likely candidates* to be unfaithful; younger women are as likely as younger men to be unfaithful.

  — 70 percent of married women and 54 percent of married men *did not know of their spouse's extramarital activity.*

  — *17 percent of divorces* in the United States are caused by infidelity.[1]

- *Trust is always earned.* Anyone who demands that others trust him without showing any trustworthy behavior or is accusatory without cause usually isn't trustworthy.

- Like trust, *a pattern of distrust develops over a period of time* and through many different painful relationships. *This pattern isn't easily changed.* For example, children instinctively trust their parents, but if parents are abusive, smothering, or absent, the child learns that home and life itself aren't safe. He may respond in extremes: by never extending trust to anyone or by being too trusting of all—even with untrustworthy people. His relationships are either enmeshed and absorbing or distant and aloof. If a person has had serial absorbing, smothering, codependent relationships in which he trusted people too much, he may come to a point of giving up and retreating emotionally, refusing to trust anybody again.

- Without trust, *people feel the need to control* themselves, other people, and any perceived threat in their environment. The methods of control vary widely: demands, anger, self-pity, frenetic action, giving in, running away, acting superior, and so on. And when it comes to healthy sexuality, without a safe, trusting relationship, sex easily becomes manipulative and self-absorbed, not something done to please a spouse.

- Learning to forgive and rebuild trust takes *time, intention, and courage.* People have to grasp their part in the problem, either as one who hasn't proven to be trustworthy enough or as one who is afraid to take risks and trust the one who has proven to be trustworthy. They need to identify small steps of progress and celebrate each one.

ASSESSMENT INTERVIEW :3

1. How is distrust affecting your relationship(s) (communication, respect, sex, and so on)?
2. What might be the root cause for your lack of trust?
3. When did the problem start? When did it begin to affect your relationship(s)?
4. When you look back over your life, what patterns of trust do you see—such as being wise about knowing whom to trust, trusting untrustworthy people, or refusing to trust even those who have done plenty to earn your trust?
5. What are some characteristics in people who are honorable and trustworthy? With these characteristics in mind, can you identify any trustworthy people in your life?
6. What honorable and trustworthy characteristics do you possess?
7. What would help you learn to trust again? (*See the first Action Step to encourage your client to learn to trust.*)

WISE COUNSEL :4

Whether we identify it in this way or not, trust is clearly *the most important factor in helping couples and individuals* build strong, lasting, loving relationships. With it, couples feel safe with each other, and they communicate what's in their heart, resolve problems, and enjoy every aspect of their relationship, including their sex life in marriage. But without it, every interaction becomes a manipulative dance to control the other person's behavior.

Help each person grasp the *"trust contract"* in which there is a trustworthy person and another who considers the person trustworthy and is willing to take the risk to trust. For a relationship to work, *both must be trustworthy and both must be willing and able to take risks to trust the other.*

Determine *long-term trust patterns*, going back to childhood, to uncover tendencies of perception, blind trust, demanding trust, or refusing to trust even trustworthy people. This history of mistrust almost certainly is playing a role in the present relational problems. In addition to family of origin trust patterns, look for experiences of premarital sex, adultery, and any nonsexual betrayal that plague the relationship.

A couple needs to *clearly identify the pattern of trust or mistrust* in the history of their relationship. Usually the current problems aren't new and different. In most cases they are a continuation of past mistrust that has, for whatever reason, mushroomed into a bigger problem. Often the ability to identify patterns of trust and distrust *puts fresh handles on a relationship* and brings new hope for progress. Teach the *skills of honest communication, attentive listening, and clarifying feedback* so they learn how to make progress on their own.

Trust must be earned. If a person *demands to be trusted*, it further erodes the bond between him and those with whom he wishes to relate.

Whether the distrust was caused by childhood abuse, abandonment, or recent betrayal, virtually *every relationship can be restored* through forgiveness, asking to be forgiven, grieving to heal wounds, perception to see things as they really are, and courage to move forward in the relationship. *The process of healing, though, takes time and attention,* just as it takes time and expert medical care to heal a badly broken bone.

Many people who can't trust others don't trust themselves. We should teach couples to trust God, trust their own intuition, and trust others.

5 ACTION STEPS

1. Discuss Your Current Level of Trust

- Evaluate your life and begin to identify areas that need improvement—pay special attention to areas related to trust issues. Be open to sharing with your counselor times you have been betrayed and hurt.
- The nature of trust requires two people: a trustworthy person and one who will take the risk to trust.
- Trusting does not happen overnight. A good analogy is the creation of a beautiful piece of pottery. It takes time, energy, precision, and effort to form the clay. However, if the pottery is dropped, it crashes to the floor in tiny pieces. Remaking it takes time. Like broken pottery, trust is cultivated over time. Start with baby steps:

  — Give yourself enough emotional and physical space to feel safe again.
  — Learn to communicate when you are not feeling safe and what you need from your spouse to feel safe again in those moments.
  — Don't allow issues to go unresolved or your emotions to be minimized.
  — Accept your spouse for who she is and don't set your expectations too high.

2. Discuss Family History

- Focus on your family history to identify patterns of trust and mistrust that have developed over your lifetime. First, think about your immediate family members and then branch out to include familial patterns passed down through generations.
- When you build or restore your ability to trust, you can hope to have more meaningful relationships with family members, and you can stop the distrust cycle in your own generation.
- As a married couple, consider incidents of premarital sex and adultery as times when trust was eroded or shattered in your marriage. Also explore the possibility that factors other than sexual indiscretions may have created distrust, things like poor handling of money, rage, avoiding responsibility, addictions, and so on.
- By building or restoring trust, you can have a stronger, more relaxed, less suspicious, and more meaningful life together. By trusting each other, you will enhance your sex life because you won't use it to manipulate each other, only to please each other.

- *It is most critical here to be sensitive to the fact that, due to abuse or abandonment, one or the other spouse may have no real experience with trust. This person may need counseling and some serious spiritual growth before he can come to a place of deeply trusting God or his spouse.*

3. Learn to Forgive

- Take responsibility for feelings, thoughts, attitudes, and actions. Learn to forgive those who have betrayed you and ask people you hurt to forgive you.
- *Forgiveness may take time, but it is essential. Help your client understand God's plan of forgiveness. Use the example of Christ, the father and his prodigal son, and the teachings in Matthew 18. In follow-up appointments, monitor his progress in communicating honestly, listening intently, and taking steps forward to build on any trustworthy trait he currently possesses as well as new traits that are developing.*

BIBLICAL INSIGHTS 6

This is love: not that we loved God, but that he loved us and sent his Son as an atoning sacrifice for our sins. Dear friends, since God so loved us, we also ought to love one another.

1 John 4:10–11

The Scriptures command us to love each other, but trust is different. Whenever trust is mentioned in the Bible, it is applied to our trust in God. Love can be given even if the person is unworthy of it, but trust in relation to others must be earned. In relationships, this means we always want the best for the other person, but until and unless he has proven he is trustworthy, the safe response is to guard our heart and innermost being until we can confirm trustworthiness.

May the God who gives endurance and encouragement give you a spirit of unity among yourselves as you follow Christ Jesus, so that with one heart and mouth you may glorify the God and Father of our Lord Jesus Christ. Accept one another, then, just as Christ accepted you, in order to bring praise to God.

Romans 15:5–7

A "spirit of unity" is a gift from God to be cherished and protected. It doesn't just happen, and we can't force it to develop. This kind of unity happens when people have proven to be honorable, gracious, and wise so that they trust each other. This occurs in the body of Christ when people focus on Christ, and it happens even more in marriage where the bond is spiritual, relational, emotional, and one-flesh sexual.

Do not let any unwholesome talk come out of your mouths, but only what is helpful for building others up according to their needs, that it may benefit those who listen. And do not grieve the Holy Spirit of God, with whom you were sealed for the day of redemption. Get rid of all bitterness, rage and anger, brawling and slander, along with every form of malice. Be kind and compassionate to one another, forgiving each other, just as in Christ God forgave you.

Ephesians 4:29–32

We grieve the Holy Spirit when we lash out at one another, blame each other, and vent our anger to intimidate others. Paul instructs us to make a choice to get rid of all of that anger and replace it with kindness and forgiveness—the traits that build trust in relationships.

Let the peace of Christ rule in your hearts, since as members of one body you were called to peace. And be thankful.

Colossians 3:15

Christian couples and individuals don't have to face the difficulties of trusting others by themselves. Christ is with them, and in fact He is in them. As people trust increasingly in Christ's love, acceptance, and strength, they sense Christ's presence, and His peace fills their hearts. Even in the process of rebuilding trust, long before the process is finished, we can experience God's presence and peace as we walk with Him. And as we build a strong foundation of trust in relationships, we can relax and enjoy each other in every way.

7 PRAYER STARTER

Father, my friends are here because they want their relationship to be the best it can be—and what You want it to be. They've come because they have difficulties trusting and they need Your help to learn to trust wisely. Help them be honorable and trustworthy, and help them have the courage to take appropriate risks to trust again . . .

8 RECOMMENDED RESOURCES

Arthur, Kay. *40 Minute Studies: Forgiveness.* WaterBrook, 2007.

Clinton, Tim, and Gary Sibcy. *Why You Do the Things You Do.* Thomas Nelson, 2006.

DeMoss, Nancy Leigh. *Choosing Forgiveness: Your Journey to Freedom.* Moody, 2006.

Glass, Shirley, and Jean Staeheli. *Not Just Friends: Rebuilding Trust and Recovering Your Sanity after Infidelity.* Free Press, 2006.

Kendall, R. T. *Total Forgiveness.* Charisma House, 2007.

MacArthur, John. *The Freedom and Power of Forgiveness.* Crossway Books, 2009.

Stanley, Charles. *The Gift of Forgiveness.* Thomas Nelson, 2002.

Worthington, Everett. *Forgiving and Reconciling: Bridges to Wholeness and Hope.* InterVarsity Press, 2003.

_____. *The Power of Forgiving.* Templeton Foundation Press, 2005.

PART 3

Sexual Addiction and Deviance

21 Sex and Romance Addiction

1 PORTRAITS

- After John kissed his two children good night and shared a glass of wine with his wife before she retired, he moved to his basement computer and logged on to one of the many porn sites that gobbled up hundreds of dollars each month from his dwindling business bank account. Since he did internet trading around the world, he had the perfect alibi for his wife, who had no idea of the masturbatory sex her husband zoned in on every night and the tens of thousands of dollars he had paid these many sites over the past couple of years.

- Cindy could hardly believe the predicament she was in. At her ten-year high school reunion, she had reunited with her old sweetheart. They were both in troubled marriages and were there without their spouses. One flaming night of sex resurfaced old feelings and recalled the wild times they had enjoyed together in high school. They met two other times that year for sex, and now her former boyfriend was leaving his wife and threatening to move to Cindy's town. She had to talk to someone about the panic she felt about his increasing compulsions and obsessive behavior. It was beginning to feel a lot like stalking.

2 DEFINITIONS AND KEY THOUGHTS

- Romance addiction, sex addiction, midday soaps, love affair movies on Lifetime, the latest novel by Danielle Steele, late-night shows on HBO, Showtime, or Cinemax. *It is clear—love and sex sell.* With a society so sexually obsessed and sex saturated, the opportunity for addiction abounds.

- An addiction is *a physical* (as to alcohol or most other drugs) *or psychological* (as to sex or gambling or shopping) *compulsion* to use a substance or activity *to cope with everyday life.* For example, without alcohol or access to a sexual partner or website, the addict does not feel "normal" and cannot function well.

- The *misuse of sexual behavior* that becomes habitual with the purpose of changing (ostensibly for improving) one's mood or psychological state classifies as an addiction to sex and/or romance. *Persons use and abuse their sexual behaviors to forget their pains or anxieties.* Substance abuse may often be combined with addictive sexual behavior, commonly referred to as co- or poly-addiction.

- An addiction is also a repetitive, compulsive behavior that is *difficult or seemingly impossible to control.* It leads to activity that is designed solely to *obtain the substance or access to the behavior and to cover up its use*—the housewife hiding her sex chat rooms on her computer, the drug addict shoplifting to support the habit, the gambler embezzling to pay off debts. Characterized by the *defense mechanisms of denial, minimization, and blame-shifting*, the addict attributes her problems to someone else or some difficult situation—the boss is too difficult or the job is too stressful, the spouse isn't affectionate enough, the kids are disobedient, or the friends are too persuasive. The addict refuses to take responsibility for her behavior and to admit the seriousness of the problem.

- *Sex addiction is the bio-psycho-social dependence* on a habitual sexual behavior—such as internet porn, sadistic or masochistic behaviors, masturbation, or a relationship with a lover. Over time the body and the brain need the sexually arousing behavior in ever-increasing amounts to cope minimally and stave off the symptoms of withdrawal.

Key Characteristics

- Mood swings are often present.
- Increasing use or pattern of behavior develops over time.
- Feelings of shame or worthlessness increase.
- There is a strong need to be liked or receive approval from others.
- Impulse control problems—especially with food, sex, drugs, or money—are common.
- The substance or behavior is used to raise a depressed mood or to reduce anxiety.
- Obsessing about the substance or behavior is common.
- Unmanageability of the addiction increases.
- Guilt, shame, fear, and anger increase.
- Efforts to control the addiction have failed.
- The addiction has caused negative consequences to self and others.

Causes of Addiction

- *Emotional.* Addicts are emotionally wounded, often experiencing severe trauma in childhood. One study of sex addicts found 81 percent to be sexually abused, 74 percent physically abused, and 97 percent emotionally abused.[1]
- *Relational.* Addictive behaviors are positively related to troublesome early life relationships. For adults, addiction causes stress in interpersonal relationships—especially marriage and family life—and leads to many social difficulties.
- *Physical.* Addicts become physically dependent on their substances or behavior of abuse, experiencing withdrawal without them.
- *Cognitive and behavioral.* Often addicts have illogical or irrational thoughts that cause them to forget their identity as children of God. Unrealistic expectations for themselves and others and reliance on quick and magical solutions are also common.

- *Spiritual.* At its core addiction is rebellion against God. In addition, whether it is drugs, alcohol, or sex, the addiction becomes a false idol to the addict. Giving up this reliant idolatry is one of the most difficult and long-term struggles for the addict.

3 ASSESSMENT INTERVIEW

Remember that a key characteristic of addiction is denial. The behavior is never an issue for the addict. Breaking down this denial is part of your job in your assessment. When interviewing the addict, focus on asking concrete questions about circumstances, events, and symptoms. If questions are asked in a nonthreatening and nonjudgmental fashion, the counselee should respond fairly honestly. If speaking with a family member, reframe these questions and ask them about the addict.

Rule-Out Questions

1. Has your use of sex to cope with life and/or obsession with romance increased or decreased over the years? Has there ever been a time when you were free of this use? Do you mix sexuality with other drugs or behaviors to keep enjoying the high it gives you? (*Tolerance, or the need for increasing amounts of the substance or behavior, is a key factor in distinguishing between a problem and a dependency. Also, you want to assess strengths, including family strengths, and find reasons for reliance on current treatment by finding out about past periods of freedom from the addiction.*)
2. Have you ever experienced a time when you did not remember what you did while engaging in sexual escape? Have you ever experienced anxiety, panic attacks, shakes, or hallucinations after not engaging in sexual practices for a while?
3. Have you ever been treated for or received counseling for this problem or for anything else? (*This is asked to assess severity of the addiction and success or failure of prior treatment, and to assess whether a mental disorder or dual disorder is at the root of the problem.*)
4. Has anyone in your family ever been hurt by your sexual behaviors or said anything to you about your being obsessed with sex and/or romance? If so, why do you think the person said that?
5. Is your spouse threatening to leave you?
6. Are you in any legal trouble as a result of your addiction? (*This is to assess the need for family help, crisis intervention, or legal referral.*)

General Questions

1. Have you ever been concerned about an addiction to sex and/or romance? If you saw that your best friend or spouse showed the same level of interest in sex and/or romance that you have, would you consider it a problem? What would you say to him or her?

2. How often do you engage in addictive sexuality or fantasize about romantic encounters?
3. Have you ever done anything while engaging in addictive sex that you later regretted?
4. Did anyone in your family of origin use sex or a substance in excess while you were growing up? Who was that? What did the person do? Did she ever break free of it? Do you remember how you felt when you saw the person in her addicted state?
5. Has your use of addictive sex and/or romance ever affected your job or your family? What happened?
6. Have you ever quit or tried to quit? How long did this last? What happened when you quit? How did you feel? How did others respond to you? What would it take now for you to quit?
7. Do you want to quit for good? If "for good" is too impossible to contemplate, how long are you willing to commit to staying sexually pure? What will/should happen if you relapse again?
8. How do you see your life improving without a sex and/or romance addiction? How will your relationships improve if you quit?
9. Do you believe that God can be a resource to turn to for strength in this struggle? How has He helped you experience freedom from sin in the past? Are you willing to do what it takes to break free now?

> **Some Causes of Sexual Addiction**
>
> - emotional wounds
> - troublesome relationships
> - dependency on behavior of abuse
> - irrational thoughts
> - unrealistic expectations
> - rebellion against God

WISE COUNSEL 4

The effects of addiction include the following:

Unmanageability. The dependency of addicts on their addiction is out of their control. They cannot manage it without help.

Neuro-chemical tolerance. God designed our bodies to adapt to what is presented to them. Therefore, addicts experience tolerance—their bodies need increasing amounts of a chemical or a behavior to procure the same effect.

Progression (often to poly-addiction). Many addicts begin by simply experimenting—trying out a drug, going to a casino, taking a puff on a cigarette, viewing porn in a magazine. However, because more of a chemical or a behavior is needed to achieve an effect, the addict will increase addictive actions in strength or frequency, eventually shifting to combining and mixing various addictive behaviors.

Feeling avoidance. The addiction is used to improve the addict's emotional or psychological state—it is a way of avoiding such feelings as loneliness, anxiety, anger, sorrow, and depression.

Negative consequences. Estrangement from God, the manifestation of habitual sin, poor health issues, chronic pain, and social and interpersonal problems are all consequences common to addiction.

Addicts need *hope and encouragement* to overcome their addiction and to know that *Christ is stronger than what pulls them down*. Have them memorize and recite biblical passages of hope and strength in God so they can recall them in the difficult times of temptation.

In addition to the Biblical Insights section of this chapter, review Psalm 44:21; 51; 1 Corinthians 6:19–20; Ephesians 5:18; and Hebrews 10:22–25 so you can use them to encourage your client. Advise her to meditate on the truth of God's Word, which will fill her mind and lead to everlasting freedom and healing.

5 : ACTION STEPS

1. Repent and Seek God's Forgiveness

- As you work through the counseling process, you will begin to see how the sinful nature can rage out of control if you are unable to recognize temptation. Sin is powerful and Satan seeks to destroy your life. Begin to take control; ask for God's forgiveness and strength to stand against temptation. He will answer and provide a way of escape to freedom in Christ!

- You may need to evaluate your relationships and assess the need to ask for the forgiveness of others in your life.

2. Be Accountable

- Make a commitment to God and the counseling process to remain consistent in attending sessions and living free of sexual sin and addiction. It would also be beneficial to write down your goals and commitment for both you and your counselor to keep as a reminder of your new vows.

- *Help your client commit to some form of accountability, at the most serious level she is willing. If she will sign a contract with you, she is serious about change.*

3. Pursue Regular Counseling

- Participate in ongoing individual counseling to begin to discover the underlying issues that perpetuate the addiction cycle in your life. Stay consistent in attendance and keep in mind that sessions may become harder before things get better. However, healing will begin to happen as you learn more positive ways of coping with life.

4. Consider Group Therapy

- Consider attending group treatment or a local support group. In a group setting, you will gain great insight and support from others who struggle with similar issues. It will help you know that you are not alone in this battle for sexual purity.

Let us draw near to God with a sincere heart in full assurance of faith, having our hearts sprinkled to cleanse us from a guilty conscience and having our bodies washed with pure water.

Hebrews 10:22

- Take a look at www.everymansbattle.com or call 800-New-Hope to locate any sexual integrity support groups that meet in your local area so you can provide a referral for your client.

BIBLICAL INSIGHTS 6

Now those who belong to Christ Jesus have crucified the flesh with its passions and desires. If we live by the Spirit, let us also walk by the Spirit.

Galatians 5:24–25 NASB

God offers hope to the addict. God wants to free His people from anything that takes His rightful place in their lives. He wants to show them that He can meet all their needs. With God's help and their accountability to compassionate believers, addicts can be set free! But it takes time, energy, determination, and accountability. Ephesians 4:19 says, "Having lost all sensitivity, they have given themselves over to sensuality so as to indulge in every kind of impurity, with a continual lust for more." Being led by the Holy Spirit, an addict can be victorious over the sin of sexual addiction. However, it takes serious discipline to stop engaging in the sexual acts that "desensitize" one from truly walking by the Spirit.

All things are lawful for me, but all things are not helpful. All things are lawful for me, but I will not be brought under the power of any.

1 Corinthians 6:12 NKJV

God gave people all things to enjoy, but Satan works tirelessly to take God's blessings and twist them into evil. Believers are allowed to enjoy many things, as long as Scripture does not forbid them. But they must never allow themselves to be controlled or "brought under the power of any."

Therefore put to death your members which are on the earth: fornication, uncleanness, passion, evil desire, and covetousness, which is idolatry. Because of these things the wrath of God is coming upon the sons of disobedience.

Colossians 3:5–6 NKJV

These verses describe some of those sinful desires that believers should "put to death." Sexual sins, evil desires, and covetousness (a form of idolatry) should have no place in a believer's heart. It takes a conscious daily decision to say no to these sinful temptations and rely on the Holy Spirit's power to overcome them.

It is God's will that you should be sanctified: that you should avoid sexual immorality; that each of you should learn to control his own body in a way that is holy and honorable, not in passionate lust like the heathen, who do not know God; and that in this matter no one should wrong his brother or take advantage of him. The Lord will punish men for all such sins, as we have already told you and warned you. For God did not call us to be impure, but to live a holy life.

1 Thessalonians 4:3–7

God desires His children to live lives that are holy as He is holy. We are His ambassadors to a world that is being ruled by evil. As Christians, we represent Christ. Therefore, we have the responsibility to be an example to others so they too might believe in God.

7 PRAYER STARTER

Dear Lord, thank You that my client has come here today to seek help for an addiction. Please help her to be open to considering that this might be a true addiction for which she needs to get help and find healing. Lead us by Your Holy Spirit to the resources that will be most helpful, and thank You for Your gift of forgiveness . . .

8 RECOMMENDED RESOURCES

Clinton, Tim. *Turn Your Life Around*. FaithWords, 2006.

Hart, Archibald D. *Healing Life's Hidden Addictions: Overcoming the Closet Compulsions That Waste Your Time and Control Your Life*. Haworth Press, 1998.

Hawkins, David. *Breaking Everyday Addictions: Finding Freedom for the Things That Trip Us Up*. Harvest House, 2008.

Laaser, Mark. *Healing the Wounds of Sexual Addiction*. Zondervan, 2004.

_____. *The L.I.F.E. Guide for Men*. L.I.F.E. Ministry, 2004.

Moore, Beth. *Breaking Free: Discover the Victory of Total Surrender*. B & H Publishing, 2007.

Schaumburg, Harry. *False Intimacy: Understanding the Struggle of Sexual Addiction*. NavPress, 1997.

Willingham, Russell. *Breaking Free: Understanding Sexual Addiction and the Healing Power of Jesus*. InterVarsity, 1999.

www.everymansbattle.com or 800-New-Hope
www.faithfulandtrueministries.com

Pornography 22

PORTRAITS 1

- Sharon couldn't shake the nagging feeling she'd been having about her husband, Paul. She finally asked him if he had ever been involved in pornography.

  He replied defensively, "I have, but I have it under control now. You have nothing to worry about."

  Sharon wept as she described her horror in finding obscene pictures on their computer that he had downloaded from the internet. "I trusted him," she said.

- Fifteen-year-old Andrew remembers the first time he viewed sexually arousing material. He was at his friend's house and was checking his email. He got a message with a file attachment from someone he didn't recognize. He opened the file and saw a photo of a man and woman engaged in sexual activity. Andrew felt flush with excitement and guilt. Soon he was going online when no one was home to view similar sites because he liked the feeling it gave him.

- Beth was a stay-at-home mom with two small children. She loved them dearly but sometimes felt as though life were passing right by her. She was bored to death. While watching a women's program about the joys of sex, she thought about how dull her life had become and decided to go online to see if she could find something to spice up her sex life with her husband. When she typed in "better sex," she entered a shocking world of pornography. She felt the dual sensations of excitement and guilt, but she was hooked. Every day she watched sexually explicit videos and chatted with strange men online.

DEFINITIONS AND KEY THOUGHTS 2

- Pornography is *sexually explicit material* that dehumanizes, objectifies, and degrades men and women for the purpose of sexual arousal. Usually it is photos or videos; sometimes it takes the form of stories or comic book drawings.

- Pornography *promotes "sex without consequences"* and serves as an aid to self-gratification. It is sometimes called "the victimless sin," but this perception doesn't account for the damage done to the person's soul and the erosion of relationships.

- Generally, *a man will come to counseling because he has been found out* by someone at work or a loved one. Or sometimes a man will seek counseling because he is weary of his feelings of guilt and shame.

- *A woman may come for counseling because she either suspects or has found evidence* that her husband has been involved in pornography and she does not know what to do. However, studies show that *increasing numbers of women* are viewing pornography as well.

- *A teenager may come in for counseling at the insistence of his parents.*

- Many married people *rationalize their behavior as "harmless"* because they think they aren't actually committing adultery.

- Eventually, pornography *loses its power to stimulate*, and the user is enticed to move from viewing sexual content to engaging in sexual behaviors involving others (usually strangers). As such, porn is increasingly considered to be a "gateway drug" to more degrading porn and to serious sexual deviancy—which may involve using prostitutes, using children, and adding sexual violence and dangerous behaviors to one's sexual routine.

- Some people use pornography as a *stress reliever that provides escape* from life's perceived hardships.

- Though the numbers continue to increase, recent studies show:

  — *pornographic websites*: 4.2 million (12 percent of total websites)
  — *daily pornographic search engine requests*: 68 million (25 percent of total search engine requests)
  — *U.S. adults who regularly visit internet pornography websites*: 40 million
  — *Promise Keepers men who viewed pornography in the last week*: 53 percent[1]

- Another survey revealed:

  — *Christians* who said *pornography is a major problem* in the home: 47 percent
  — average age of *first internet exposure to pornography*: 11 years old
  — *8–16-year-olds having viewed porn online*: 90 percent (most while doing homework)[2]

- Pornography use is usually *a symptom of a deeper issue* (low self-esteem, loneliness, past sexual abuse).

- Many use pornography *to avoid emotional and/or sexual intimacy* with their spouse.

- Consistent use of pornography promotes the notion that *women and one's spouse are to be viewed as mere objects* and that *sex is unrelated to love, commitment, and marriage.*

- Viewing *pornography increases the likelihood of developing a sexual addiction* and sexual pathology. At the very least, the use of pornography will create conflict and dissatisfaction in the marriage due to *unrealistic sexual expectations* of one's spouse.

- The user of pornography will *struggle consistently* with anger, guilt, shame, increasing anxiety, and oppressive memories.

- It is not uncommon for many people to have their *first exposure* to pornographic material during the *junior high school years*.
- Many adolescents begin viewing pornography because of *curiosity* and as a release for hormonal tension.
- For the sake of clarity, we'll refer to the person using pornography as a male, but it is certainly possible for a woman to view porn as well.

ASSESSMENT INTERVIEW 3

Interviewing the Person Viewing Pornography

Recognize that people who are struggling with this issue may feel a *great deal of shame* and be reluctant to speak about it. They usually deny their involvement for months or even years, and when they are confronted, they often react defiantly and defensively.

It is important for the counselor to *communicate acceptance of the client as a person* and a willingness to understand the struggle that has been occurring. Approach the person with *grace rather than judgment. Be patient* as you encourage the person to relate how the struggle began, how it progressed, and what is currently happening.

In the assessment process, *evaluate the length of time* the person has been involved in this activity and *the extent of the involvement.* (Is it daily or sporadic? Does the client feel as though it is becoming an addiction—a controlling issue in his life? Is it affecting his work or home life?) In addition, it is important to evaluate the degree to which the person feels *sorrow and regret and to test his willingness to change.*

1. When was the first time you viewed pornography? How old were you?
2. How long has this pattern been going on?
3. What prompted you to start?
4. When do you find you most often engage in viewing pornography (at night, when stressed, when you are on the computer and no one is around, or some other time)?
5. Have you tried to stop? What happened?
6. How do you feel about admitting that you use pornography?
7. How is viewing pornography affecting your relationships?
8. How is it affecting your heart and your relationship with God?
9. Have you progressed into other forms of sexual acting out, such as visiting strip clubs, paying prostitutes for sex, or having an affair? Are you tempted to do these things?
10. How do you hope counseling will benefit you?

Interviewing the Spouse Seeking Counsel

If the client is the spouse of someone suspected of using pornography, the client will probably *express a variety of emotions* from anger to shame to guilt (feeling as if she is somehow at fault).

In the initial interview, you will need to show a willingness to *listen and provide hope* that God will show a way through this difficult experience.

It will be important to *evaluate what specifically she wants to do*. She may be dealing with fear of confronting her husband. She may be struggling with thinking clearly about this situation and need to talk it through with you.

1. When did you find out about this problem?
2. How did you find out?
3. Have you made any attempts to talk with your husband about this?
4. If not, why not? Are you afraid of his reaction?
5. If so, how did you approach it, and what did you say?
6. How did he respond?
7. Have you seen any unusual changes in his behavior lately?
8. How are you feeling in regard to this situation?
9. How specifically can I help you?
10. Would you like me to talk to your spouse? Do you think he will be willing to come in and talk to me?

4 : WISE COUNSEL

For the Person Viewing Pornography

Evaluate how *honest* the person is being with himself and you. Determine *how willing he is to take steps to change*. Honest confession and repentance are pivotal to begin the process of change. *Repentance is a crucial spiritual component* in the healing of sexual sin. You may wish to investigate with the person David's confession of sin in Psalm 51.

It is important to *identify the triggers* that are involved in tempting the person to use pornography. Some therapists summarize the main triggers with a simple acronym: HALT, which stands for:

Hungry

Angry

Lonely

Tired

Provide hope that the client will be able to experience victory over this problem. Let him know that there will be times of temptation and possible setbacks, yet God is faithful to forgive and restore. Assure him of your continued support through this process.

Instruct the person on the importance of *a system of accountability*, and help him structure one through the help of a trusted friend.

For the Spouse or Parent

Help the spouse or parent realize that even if the person stops viewing pornography immediately, *rebuilding trust will take time, attention, and courage* from both of them.

Invite the offended person to be honest about her anger, guilt, shame, and sense of betrayal.

Explain the importance of *grieving emotional wounds and forgiving offenses*. Help the person understand that forgiveness is both a choice and a process. People may need time to understand what forgiveness means in this situation, and they also need to grasp the fact that trust must still be earned.

The vast majority of offended parties *have been lied to* about the pornography, so talk about the need for the offender to be held accountable.

ACTION STEPS 5

For the Person Viewing Pornography

1. Identify the Damage

- You will need to see how viewing pornography has been affecting your life, including obsessive thoughts that distract from more wholesome pursuits, distance in family relationships, and guilt. (*If a sense of guilt and shame isn't present, the person won't see any need to repent.*)

2. Identify Patterns of Temptation

- Identify all the locations and activities that provide temptation.
- Avoid stores that sell pornographic magazines.
- Use the computer only when someone else is in the room.
- Purchase software that blocks access to undesirable internet sites and become accountable to someone you trust.

3. Identify Emotional Triggers

- Are there work associates, times of the day, or particularly stressful situations that trigger the temptation?
- Identify which part of HALT (hungry, angry, lonely, tired) is your strongest trigger.
- Take specific steps to minimize the triggers.

4. See It as Sin

- It is important to see the behavior as sin and no longer justify it. Remember that even looking on the opposite sex lustfully is sinful, creating brokenness with God.
- With your counselor, think about how God views sin, the nature of forgiveness, and God's unconditional love. How do you see yourself in relationship to how God sees you?

5. Refocus on Christ

- Develop a plan to strengthen and deepen your relationship with Jesus Christ. Be accountable to someone for daily Scripture reading and prayer.
- Memorize Scripture so that you can bring "every thought into captivity to the obedience of Christ" (2 Cor. 10:5 NKJV).
- We have all been created and are loved by God. Try to view others as sons and daughters of the King. With your counselor's help, train your eyes—including the eyes of your heart—to see people as God sees them, not as sexual objects.

6. Find Support and Accountability

- Become involved in a local Christian ministry that supports men or women who are experiencing this struggle.

7. Consider the Impact on the Marriage

- *Evaluate the client's relationship with his spouse (if married) and provide an invitation to meet with both to explore the effects of this behavior on their relationship and to find healing for wounds. Help him build sexual and emotional intimacies with his spouse.*

8. See a Therapist Trained in Sexual Addiction Recovery

- Pornography use can lead to devastating, long-term problems, such as affairs, divorce, other forms of promiscuity, and sexually transmitted diseases.
- *If this has been a long-standing pattern with a high degree of involvement, it is important to enlist the support of professionals trained in the area of sexual addiction and/or encourage the person to become involved in a local 12-step recovery group.*

For the Spouse Seeking Counsel

If the husband will not come in and talk with you, or if the wife doesn't want him to know about her conversation with you, you will only be able to offer encouragement to the wife.

1. Watch for Triggers

- You can identify the locations and activities that provide temptation.

- Help your husband avoid stores that sell pornographic magazines (for example, don't send him late at night to the local gas station on an errand).
- Move the computer out of isolation. If your husband is willing to be helped, he should go along with this. If not, you can explain that you don't want the kids to find pornography.
- Purchase software that blocks access to undesirable internet sites.

2. Identify Emotional Triggers

- Do you sense that there are work associates, times of the day, or particularly stressful situations that trigger the temptation? What can you do to help?
- Which part of HALT (hungry, angry, lonely, tired) is the strongest trigger? What can you do to offset it?
- If your husband is willing to be helped, you can talk to him about these triggers and how you can be his ally in minimizing them.

3. Continue to Love Him

- Nagging, anger, or humiliation won't work. Continue to love your husband. It will be difficult because you will feel "cheated on," but ask God to help you choose to love him through this.
- Let him know you want him back from the darkness and you want your marriage unhindered by these "other women."
- Tell him how you feel when he views pornography.
- Ask him if he wants his children similarly enslaved when they are older.
- Explain that eventually pornography will no longer satisfy, and he will need more and other types or will be led into an affair.

> One out of every 6 women, including Christians, struggles with an addiction to pornography. That's 17 percent of the population who truly believe they can find sexual fulfillment on the internet.
>
> Today's Christian Woman

4. Pray

- Pray that your husband will be sickened by what he sees and will choose to turn away.
- Ask God to work in your husband's life.

5. Encourage Support

- Encourage him to engage in counseling or to join a support group or men's Bible study that will provide accountability.
- Do whatever it takes to free him up to attend such a group.
- Consider joining a support group for spouses with sexually addicted partners.

6. Determine Your Bottom Line

- What will you do if he won't stop?

6 BIBLICAL INSIGHTS

You have heard that it was said to those of old, "You shall not commit adultery." But I say to you that whoever looks at a woman to lust for her has already committed adultery with her in his heart.

Matthew 5:27–28 NKJV

Here is the penultimate verse revealing that sin begins (and often ends) in the mind. It is not just the behavior that is sinful but the thoughts as well (and therefore we do not avoid sin simply by refusing to act on our sexual thoughts). Also, the mental fantasy of playing out sexual scenarios with attractive people loads the heart with sin. It takes little reasoning to infer from this verse and make it a tenet of our theology that it is impossible to avoid these sinful fantasies without God's power. How necessary is the sanctifying transformation of the heart and mind for pure living before God!

When tempted, no one should say, "God is tempting me." For God cannot be tempted by evil, nor does he tempt anyone; but each one is tempted when, by his own evil desire, he is dragged away and enticed. Then, after desire has conceived, it gives birth to sin; and sin, when it is full-grown, gives birth to death.

James 1:13–15

Sin is progressive. It begins with an attractive and seemingly benign temptation to barely cross the line, but soon it leads to sinful desires and behaviors that destroy the person and harm every relationship.

While Israel was staying in Shittim, the men began to indulge in sexual immorality with Moabite women.

Numbers 25:1

Sexual sin always progresses, drawing people farther and farther from God. What may start as an "innocent" flirtation with sin can lead to deadly consequences. While dabbling around the edges of sexual sin, a person can be snared and ultimately consumed, leading to pain and brokenness.

It is God's will that you should be sanctified: that you should avoid sexual immorality; that each of you should learn to control his own body in a way that is holy and honorable, not in passionate lust like the heathen, who do not know God.

1 Thessalonians 4:3–5

The Bible is very clear about sexual sin. God created sex as a beautiful expression of love in marriage. Satan took that beauty and distorted it.

Believers must have no part in sexual sin. God knows its power to destroy people. His commands are for our good.

Sexual sin encompasses a wide range of activities that God forbids. No matter what society allows, believers must look to God for instruction in this serious matter.

Christians need to avoid activities or thoughts that distort or destroy what God intended for building oneness in marriage.

I am he who searches hearts and minds, and I will repay each of you according to your deeds.

Revelation 2:23

Sometimes people think they can hide portions of their lives from everyone. Christ searches minds and hearts. Nothing is hidden from Him. No sexual sin can escape His notice. People may think they are getting away with it, but God knows.

God sees everywhere we go; He knows everything we say, think, or do. Understanding this should help us steer clear of sexual sin.

PRAYER STARTER 7

Oh, Lord, this family is being devastated by a distortion of sexual desire—something You created to be good and wholesome. Help this family deal with the pain that pornography is causing. We ask that You strengthen Your child to stand firm in his commitment to be free from the addictive power of pornography . . .

RECOMMENDED RESOURCES 8

Crosse, Clay, and Renee Crosse. *I Surrender ALL: Rebuilding a Marriage Broken by Pornography*. NavPress, 2005.

Laaser, Debra. *Shattered Vows: Hope and Healing for Women Who Have Been Sexually Betrayed*. Zondervan, 2008.

Laaser, Mark. *Healing the Wounds of Sexual Addiction*. Zondervan, 2004.

Rogers, Henry J., and Norm Miller. *The Silent War: Ministering to Those Trapped in the Deception of Pornography*. New Life Press, 2000.

Video Series

Arterburn, Steve. *Every Man's Battle: Pornography*. American Association of Christian Counselors Life Enrich Video Series, 2003.

Feree, Marnie. *Female Sex Addiction*. American Association of Christian Counselors Life Enrich Video Series, 2003.

Laaser, Mark. *Male Sex Addiction*. American Association of Christian Counselors Life Enrich Video Series, 2003.

Also see Stephen Arterburn, Fred Stoeker, and Mike Yorkey, *Every Man's Battle: Winning the War on Sexual Temptation One Victory at a Time*. The Every Man Series. WaterBrook; Shannon Ethridge, *Every Woman's Battle: Discovering God's Plan for Sexual and Emotional Fulfillment*. The Every Man Series. WaterBrook.

23 Polyamory and Group Sex

1 PORTRAITS

- Bob and Carol had been friends with Ted and Alice for most of their adult lives. They often spent weekends together and now were all involved in parenting and supporting each other's children—the families spent a lot of time together as well. Bob and Carol know that their friends are more liberal than they are about sex and expressing their sexuality, so it did not completely shock them when Ted and Alice proposed that they do some wife-swapping and that all four of them share one another sexually.

- Finally Claire yielded to her husband's constant pressure to engage in a ménage à trois. Soon he brought home a beautiful young woman from the club they attended. The reality of it was far from the fantasy, however. Not only did Claire feel strange engaging in lesbian sex, which her husband loved to watch, but watching her husband have wild and uninhibited sex with a strange woman—including anal sex, which she never wanted to do—was completely unnerving to her. She was determined to tell her husband she did not want to do this again, but she anticipated both his disappointment and anger for drawing a line here.

- Jack and Jill had been into "swinging" for many years, and it had become a routine part of their sex life. They had even gone on numerous swinging vacations where their club had taken over an entire hotel on some Caribbean beach island. Imagine the shock to them both, however, when Jill received notice from her physician that she had contracted a serious sexually transmitted disease during their last sex vacation.

2 DEFINITIONS AND KEY THOUGHTS

- *Group sex or swinging* involves inviting other partners or couples into the marital sex system, so that *both partners are involved sexually with others*. Often the justification is that there is no secrecy and no illicit affairs are being carried on behind the other spouse's back.

- *Polyamory* is a politico-social-sexual identity that supports "marriage" and family building *among any number of consenting adults*. Three or four or five people may be involved in a nonlegal "marriage" with any combination of genders in the mix. Polygamy with any number of wives is a form of polyamory, which may also include one woman with many sex partners referred to as her "husbands."

- *Fantasies of group sex are common among both men and women.* In major studies, between 54 and 88 percent of people fantasize about watching others have sex, between 40 and 42 percent fantasize about being watched by others, and between 39 and 72 percent fantasize about bondage.[1]

ASSESSMENT INTERVIEW 3

Be patient in encouraging the person to relate how the struggle began, how it progressed, and what is currently happening. In the assessment process, evaluate the length of time the person has been involved in this activity and the extent of the involvement. In addition, it is important to evaluate the degree to which the person feels sorrow and regret, and to test her willingness to change.

1. What brings you here? How do you hope counseling will benefit you?
2. How long has this pattern been going on? Is it something you do frequently or sporadically? Is it affecting your work or home life?
3. What prompted you to start swinging? When do you most often engage in swinging? Do you and your spouse plan your week or weekends around swinging events?
4. Have you tried to stop? What happened? How do you feel about admitting that you engage in swinging?
5. Does it feel as though swinging is becoming an addiction, that it is beginning to be the controlling issue in your life?
6. Do you have children? If so, are they aware of this behavior? Do any other family members know about or participate in the swinging lifestyle?
7. How has swinging affected your marriage? What is your current opinion of your spouse? What is your current view of yourself?
8. How is this affecting your heart and your relationship with God?
9. Do you want to be free of this behavior? Do you desire to stop the swinging lifestyle? Are you willing to do whatever it takes to quit?

> Create in me a pure heart, O God, and renew a steadfast spirit within me. Do not cast me from your presence or take your Holy Spirit from me. Restore to me the joy of your salvation and grant me a willing spirit, to sustain me.
>
> *Psalm 51:10–12*

WISE COUNSEL 4

Rarely do adherents to group sex or polyamory engage in counseling to address these issues. Usually some other problems bring them, and they may stubbornly resist connecting their anxiety, guilt, or depression to this lifestyle. When they do come for counseling to address these problems, it is usually because they are in some kind of crisis as a result of living this way, such as contracting a sexually transmitted disease. Therefore, it may be wise to consider them involuntary clients, whose motivation may wane once the crisis is passed.

Repentance is a crucial spiritual component in the healing of sexual sin. You may wish to read and explore David's confession of sin in Psalm 51 with your client(s). In this passage David is crying out to God for mercy and cleansing. God's plan is that sexual enjoyment and fulfillment be experienced within the bond of marriage between one man and his one wife.

Evaluate how *honest* the person is being with herself and you. Determine how *willing she is to take steps to change.* Honest confession and repentance are pivotal to begin this process of healing. God is faithful to forgive and restore.

Assure the client that she can experience freedom and victory. Yes, there may be times of relapse. Temptation may get the best of her, and she may engage in the swinging lifestyle again. Change takes time, and healing is a journey. But if she is willing to seek God's help and wisdom along with engaging in the counseling process, she can turn her life and marriage around. She can experience a life of sexual purity—the way God intended.

Accountability is key. Encourage your client to seek the support of a trusted friend. Encourage her to meet regularly with someone who will ask the hard questions and keep her accountable to a sexual lifestyle that pleases God.

5 ACTION STEPS

1. Identify and Resolve the Crisis

- Talk about the current status of your life, your marriage, and your family. Are there any medical issues present at this time? Are there any crises that need to be resolved right now? Be open to sharing your concerns and exploring the possibility of new thinking. Change is always difficult but can happen if you are willing to work.

- *If clients will concentrate on whatever the crisis may be, help them resolve it. Help them stabilize their life and their marriage/family system. By doing so you will be touching on the source of their group sex troubles and may be invited to further explore the taboo places in their lives.*

2. Get a Thorough Medical Checkup

- A medical exam will rule out any medical problems caused by group and multiple-partner sexual practices. A doctor will also be able to help in the treatment of any STD that may have been acquired.

- *Be prepared to offer your client a referral to Christian doctors in your area who will help complete the medical evaluation. They may not feel comfortable going to their primary care physician for this kind of assessment.*

3. Make a Commitment to Change and Accountability

- Make a commitment to God and the counseling process to remain consistent in attending sessions and keeping your life free from sexual sin. It would also be beneficial to write down your goals and commitment for both you and your counselor to keep as a reminder of your new vows.

- Find a trusted friend of the same sex who can keep you accountable to the new lifestyle of purity you desire. Meet regularly with this individual and be honest with her.
- *Help your client commit to some form of accountability and help. If she will sign a contract with you that she will stop having group sex and multiple-partner sex, she is serious about change and is more likely to remain consistent in attending counseling sessions and receiving help.*

Additional notes for the counselor:

- *There may be numerous threads connecting the crisis that brought the client to counseling and her practice of swinging or group sex. Also, it is likely that she may be in denial and unable to see these connections (though maybe one of the marital partners "sees the light" and is ready to forsake wild living for a more safe and conventional sex life). Either way, reinforce these connections in a way that challenges the lies she has embraced that group sex and swinging are good and desirous.*
- *Since the corollary lie is that conventional sex is dull and boring, you must also raise the bar by praising sex with one's spouse. Talk about how marital sex can offer a lifetime of discovery and a good marriage can provide joy and contentment that is never found in spreading oneself thin with multiple sex partners.*

BIBLICAL INSIGHTS 6

Therefore if the Son makes you free, you shall be free indeed.
John 8:36 NKJV

God alone can provide lasting comfort, joy, and freedom from the bondage of sexual sin. God has a beautiful and perfect plan for sexuality in its purest form. When we seek Him and lean on His strength, we come to know and desire His way.

Even so consider yourselves to be dead to sin, but alive to God in Christ Jesus. There-fore do not let sin reign in your mortal body so that you obey its lusts, and do not go on presenting the members of your body to sin as instruments of unrighteousness; but present yourselves to God as those alive from the dead, and your members as instruments of righteousness to God. For sin shall not be master over you, for you are not under law but under grace.
Romans 6:11–14 NASB

Paul warns us not to allow sin to have control in our lives. He encourages the believer to stand strong against the temptation of evil and lust. We are called to righteousness, and we can achieve this through Jesus Christ and His sacrifice on the cross—His victory over sin! Clients need to determine to change, replace the sinful behavior with something more wholesome, and then finally find a different way to meet their need.

Therefore put to death your members which are on the earth: fornication, uncleanness, passion, evil desire, and covetousness, which is idolatry. Because of these things the wrath of God is coming upon the sons of disobedience.

Colossians 3:5–6 NKJV

These verses describe some of those sinful desires that believers should "put to death." Sexual sins, evil desires, and covetousness (a form of idolatry) should have no place in a believer's heart and life. It takes a conscious daily decision to say no to these sinful temptations and rely on the Holy Spirit's power to overcome them.

Read David's prayer of repentance in Psalm 51:1–12.

7 PRAYER STARTER

Dear Lord, this marriage has been so hurt by a distortion of sexual desire—something You created to be good and wholesome. Help this family deal with the pain that group sex and swinging are causing. We ask that You strengthen this couple to stand firm and be free from the addictive power that this kind of sexual enslavement can hold over a couple. You, Lord, are able to give and maintain this kind of strength . . .

8 RECOMMENDED RESOURCES

Laaser, Debra. *Shattered Vows: Hope and Healing for Women Who Have Been Sexually Betrayed.* Zondervan, 2008.

Laaser, Mark. *Healing the Wounds of Sexual Addiction.* Zondervan, 2004.

Video Series

Arterburn, Steve. *Every Man's Battle: Pornography.* American Association of Christian Counselors Life Enrich Video Series, 2003.

Feree, Marnie. *Female Sex Addiction.* American Association of Christian Counselors Life Enrich Video Series, 2003.

Laaser, Mark. *Male Sex Addiction.* American Association of Christian Counselors Life Enrich Video Series, 2003.

Exhibitionism and Voyeurism **24**

PORTRAITS : 1

- Daniel is a respected businessman in his community. He says, "I can't believe I did what I did. I was as shocked as they were." Then he describes driving his car by two school-aged girls, yelling to get their attention, and exposing his genitals.
- Craig travels for work so he spends a lot of time in hotels. No matter what city he is in, he always seems drawn to standing naked in front of the large hotel room window. As he stands there, he hopes someone will look up and see him.
- "You don't understand. I live in New York City—everyone looks!" protests Bob at his court-appointed counseling session. "I'm not the only person with a telescope in his apartment, and if people cared, even a little, they would draw their blinds!"

DEFINITIONS AND KEY THOUGHTS : 2

- Exhibitionism is a psychological disorder characterized by a pattern of behaviors that involve the *exposure of body parts—often the genitals, buttocks, or breasts—to others.* This exposure may be of an extravagant nature and usually involves some sexual suggestions.
- Voyeurism is a mirror disorder of exhibitionism. The voyeur experiences *sexually arousing fantasies or behaviors through observing an unsuspecting person who is naked, in the process of disrobing, or engaging in sexual activity.*
- Exhibitionism is classified in the DSM-IV-TR under the category of paraphilias, which are patterns of sexual behavior involving *unusual and socially unacceptable practices.* The American Psychiatric Association also classifies voyeurism as a paraphilia.
- A person who practices voyeurism is known as a voyeur or Peeping Tom. *Two criteria are required to make a diagnosis of voyeurism:*

  — Over a period of at least six months, an individual must experience recurrent, intense, sexually arousing fantasies, sexual urges, or behaviors that involve the act of observing an unsuspecting person who is naked, in the process of disrobing, or engaging in sexual activity.

171

— The fantasies, sexual urges, or behaviors must cause *clinically significant distress or impairment in social, occupational, or other important areas of functioning.*[1]

• A research team once asked a sample of 185 exhibitionists, "How would you prefer a person to react if you were to expose your privates to him or her?" The most common response was *"would want to have sexual intercourse"* (35.1 percent), followed by "no reaction necessary at all" (19.5 percent), "to show their privates also" (15.1 percent), "admiration" (14.1 percent), and "any reaction" (11.9 percent). Very few exhibitionists chose "anger and disgust" (3.8 percent) or "fear" (0.5 percent).[2]

• Exhibitionism is known by several names, including: flashing, apodysophilia, and Lady Godiva syndrome. It has been called a *"hands-off" paraphilia*. This descriptive term is in contrast with the "hands-on" paraphilias that involve physical contact with others. In some cases, an *exhibitionist will masturbate* while exposing himself.

• Some exhibitionists have *a conscious desire to shock or upset* the person or persons to whom they are exposing themselves. In contrast, a high percentage of exhibitionists hope or fantasize that the target of their exposure will *become sexually aroused and want to engage in sexual activity with them.*

• Voyeurs often *fantasize about engaging in sexual activity* with the target. A voyeur derives *sexual pleasure from secretly observing* (either directly or by recording) another person nude or partially nude. Some voyeurs attempt to see others bathing, defecating, or engaging in sexual activity. Some experts have observed that the United States is becoming a more voyeuristic culture with the introduction of *"reality television."*

• A variant form of voyeurism involves *secretly listening to erotic conversations* or other persons engaged in sexual activity. This practice has gained many new adherents through the use of internet chat rooms.

• Legal statutes vary greatly between states in regard to the seriousness of voyeurism. However, *international laws have been becoming stricter* against voyeurism.

3 ASSESSMENT INTERVIEW

Interviewing the Exhibitionist

1. What kind of exhibitionism are you participating in now? When did you first begin thinking about exhibitionistic behaviors? Explain your history of exposing yourself.
2. How frequently have you exposed yourself to others in the past year, and how does the exposure usually occur?
3. Are you masturbating when you expose yourself? Have you done so in the past?
4. Do you ever try to make physical contact with the targets of your exhibitionism?

5. Have you been arrested or have the police ever responded to a complaint brought on by your exposing yourself?
6. Are you experiencing any other odd sexual behaviors or fantasies?
7. Have you attempted to change your behavior and stop this practice? If so, what were the results?
8. How is this behavior affecting your relationships (directly or indirectly)?
9. Are you ready to give up exhibitionism? What will be the benefits of change for you?

Interviewing the Voyeur

1. When did you begin peeping or spying on others?
2. Describe your first experience. How did you feel?
3. How did you cover up your behavior?
4. Have you ever been caught?
5. Are there certain places where you are more tempted to peep?
6. Are there certain times or places where it is easier for you to avoid the temptation?
7. Do you know the people you spy on? If not, do you try to make contact with them in some way?
8. How has your behavior affected your life and your relationships (directly or indirectly)?
9. How would your life benefit if you were able to put voyeurism behind you?
10. Has anything or anyone ever helped you with your problem in the past? If so, what were the results?

WISE COUNSEL 4

Several theories have been proposed about the *causes of exhibitionistic and voyeuristic tendencies.* While the following theories are not conclusive, they may offer significant insight into determining the origin of a person's disorder.

Biological cause. It has been found that unusual levels of the hormone testosterone increase the susceptibility of males to develop deviant sexual behaviors.

Childhood abuse. Numerous studies have shown that emotional or physical abuse occurring in a person's childhood increases the risk of his developing exhibitionism.

Traumatic brain injury. A number of documented cases have shown that traumatic brain injury (TBI) can precede sexually deviant behavior (including exhibitionism) in persons with no prior history of such offenses.

These disorders are *sexual and social problems* that negatively affect both the person with the disorder and the target of the exposure. The ways of acting out these tendencies and the sites for the deviant behavior are steadily increasing throughout

America—it is not just a "big city" problem anymore. For example, the continued suburban sprawl has led to action in the malls of America and in mall parking lots.

An *important part of recovering from this paraphilia includes repenting* of this behavior in public. If possible or appropriate, it may be important to ask forgiveness of the persons who have been the target of this behavior.

Both exhibitionism and voyeurism are sexual paraphilias and, *to those who suffer with these disorders, they can feel and cause behavior like addictions*. A combination of individual counseling, group therapy, and medication can help. The possibility of exposure and embarrassment may deter some sufferers.

Voyeurism and exhibitionism are criminal acts in most jurisdictions. They are *usually classified as misdemeanors*, and as a result, legal penalties are minor. It is not easy to prosecute voyeurs because intent to watch is difficult to prove. In their defense statements, voyeurs typically claim that the observation was accidental.

5 ACTION STEPS

1. Cultivate the Desire to Change

- The first step to overcoming exhibitionism or voyeurism is having a desire to leave the practice behind, which, like overcoming an addiction, is a challenging motivational problem.

- Preventing exhibitionism or voyeurism while in the early stages, or before the behavior has become habituated with urges and fantasies, is the most effective treatment. Early intervention involves psycho-education, accountability, and seeing the behavior as a sin that, with confession and repentance, God will provide power to overcome.

- *Most exhibitionists and voyeurs never seek treatment out of embarrassment or because they do not want to change. For this reason a large percentage of people who seek treatment for exhibitionism and voyeurism do so after being prosecuted and subject to a court order.*

2. Limit Exposure to Triggers

- You must identify your emotional triggers and avoid places where you will be tempted to participate in exhibitionist or voyeuristic practices.

- *Honesty and comprehensive analysis are needed here, as the paraphilic who secretly wants to maintain his habit will not reveal important cues and places to any accountability person or group.*

3. Increase Thought and Impulse Control

- Through individual counseling you will learn coping mechanisms for resisting the urge to expose your body to others or secretly watch others in private moments.

- You need to learn how your thoughts affect your emotions, how negative emotions can lead to sexually deviant behaviors, and how you can stop triggered fantasy by substituting different thoughts and pursuits. Also, you are encouraged in counseling to identify and challenge any reasons you use to justify your inappropriate behavior.

- One technique, known as "orgasmic reconditioning," involves the process of replacing the fantasies of exposing yourself or viewing another person with fantasies of acceptable sexual behavior.

Faithful and True
Ministries
15798 Venture Lane
Eden Prairie, MN
55344
faithfulandtrueminis
tries.com

4. Consider Group Therapy and Support Groups

- Group therapy and support groups can be very effective and can become a necessary source of accountability. One of the most beneficial aspects of group therapy is that you will learn that you are not alone in your problem of exhibitionism or voyeurism.

- *Be prepared to provide your client with a list of referrals to group treatment within your area. By attending a 12-step support-group program (such as Sex Addicts Anonymous or Sexaholics Anonymous), a person can learn from and even be mentored or "sponsored" by others who have successfully stopped participating in these behaviors. Having a Christ-centered sponsor can also reinforce the needed accountability that is completely lacking when struggling alone.*

BIBLICAL INSIGHTS 6

Love must be sincere. Hate what is evil; cling to what is good. Be devoted to one another in brotherly love. Honor one another above yourselves. Never be lacking in zeal, but keep your spiritual fervor, serving the Lord. Be joyful in hope, patient in affliction, faithful in prayer. Share with God's people who are in need. Practice hospitality.

Romans 12:9–13

Exhibitionism and voyeurism are selfish and sinful behaviors—the perpetrator cares more about sexual titillation and sensationalism than the welfare of the victim. Those who have engaged in these behaviors need to understand the damage they do to their victims, their own families, and themselves. Like all of us, they can be forgiven and learn to love others out of an overflowing heart of thankfulness to God.

My dear children, I write this to you so that you will not sin. But if anybody does sin, we have one who speaks to the Father in our defense—Jesus Christ, the Righteous One. He is the atoning sacrifice for our sins, and not only for ours but also for the sins of the whole world.

1 John 2:1–2

175

The sins of exhibitionism and voyeurism aren't outside the grace of God. Christ's forgiveness extends to those who commit sexual sins, just as it applies to everyone else. But forgiveness isn't just a legal statement of "not guilty"; it means we have a relationship with Christ that can be transformative if we learn to become intimately related to our Savior and friend.

Let your eyes look directly ahead and let your gaze be fixed straight in front of you. Watch the path of your feet and all your ways will be established. Do not turn to the right nor to the left; turn your foot from evil.

Proverbs 4:25–27 NASB

In this passage Solomon reminds us of the importance of guarding the focus of our attention. If we pursue Christ and live a life that's fixed on doing what is right in the eyes of God, all of our ways will be established. We must stand strong against the temptation to veer toward the path of evil. Exhibitionism and voyeurism will lead only to the destruction of the lives of the perpetrator and his victims.

7 PRAYER STARTER

Father, thank You for Your amazing grace. You forgive every sin, including the sins of exhibitionism and voyeurism. Give my friend confidence that You care, that You are present, and that You still change lives today. Give him courage to face and overcome the urges that have led to these problems, and help him rebuild trust with those he loves . . .

8 RECOMMENDED RESOURCES

Beers, Mark H., MD, and Robert Berkow, MD. "Exhibitionism." Chapter 192 in *The Merck Manual of Diagnosis and Therapy*. Merck Research Laboratories, 1999.

Carnes, Patrick J. *Out of the Shadows: Understanding Sexual Addiction*. Hazelden, 2001.

Charlton, Randolph, and Irvin D. Yalon. *Treating Sexual Disorders*. John Wiley and Sons, 1997.

Laaser, Mark. *Healing the Wounds of Sexual Addiction*. Zondervan, 2004.

_____. *L.I.F.E. Guide for Men: A Workbook for Living in Freedom Everyday in Sexual Wholeness and Integrity*. Life Ministries, 2007.

Course

"Treating Sexual Addiction," Certificate Training Program. Light University/AACC DVD Course; www.aacc.net.

Fetishism **25**

PORTRAITS :1

- Kate loves leather—beyond any healthy attachment. She has leather pants, leather shirts, and of course, leather jackets. She even has leather bed sheets. Leather is such an important part of her sex life that without it, sex seems dull and unappealing.

- Keith is what you might call a "foot man." He commented, "I don't know if a woman is attractive until I see her feet. I've got to see her feet." Even in the winter, he asks his wife to wear her high-heeled sandals.

- Something about the smell of rubber has always turned Megan on. She shyly admits this to her friends one day. "Is that weird or what?" she says. She was shocked when her friend responded, "My sister is into rubber big time. She goes to parties where she wears these tight rubber suits and has sex with guys she refers to as 'rubber band men.'"

DEFINITIONS AND KEY THOUGHTS :2

- Fetishism is *the sexual attraction to materials or objects not conventionally viewed as being sexual in nature.* When a body part is the subject of a person's fetish (known as *partialism*), the body part often takes sexual precedence over the rest of the other person's body.

- Fetishism is more accurately called sexual fetishism or erotic fetishism. One who has a sexual fetish is known as a fetishist. Alfred Binet, the famous psychologist best known for developing the IQ test, first introduced the term *sexual fetish*.[1]

- The American Psychiatric Association categorizes fetishism as a paraphilia, a sexual disorder characterized by *abnormal or socially unacceptable sexual behavior.* Other paraphilias include voyeurism and exhibitionism.

- According to the International Classification of Diseases (ICD), fetishism is the *use of inanimate objects as a stimulus to achieve sexual arousal and satisfaction.*

- Many people *never seek treatment* for their sexual fetishes but instead embrace or even celebrate them. They believe their fetishes enhance their sexual relationship and pleasure. This is a primary reason that treating and providing education to others regarding fetish control is so difficult.

3 ASSESSMENT INTERVIEW

Initial Questions for Assessment

1. How long have you experienced sexual fetishism?
2. What is your fetish?
3. Do you become aroused without the fetish object?
4. Is your spouse comfortable with your sexual fetish? Explain your answer.
5. Why are you seeking to overcome your sexual fetish now?
6. Have there ever been periods of time when you were not experiencing sexual fetishism?

Questions on Concerns about a Fetish

Today many psychologists and medical doctors regard a fetish as an *accepted variation of human sexuality*. The practice of incorporating a fetish into sexual practice is often understood to be *unobjectionable as long as the people involved feel comfortable*. However, there are issues that are often overlooked in this type of permissive assessment, so the following questions should be asked.

1. Has this fetish become a personal obsession that interferes with the relational dimensions of sex or your ability to know and enjoy sexual intimacies with your spouse?
2. Have you made the fetish more important than your spouse and the sexual health of your marriage?
3. Is involvement with your fetish the only way you enjoy sex or the only way you are able to come to an orgasm with your spouse?
4. Is your fetish part of a sexual or personal abuse issue that has not been appropriately resolved?
5. Has anything helped you put the fetish behind you?
6. Have you ever sought treatment for sexual fetishism? If so, what were the results?
7. What are your treatment goals now?

4 WISE COUNSEL

Sexual fetishism—whether it is a preoccupation with an item, such as leather or foam, or a preoccupation with some part of a partner's body, such as feet or a belly button—*can distract from the significance of the union between man and wife*. God made husband and wife to share their bodies with one another and to keep the marriage bed undefiled. If the fetish becomes a barrier to sexual intimacy between the couple and violates feelings of safety for either spouse, these feelings need to be communicated and addressed.

The *causes* of this disorder *haven't been clearly determined*. Abnormalities in hormonal levels, childhood abuse, and a history of brain injury are being investigated.

Some counselors have attempted to treat sexual fetishism with *cognitive behavioral therapy* (which helps people see how their thoughts affect their emotions) or through *psychoanalysis* (which could look into the origins of fetishism by seeking out a trauma from a person's past). However, treatment may be more successful if it focuses on keeping a fetish under control and making sure the spouse is comfortable with their sexual intimacy.

Aversive conditioning has been shown to reduce unwanted behaviors. This is a process that involves using stimulation detested by the individual at the time that she is engaging in fantasizing about the object of her fetish. The goal is for the individual to begin to associate the fetish with the detestable stimulation, thus decreasing the appeal of the fetish.

Thought stopping is a cognitive behavioral technique that has also been useful in controlling unwanted impulses. The client is asked to begin to fantasize about engaging in fetishism. After a few moments, the counselor yells, "Stop!" The client's thinking pattern associated with the fetish is stopped, and she is asked to immediately replace her thought with a more positive and appropriate fantasy. It may take several attempts by the counselor to teach the client to engage in thought stopping on her own, away from the session.

Our thoughts are so important that there is much teaching in the Bible concerning them. For example, Paul told the Ephesians to be made new in the attitude of their minds (Eph. 4:23). Jesus said, "For out of the heart come evil thoughts, murder, adultery, sexual immorality, theft, false testimony, slander. These are what make a man 'unclean'" (Matt. 15:19–20). Therefore, it is vital that we understand Paul's warning to the Corinthians: "The weapons we fight with are not the weapons of the world. On the contrary, they have divine power to demolish strongholds. We demolish arguments and every pretension that sets itself up against the knowledge of God, and we take captive every thought to make it obedient to Christ" (2 Cor. 10:4–5). It takes practice, discipline, and accountability, but this is the way toward freedom.

Fetishes always have symbolic value. They may be an attempt to work out trauma, woundedness, or some associations from the past. We call it the "arousal template." One way to deal with them is to understand the meaning of the fetish.

> A review of the files of a teaching hospital revealed 48 cases over a 20-year period that met the criteria for fetishes. The objects of their fetishes included clothing (58.3%), rubber and rubber items (22.9%), footwear (14.6%), body parts (14.6%), leather and leather items (10.4%), and soft materials and fabrics (6.3%).
>
> British Journal of Psychiatry

ACTION STEPS 5

1. Keep It under Control

- Commit to yourself, your spouse, and your counselor that you are going to do what it takes to learn how to keep this behavior under control, since it is negatively affecting intimacy in your marriage.
- Shut out any fantasy obsessions with the object of the fetish and focus instead on parts of your spouse's body that are customarily sexual in nature. Learn to become sexually aroused by all parts of your spouse's body; take time to appreciate his entire body and not just one particular part.

- *If sexual arousal is contingent on the fetish, set up a program of systematic desensitization during which the fetish loses more and more focus as sexual experiences shared together are emphasized.*
- *Use sensate focus exercises to reinforce new arousal patterns so the client learns to become eroticized by different things in her spouse and in the experience.*

2. Establish Comfort in the Sexual Relationship

- Talk to your spouse. Find out what pleases each of you the most sexually. Discuss ways to incorporate practices that will comfortably increase sexual arousal for both of you during intimacy.
- Communication with your spouse is essential if you are to understand one another and take steps toward a rich and satisfying sex life.

3. Participate in Individual Counseling and Group Support

- Individual counseling will be very helpful in teaching you new coping mechanisms. You will learn how your thoughts affect your emotions and how negative emotions can lead to sexually deviant behaviors. Also, you will be encouraged to identify any reasons you may often use to justify an obsessive thought life.
- One of the most beneficial aspects of group therapy is that you will learn that you are not alone in your struggle with sexual fetishism. You will be able to learn from, encourage, and help others work through issues surrounding fetish addiction.
- In a 12-step support-group program (try to find a Christ-centered Sex Addicts Anonymous or Sexaholics Anonymous program), you can learn from and even be mentored or "sponsored" by others who have successfully stopped participating in sexual fetishes.

6 BIBLICAL INSIGHTS

Since we have these promises, dear friends, let us purify ourselves from everything that contaminates body and spirit, perfecting holiness out of reverence for God.
2 Corinthians 7:1

Anything that gets our focus off God and His purposes for us "contaminates" our body and spirit. Sexual fetishism may seem innocent fun to some people, or it may seem kinky to others. The primary point of this passage is that we need to be ruthlessly honest about how our behaviors affect our relationship with God and with other people. Anything that gets in the way needs to be changed.

So whatever you believe about these things keep between yourself and God. Blessed is the man who does not condemn himself by what he approves. But the man who has doubts is condemned if he eats, because his eating is not from faith; and everything that does not come from faith is sin.

Romans 14:22–23

Our conscience is a God-given tool to give us an indication of right and wrong. When the Holy Spirit pricks our conscience and causes us to sense conviction that our words, attitudes, or behavior are less than God's best, we need to pay close attention. If we can't thank God for an experience, we probably should repent and refrain from being involved in it again.

When I kept silent, my bones wasted away through my groaning all day long. For day and night your hand was heavy upon me; my strength was sapped as in the heat of summer. Then I acknowledged my sin to you and did not cover up my iniquity. I said, "I will confess my transgressions to the LORD"—and you forgave the guilt of my sin.
Psalm 32:3–5

God's forgiveness is strong and available for us to experience. When we keep silent about our sin, we suffer emotionally, relationally, spiritually, and sometimes physically. But when we respond to conviction with honesty and repentance, God graciously forgives and restores.

PRAYER STARTER 7

Dear Lord, You write that husband and wife should share their bodies with each other, but an obsession has come into my friend's life that separates her and her spouse instead of building bonds of closeness. Help her refocus her sexual interest and energy so that they become wholesome, constructive, and pleasant for her and her spouse . . .

RECOMMENDED RESOURCES 8

Carnes, Patrick J. *Out of the Shadows: Understanding Sexual Addiction*. Hazelden, 2001.

Charlton, Randolph, and Irvin D. Yalon. *Treating Sexual Disorders*. John Wiley and Sons, 1997.

Laaser, Mark. *Healing the Wounds of Sexual Addiction*. Zondervan, 2004.

_____. *L.I.F.E. Guide for Men: A Workbook for Living in Freedom Everyday in Sexual Wholeness and Integrity*. Life Ministries, 2007.

Weinstein, Estelle, and Efrem Rosen. *Sexuality Counseling: Issues and Implications*. Thomas/Brooks Cole, 1988.

Course

"Treating Sexual Addiction," Certificate Training Program. Light University/AACC DVD Course; www.aacc.net.

26 Frotteurism

1 PORTRAITS

- With a loving wife, two children, and a thriving business, Dale is a respected pillar of his community. But there are strange rumors going around that he has groped women while passing them in restaurants or walking by them at the office.

- Chris lives in Lower Manhattan and takes the subway every morning and evening. He looks forward to the commute—the more crowded the better. On the train he holds his briefcase in such a way that others won't see him rubbing women's rears. He knows what he does is wrong, but many of the women don't even seem to notice.

- Tan is a nineteen-year-old college student who was at a packed concert. He reached past a friend to touch a woman's breast. She grabbed his hand and called for the police. A few minutes later security guards took him away.

2 DEFINITIONS AND KEY THOUGHTS

- Frotteurism is *the nonconsensual touching of, groping of, or rubbing against another person as a means to achieve sexual arousal.* The most commonly practiced form of frotteurism is rubbing one's genitals against the victim's thighs or buttocks. A common alternative is to rub one's hands over the victim's genitals, rear end, or breasts. Most people who engage in frotteurism fantasize that they have an exclusive and caring relationship with their victim during the moment of contact. However, once contact is made and broken, the frotteur realizes that escape is important to avoid prosecution.

- The American Psychiatric Association (in the DSM-IV-TR) categorizes frotteurism as a paraphilia: *a pattern of socially unacceptable sexual behavior.*

- The term *frotteurism* is derived from the French verb *frotter*, which means "to rub." The designation *frotteur* comes from a French word literally meaning "rubber" or "one who rubs." During an act of frotteurism, the frotteur will usually make contact with the target *using his hands or genitals*. A frotteur tends to *touch people in crowded places*, such as at a concert or on a crowded train.

- The APA diagnostic criteria for frotteurism are:

— *Recurrent, intense, or arousing sexual urges or fantasies* that involve touching and rubbing against a nonconsenting person. A person who practices frotteurism is known as a frotteur.

— Acting on these sexual urges or fantasies, or being significantly distressed by them to a degree that is *disruptive to everyday functioning.*[1]

- The *majority of frotteurs are male*, and the majority of frotteurism targets are female (however, male-male, female-female, and female-male incidents do occur).

- Frotteurism is *a criminal offense* and is considered a form of sexual assault. Frotteurism directed toward a child by an adult is considered *sexual abuse of a child and is a mandated reportable offense. **In the SH (or SA) community we refer to this as "indecent liberty."***

ASSESSMENT INTERVIEW 3

1. When did you begin to find sexual pleasure touching others without their consent?
2. What are your healthy relationships with friends and family like? Are you romantically involved with someone?
3. Describe the pleasure and thrill you enjoy from touching people.
4. Have you ever been caught groping another person? If so, what were the consequences? Have you ever been arrested or had any legal problems due to frotteurism?
5. Are you experiencing any other similar sexual desires or behaviors? If so, describe them.
6. Have you experienced any physical or sexual abuse in your past?
7. How has frotteurism caused you embarrassment or pain?
8. What will be some of the benefits of learning to overcome this problem?

WISE COUNSEL 4

Frotteurism is a serious sexual offense. Clients who are currently committing or have committed frotteurism need to *acknowledge their obsessive thoughts and compulsive actions.* And they need to repent of the wrong they have done to others. This problem is, by its nature, secretive, so those who practice it *go to great lengths to hide their behavior and deny their involvement.* Typically they won't quit or even have any desire to quit until they are confronted by a victim and face legal trouble. Even then, many frotteurs can't wait until they can return to their compulsive behavior.

Since this is a sexual paraphilia, a combination of individual counseling, group therapy, and medication can help. *Cognitive-behavior therapy is commonly used to treat frotteurism.* The frotteur must learn to stop the mental/sexual fantasy and to control the impulse to touch nonconsenting victims. Medroxyprogesterone, a female hormone, is sometimes prescribed to decrease sexual desire.

The *causes of this disorder haven't been clearly determined*. Most experts attribute the behavior to an initially random or accidental touching of another's genitals that the person found sexually exciting. Successive repetitions of the act tend to reinforce and perpetuate the behavior.

Frotteurism is *classified as a criminal misdemeanor* in many jurisdictions. As a result, legal penalties may be minor. It is also not easy to prosecute frotteurs because intent to touch is difficult to prove. In their defense statements, the accused often claim that the contact was accidental.

Sexual behavior toward a minor child is a criminal offense and *must be reported to appropriate authorities* by mandated reporters (which, in most cases, is any individual providing counseling-related services, an educational representative, or law enforcement personnel). Be sure to consult your local state laws about your duty to report.

5 ACTION STEPS

1. Avoid Places of Temptation

- Avoiding places of temptation is important but will not prevent you from further frotteurism. It's the equivalent of getting the beer out of an alcoholic's house. Do not go to places where you have engaged in frotteurism or places you've thought would offer opportunities to indulge in it.
- If you avoid busy trains, lines in stores, or places with dense crowds, you may be able to resist the temptation of inappropriately touching another person. Make a list, with your counselor's help, of places you can visit and places you cannot.

2. Identify Emotional Triggers

- There may be internal triggers that encourage your frotteurism. Some common ones include being hungry, angry, lonely, stressed, depressed, or tired. Identifying triggers and being aware of them will help you avoid frotteuristic behaviors when urges arise.
- With your counselor's help, identify and acknowledge recurring times, situations, and internal experiences that make it more difficult to avoid frotteurism. When you sense these triggers, stop and pray or read some pre-chosen Scripture or pull out your cell phone and call your sponsor, your accountability partner, or your trusted friend.

3. Identify Strengths and Assets

- It is important to think about the times you had the opportunity to engage in frotteurism but chose not to. Where were you? What happened? Why did you choose not to engage? Remember those times as often as you can to reinforce your decision not to engage in the behavior and to increase the habit of refraining from engagement in the future.

- What relationships or behaviors have been helpful in the past in preventing your frotteurism? Perhaps feeling connected with friends, having things to look forward to, or some other internal stimulus has been helpful.

4. Consider Group Support

- One of the most beneficial aspects of group therapy is that a person learns he is not alone in suffering from this problem. Moreover, being challenged by peers, who are not experts or leaders, to own your problem and to change can be a powerful inducement.
- Call today to find out the logistics of joining group therapy and make every effort to get to the next meeting.
- *Be prepared to offer a list of possible support groups in your area that can be an avenue for change in the life of your client.*

Additional note to the counselor:
- *Recommend that your client get an evaluation with his primary care physician or another doctor. In some cases, drugs and hormones, such as medroxyprogesterone, have been prescribed to decrease frotteur urges. Testosterone-lowering drugs have been found to be quite effective in reducing aberrant sexual fantasy and behavior.*

5. Confess, Repent, and Ask God for Divine Help

- Consistent with any other sexual sin, take your issue before God. Cry out Psalm 51 and ask God for daily strength.

BIBLICAL INSIGHTS 6

For though we live in the world, we do not wage war as the world does. The weapons we fight with are not the weapons of the world. On the contrary, they have divine power to demolish strongholds. We demolish arguments and every pretension that sets itself up against the knowledge of God, and we take captive every thought to make it obedient to Christ.

2 Corinthians 10:3–5

The battle for moral purity is waged in the mind, but we don't have to fight alone—indeed we cannot. The Spirit of God reveals thoughts that are destructive and distracting, and He gives us the power to fight them with the truth of God's Word. Deviant sexual practices are supported by entrenched thought patterns that have plagued the person for a long time. They don't give up easily, but the combination of God's Word, God's Spirit, and the encouragement and accountability of God's people can change lives.

Put to death, therefore, whatever belongs to your earthly nature: sexual immorality, impurity, lust, evil desires and greed, which is idolatry. Because of these, the wrath of God is coming. You used to walk in these ways, in the life you once lived. But now you must rid yourselves of all such things as these: anger, rage, malice, slander, and filthy language from your lips. Do not lie to each other, since you have taken off your old self with its practices and have put on the new self, which is being renewed in knowledge in the image of its Creator. Here there is no Greek or Jew, circumcised or uncircumcised, barbarian, Scythian, slave or free, but Christ is all, and is in all.

Colossians 3:5–11

The process of change isn't mysterious. Paul instructs the Colossian believers to recognize behaviors that displease God and get rid of them. But that's not all. He tells them to replace those behaviors with truth, righteousness, and a new identity based on God's love, forgiveness, and purposes.

Therefore, there is now no condemnation for those who are in Christ Jesus, because through Christ Jesus the law of the Spirit of life set me free from the law of sin and death. For what the law was powerless to do in that it was weakened by the sinful nature, God did by sending his own Son in the likeness of sinful man to be a sin offering. And so he condemned sin in sinful man, in order that the righteous requirements of the law might be fully met in us, who do not live according to the sinful nature but according to the Spirit.

Romans 8:1–4

God is more than willing to forgive the sin of frotteurism. He delights in people turning to Him and experiencing His cleansing love. He sets us free to live for Him instead of indulging our lusts, and He gives us His Spirit to enable us to take steps toward wholeness in our relationships—with those we know and with those we don't know but pass by each day.

7 PRAYER STARTER

Heavenly Father, thank You for Your mercy and grace. You are always with us, God, even when we have done wrong. Please help my friend as he comes to You to find sexual healing and spiritual growth. Remind him of Your love, Your forgiveness, and Your purposes for his life. Help him take steps today to avoid groping and frotteurizing people. Fill his life with the desire to please You and enjoy healthy relationships . . .

8 RECOMMENDED RESOURCES

Carnes, Patrick J. *Out of the Shadows: Understanding Sexual Addiction.* Hazelden, 2001.

Charlton, Randolph, and Irvin D. Yalon. *Treating Sexual Disorders.* John Wiley and Sons, 1997.

Eiguer, A. "Cynicism: Its Function in the Perversions." *International Journal of Psychoanalysis* 80, no. 4 (1999): 671–84.

Kohut, J. J., and Roland Sweet. *Real Sex: Titillating but True Tales of Bizarre Fetishes, Strange Compulsions, and Just Plain Weird Stuff.* Plume, 2000.

Laaser, Mark. *Healing the Wounds of Sexual Addiction.* Zondervan, 2004.

_____. *L.I.F.E. Guide for Men: A Workbook for Living in Freedom Everyday in Sexual Wholeness and Integrity.* Life Ministries, 2007.

Rosler, A., and E. Witztum. "Pharmacotherapy of Paraphilias in the Next Millennium." *Behavioral Science Law* 18, no. 1 (2000): 43–56.

Seelig, B. J., and L. S. Rosof. "Normal and Pathological Altruism." *Journal of the American Psychoanalytic Association* 49, no. 3 (2001): 933–59.

Weinstein, Estelle, and Efrem Rosen. *Sexuality Counseling: Issues and Implications.* Thomas/Brooks Cole, 1988.

DVD

Laaser, Dr. Mark, Dr. Patrick J. Carnes, and Dr. Daniel Amen. *Freedom Begins Here: Diagnosis and Treatment of Sexual Addiction.* 2005.

27 Sadism and Masochism

1 : PORTRAITS

- Since he was a teenager, Carl has had recurring fantasies about being restrained, humiliated, or abused in a sexual way. His fantasies became reality when he found a group of others who routinely participate in these behaviors.

- Jenny was reading the personals section of the classifieds when she came across an ad from a person requesting a "sex slave." She ignored the ad but then found that she was excited by it and drawn back to it. She made the call and for the past several months has been secretly seeing the man who placed the ad. Now she wants out, but his threats keep her locked into an increasingly degrading relationship with him.

- "Sex isn't the same for me as it is for other people," Ryan explains. "I can't get aroused with normal sexual touching. I need to dominate another person to feel anything. I want the chains, handcuffs, you know, whatever—that's what gets me going. They love it too!"

2 : DEFINITIONS AND KEY THOUGHTS

- *Sadism and masochism are characterized by feelings of sexual pleasure or gratification when inflicting suffering on another person, or when having it inflicted on oneself.*

- *It's not unusual for the sadist's acts, performed or fantasized, to reflect a desire for sexual or psychological domination of another person.* These acts range from behavior that is not usually physically harmful, although it may be humiliating to the other person (such as being urinated on), to criminally harmful and potentially deadly behavior.

- Sexual sadism and sexual masochism are two separate psychological disorders, and each is categorized by the DSM-IV-TR as a paraphilia, which is a sexual disorder characterized by *socially unacceptable preoccupations or behaviors* (other paraphilias include voyeurism, exhibitionism, and fetishism). Sexual sadism with consenting partners is more common than with nonconsenting partners. More people consider themselves masochistic than sadistic.

- The DSM-IV-TR criteria for *sexual sadism* are:

188

— Over a period of at least six months, recurrent, intense sexually arousing fantasies, sexual urges, or behaviors involving acts (real, not simulated) in which the psychological or physical suffering (including humiliation) of the victim is sexually exciting to the person.

— The person has *acted on* these urges with another person, or the sexual urges or fantasies cause marked distress or interpersonal difficulty.[1]

- The DSM-IV-TR criteria for *sexual masochism* are:

— Over a period of at least six months, recurrent, intense sexually arousing fantasies, sexual urges, or behaviors involving the act (real, not simulated) of being humiliated, beaten, bound, or otherwise made to suffer.

— The fantasies, sexual urges, or behaviors cause clinically significant distress or impairment in social, occupational, or other important areas of functioning.[2]

- A person with a *diagnosis of sexual sadism* is known as a *sadist*. The name is derived from Marquis Donatien de Sade (1740–1814), a French aristocrat who became famous for writing novels around the theme of inflicting pain as a source of sexual pleasure.

- A person with a diagnosis of *sexual masochism* is known as a *masochist*. The term *masochist* is derived from Leopold von Sacher-Masoch (1836–95), an Austrian novelist who described the disorder in his works.

- The term *sadomasochism* is used to describe either the *co-occurrence of sadism and masochism* in one individual or as a replacement for both terms.

- In 1905 Sigmund Freud described sadism and masochism in his *Drei Abhand-lungen zur Sexualtheorie* (*Three Papers on Sexual Theory*) as disorders resulting from an incorrect development of the child psyche.

- In some extreme cases, sexual sadism can lead to serious injury or death for the target of the sadistic behaviors. According to the DSM-IV-TR, these occurrences are most likely *when the paraphilia is diagnosed as severe*, and when *antisocial personality disorder is also present*.

- A practicing sadist will find either a willing partner to participate in these behaviors or a sexual victim.

- Some acts of sadism are *not physically harmful* but are *aimed at humiliation*. However, when considering the range of sadomasochistic behaviors, one may classify these actions according to the degree of risk or harm to the other person who is the object of such abuse. From the least to the most risky, these behaviors may include:

— insults, private or public
— restraining a person with handcuffs, chains, ropes, or cages
— spanking or paddling
— whipping
— biting

— beating
— urinating or defecating on the other person
— administering electrical shocks
— cutting and burning
— physical mutilation
— rape
— murder

3 : ASSESSMENT INTERVIEW

For the Sadist or Masochist

1. How long have you had thoughts that are sadistic/masochistic in nature?
2. Have you performed these acts or have you allowed anyone to perform them on you?
3. Are you currently participating in any of these behaviors?
4. Why do you seek treatment or help for sadism/masochism?
5. Have you ever been arrested for committing sadistic practices?
6. Are others in danger because of your present sadistic tendencies? If so, explain.
7. What are some benefits you'll experience by stopping these practices and having a healthy sex life?

For the Victim of a Sadist or Masochist

1. Are you currently in a sadistic/masochistic relationship?
2. When did these behaviors begin?
3. Have you spoken about how you feel to your spouse? If so, how did he react? If not, what fears do you have in disclosing how you feel? Do you fear for your personal safety? (*If the answer is yes to this question, you will need to immediately construct a safety plan that may include a local domestic violence shelter or assistance from other treatment professionals.*)
4. Do you believe you deserve this kind of treatment? If so, why?
5. What are some benefits you'll experience by sharing how you feel and seeking safety from these practices?
6. Do you believe that if these behaviors were ended, you and your spouse would benefit from a healthy sex life?

4 : WISE COUNSEL

True love and healthy sexuality are based on respect, honor, and pure intimacy between a husband and wife. The sexual sadist's desire is for domination, manipulation, control, and the infliction of pain on another. This is at the core of his behavior. The masochist, on the other hand, desires to have pain inflicted on himself, whether self-inflicted or inflicted by someone else. *A desire for domination, manipulation, and control* is at the core of the sexual sadist's and/or masochist's behavior. With sadism and masochism, *a beautiful expression of love that is to exist between husband and wife is severely tarnished.*

Rarely do sexual sadists or masochists volunteer to come for treatment. They may be afraid of being reported to the police. In most cases, they come because the court refers them after their arrest and conviction, or perhaps a victim or family member may come for help.

The practice of sexual sadomasochism can lead to *health problems*, not only through harm to the human body but also through contracting sexually transmitted diseases, due to the release of blood, urine, or other body fluids. For the victim of sadism, *severe physical injury* is also a concern.

Those who engage in sexual sadism and/or masochism *experience the tolerance effect*, like an alcoholic who needs more to get high. Typically sadomasochists *become increasingly violent and bizarre* to achieve the same level of stimulation and excitement.

As the counselor, it is important to help the client(s) realize the *immense love God has for every person*—including him. God also instructs us to show love toward one another through respect, kindness, and compassion. The main task for those struggling with sadistic and masochistic urges will be to train their mind to believe in this kind of love. *They will need to repent and surrender to God's plan for healthy sexuality.*

Sadism and masochism is usually an attempt to work out early experiences of sexual and physical abuse. Trauma therapy is a key.

> Sexual violence victims exhibit a variety of psychological symptoms that are similar to those of victims of other types of trauma, such as war and natural disaster.
>
> *National Research Council, 1996*

ACTION STEPS 5

For the Sadist or Masochist

1. Renounce and Replace Violent Behaviors

- Sadistic behaviors can include a wide range of violent behavior. Some sadistic behaviors are focused on humiliation and mild pain, while others are aimed toward severe pain. Evaluate your current sexual practices and seek to replace violent behaviors with those that honor and respect your partner and please God.

- As a couple, commit to practices that are not harmful or hurtful, and find ways to ensure the safety of both of you. When you accomplish this step, go further and explore sexual behaviors and styles that honor God.

2. Gain Knowledge of God's Design for Sex

- Spend time researching and reading information related to healthy sexuality. Study God's Word and His design for sex. Identify and focus on sexual practices that are gratifying but do not incorporate sadistic or masochistic behaviors.

- As God designed us, every person has strengths, assets, and tendencies toward normal sexual behavior. As a couple, discuss several sexual practices that are acceptable and develop a plan for incorporating these practices into your sex life as husband and wife.

3. Take Action and Commit to Change

- Even if you continue to fantasize about sadism or masochism, you can make a conscious commitment to avoid participating in such behaviors. You may need to take an additional step of putting your commitment down in writing for both you and your counselor to sign/witness for added confirmation.
- With your counselor's help, focus on the innate value of other people and think about how to treat all people with respect and care. This understanding of another person's value can overcome any desire to practice violent or humiliating acts against her. Similarly, seeing yourself as valuable should supersede your sadomasochistic desire to have violent or humiliating acts inflicted on you.

4. Participate in Regular Counseling Support

- You do not have to go through this alone. It will be a great benefit to express your thoughts and feelings to another person, such as a mentor or counselor. Due to the nature and intensity of these urges and behaviors, it is recommended that you meet on a consistent basis with someone who has counseling experience and training for ongoing support throughout the healing process.

For the Victim of Sadomasochistic Behaviors

1. Develop a Personal Safety Plan

- For your own personal safety, you may need to seek shelter from a trusted friend or local program designated for victims of abuse.
- *Be prepared to provide a list of appropriate referrals that can help to ensure the client's safety as necessary.*

2. Ask God for Strength and Wisdom

- Ask God for strength to overcome any fears you may have and wisdom to get out of an abusive relationship.
- A time of separation from your spouse may be needed to work through issues of trust and respect.
- If a time of separation from the marriage is needed, discuss with your counselor a plan for the care of any children involved and for meeting financial concerns.
- As a couple, you will need to begin at square one to get to know one another and reestablish trust in your relationship.

3. Seek God's Blessing

- Abuse has no place in any relationship, and it is certainly not God's design for your marriage. God will bless those who desire righteousness and seek to honor Him in all their ways.

4. Consider Participation in Group Support

- One of the most beneficial aspects of group therapy is that the client learns he is not alone in his problems. We are created for relationship with others. As we go through life, we all have experiences that we can learn from, and then we can use what we have learned to help others navigate along a similar journey.

BIBLICAL INSIGHTS 6

Submit yourselves, then, to God. Resist the devil, and he will flee from you. Come near to God and he will come near to you. Wash your hands, you sinners, and purify your hearts, you double-minded. Grieve, mourn and wail. Change your laughter to mourning and your joy to gloom. Humble yourselves before the Lord, and he will lift you up.

James 4:7–10

Treating others with blatant disrespect and the desire to dominate them is sinful behavior—against the victim and against God. In this passage, James promises that God will draw near to us if we repent and draw near to Him, but this attitude of submission requires genuine conviction, healthy regret, and repentance.

This is the message we have heard from him and declare to you: God is light; in him there is no darkness at all. If we claim to have fellowship with him yet walk in the darkness, we lie and do not live by the truth. But if we walk in the light, as he is in the light, we have fellowship with one another, and the blood of Jesus, his Son, purifies us from all sin. If we claim to be without sin, we deceive ourselves and the truth is not in us. If we confess our sins, he is faithful and just and will forgive us our sins and purify us from all unrighteousness. If we claim we have not sinned, we make him out to be a liar and his word has no place in our lives.

1 John 1:5–10

A number of long-lasting symptoms and illnesses have been associated with sexual victimization, including chronic pelvic pain, premenstrual syndrome, gastrointestinal disorders, and a variety of chronic pain disorders, such as headache, back pain, and facial pain.

Justifying, excusing, or denying sinful behavior doesn't lead to forgiveness—only to more darkness and heartache for the victim and the perpetrator. This wonderful promise is that if we confess our sins, God is gracious and will forgive us. Confession means to agree, so we agree that our actions are sinful, that Christ has paid the price for them, and that we choose not to be involved in the behavior again.

For the grace of God that brings salvation has appeared to all men. It teaches us to say "No" to ungodliness and worldly passions, and to live self-controlled, upright and godly lives in this present age, while we wait for the blessed hope—the glorious appearing of our great God and Savior, Jesus Christ, who gave himself for us to redeem us from all wickedness and to purify for himself a people that are his very own, eager to do what is good.

Titus 2:11–14

Repentance is a choice to say yes to God and no to sin. The struggle to overcome sexual sadism or masochistic behavior can be difficult, but if the person wants to make progress, he can be assured that God gives hope, strength, and wisdom all along the way.

7 PRAYER STARTER

Father in heaven, thank You for the gift of sexuality. We come to You today because my friend is struggling with sadomasochism. We know and understand that You hate violence and call us to a life of love toward each other. Please help him walk in Your light and truth and guide him to a place of true restoration and healing. Give him courage to face the tough issues in his life that have led to the desire for this kind of sexuality . . .

8 RECOMMENDED RESOURCES

Carnes, Patrick J. *Out of the Shadows: Understanding Sexual Addiction*. Hazelden, 2001.

Charlton, Randolph, and Irvin D. Yalon. *Treating Sexual Disorders*. John Wiley and Sons, 1997.

Dutton, Donald. *The Abusive Personality: Violence and Control in Intimate Relationships*. 2nd ed. Guilford Press, 2008.

Laaser, Mark. *Healing the Wounds of Sexual Addiction*. Zondervan, 2004.

_____. *L.I.F.E. Guide for Men: A Workbook for Living in Freedom Everyday in Sexual Wholeness and Integrity*. Life Ministries, 2007.

Weinstein, Estelle, and Efrem Rosen. *Sexuality Counseling: Issues and Implications*. Thomas/Brooks Cole, 1988.

Wilson, Sandra. *Turn In Your Captivity: Ending Abuse in Marriages and Relationships the Jesus Way*. Tate Publishing, 2008.

DVD

Laaser, Dr. Mark, Dr. Patrick J. Carnes, and Dr. Daniel Amen. *Freedom Begins Here: Diagnosis and Treatment of Sexual Addiction*. 2005.

Sexual Violence and Rape 28

PORTRAITS 1

- Jane and her husband were part of a church with a very rigid theological viewpoint that men were the indisputable "head of the household" and wives "must be submissive in all things." When her doctor inquired about the bruising on her face and shoulders, she went numb and told him that it was her fault. If she could only learn to be more submissive, her husband would stop beating her and forcing her into rough sex. Their pastor had been counseling them both and strongly advised against Jane's leaving the home and marriage, even though this would provide for her safety and sanity. To her husband and her pastor, her leaving would be a selfish act of abandonment.

- Nancy was a freshman at the university, and she really wanted to fit in. She was invited by a handsome young man to go to a fraternity party. After a few drinks, he led her into a back room where other couples were engaged in various stages of sexual acts. She protested, but in a drunken rage he overpowered, violated, and raped her.

- Daniel and Bethany have been married for almost two years. Bethany reports that about one year into their marriage, Daniel became very rigid in his desire for certain sexual practices that she is very uncomfortable performing. At first she thought that it was just a phase of experimentation that he would get over. During a recent visit to her gynecologist, however, Bethany was told that she may never be able to have children due to the injury she received after the most recent sexual encounter with Daniel.

DEFINITIONS AND KEY THOUGHTS 2

- *Sexual violence is defined as* any sexual act, attempt to obtain a sexual act, unwanted sexual comments or advances, or acts against a person's sexuality using *coercion by any person* regardless of their relationship to the victim, in any setting, including but not limited to home and work.[1]

- *Rape is defined as* sexual intercourse, or other forms of sexual penetration, by one person ("the accused" or "the perpetrator") with or against another person ("the victim") without the consent of the victim.[2] "Rape may be heterosexual (involving members of opposite sexes) or homosexual (involving members of the same sex). Legal definitions of rape may also include forced oral sex, date rape, gang rape and other sexual acts."[3]

- Historically, marriage has been a defense against being charged by one's spouse with sexual violence. However, in the past forty years, a growing number of states have criminalized sexual violence in marriage. Trends in the law clearly indicate that such violence will no longer be tolerated in the United States.

- The Centers for Disease Control report that sexual violence and rape are *significant problems in the United States*:

  — Among high school students surveyed nationwide, about *8 percent reported having been forced to have sex*. Females (11 percent) were more likely to report having been forced to have sex than males (4 percent).

  — An estimated *20 to 25 percent of college women* in the United States experience attempted or completed rape during their college career.

  — In the United States *one in six women and one in thirty-three men* reported experiencing an attempted or completed rape at some time in their lives.

  — These numbers underestimate what many experts consider to be a problem plagued by *secrecy and failure to report*. Many cases are not reported because victims are afraid to tell the police, friends, or family about the abuse. Often they are *threatened with further violence* or violence against their children, or they are simply afraid that telling will cause the breakup of their family and they'd be left destitute and without financial resources to raise their children.

  — Also, victims think that *their stories of abuse will not be believed and that police cannot help them*. And intense feelings of *shame and embarrassment* can be too painful to expose.

  — Sexual violence may be linked to *risky behaviors* that affect physical health. For example, victims are more likely to smoke, abuse alcohol, use drugs, and engage in unsafe sexual activity.

- The U.S. Department of Justice reports:

  — *Every two minutes someone in the United States is sexually assaulted.*

  — Sexual assault is one of the most underreported crimes, with *60 percent being left unreported*. Males are the least likely to report a sexual assault, though they make up about 10 percent of all victims.

3 ASSESSMENT INTERVIEW

1. What has happened that has brought you here today?
2. Is this the first time you've sought help as a victim of sexual violence/rape?
3. Tell me about your family. How are things going at home?
4. Tell me about your past. Have you had any painful or unusual things happen— even a long time ago?

5. Can you tell me who has abused or is currently abusing you? (*If the person seems reticent, explain that you need to know to help her, others who might be abused, and the abuser himself. In addition, if your client is a minor and still in contact with the abuser, immediate reporting action may need to be taken.*)

6. How long has the abuse been going on?

7. Do you know if others are being abused?

8. What problems are you currently having as a result of what happened? (*Listen to how the abuse affected her. No two people are alike in what happened to them or the consequences of sexual violence/rape. Be aware that victims tend to minimize the impact of the abuse.*)

9. Tell me how you feel about what has happened to you. (*The client needs to have permission to feel her true emotions.*)

10. Do you feel responsible for the abuse? (*Reassure her that she is not alone and that she is not responsible for the abuse.*)

11. What do you believe about yourself? (*Uncover unhealthy beliefs that have developed as a result of abuse. For example, what does she think about herself that she would allow this abuse to continue?*)

12. What do you believe about the person who raped (abused or is abusing) you? (*Listen for rationalizations, such as "He couldn't help it; he was drunk." These defenses have helped the client cope but have also made her less capable of seeing herself as a true victim of abuse.*)

13. Have you ever tried to stop the abuse? What happened?

14. What would you like to have happen as a result of our meeting today?

15. What kinds of boundaries do you think need to be set up to protect you? What do you need if you are to heal from this?

16. Who else knows about this?

17. How did that person respond when you told her?

18. Do you have a personal support system in your life?

19. Where do you think God has been in all of this?

National Center for Victims of Crime
2000 M Street NW, Suite 480
Washington, DC 20036
Toll-free help line:
800-FYI-CALL
Office hours: Mon–Fri, 8:30 a.m.–8:30 p.m. ET
www.ncvc.org

RAINN (Rape, Abuse and Incest National Network)
800-656-HOPE
www.rainn.org

WISE COUNSEL 4

Shame, humiliation, fear, pain, and confusion are among the myriad feelings encircling a victim of sexual violence and rape. These victims have been violated and assaulted in the most demeaning way possible. *Personal boundaries were disregarded* as the victim lost control over her own body, leaving scars that run deep.

It is the responsibility of the counselor to *establish safety and trust* with the client before engaging in any kind of treatment strategy. The *counselor-client relationship must be viewed as the primary initial intervention of utmost importance.* Establishing rapport and creating safety take time and the process cannot be forced.

Reasons a victim may seek the help of a counselor include:

- fear for the safety of her life or the lives of her children

- depression, anxiety, panic, or other mental health symptom that is presently preventing the client from daily functioning
- referral by a pastor, mentor, doctor, family member, or trusted friend
- requirement of a court due to a pending legal case against the perpetrator

A thorough assessment and an evaluation are needed to determine the *level of impairment and current dysfunction*. Areas to assess include personal history, current functioning or impairment, level of safety in current living arrangement, family history, abuse history, medical history, and suicidal or other self-harm ideation.

If danger is still present and the client's personal safety is an issue, you will need to *develop a safety plan* with her. This may include deciding on alternate living arrangements with a family member, trusted friend, or local safety shelter.

Dr. Judith Herman wrote these words in her book *Trauma and Recovery*: "The core experiences of psychological trauma are disempowerment and disconnection from others. Recovery, therefore, is based upon the empowerment of the survivor and the creation of new connections. Recovery can take place only within the context of relationships; it cannot occur in isolation."[4]

Although Dr. Herman did not write her book from a Christian viewpoint, her insight is still valuable and can be aligned with Solomon's words in Ecclesiastes 4:9–10: "Two are better than one. . . . If one falls down, his friend can help him up. But pity the man who falls and has no one to help him up!"

We are *created for relationships*. Beginning with a counselor-client relationship that fosters empowerment, and then in reconnecting with others who are safe, victims of sexual violence and rape can discover God's healing power.

5 : ACTION STEPS

1. Reconnect

- You will begin to find healing when you allow yourself to open up and talk about your feelings to another safe person, such as a counselor. When you were victimized, your ability to control and protect your own body was taken away. This is the gravest of violations for most people and can wreak emotional and relational havoc for years to come if not dealt with in the context of a safe environment. It is important to begin to find your "voice" again and become empowered to overcome the pain this has caused in your life.

- *It is important for the counselor to move slowly and allow the client to explore her feelings at her own pace. She has suffered severe personal boundary violation and needs to feel that she is worthy of respect and honor again. Be a refuge of safety for her.*

- *Many victims will report feelings of guilt and/or shame, believing that they could have done something to prevent the abuse or that they deserved the abuse. Validate your client's feelings, yet reassure her that the abuse was not her fault. Challenge irrational thought patterns and discuss the importance of placing responsibility on the offender.*

2. Develop a Plan for Safety

- If you are still in danger, develop a plan with your counselor as to how you can establish physical and emotional safety for yourself and, if applicable, for your children. Write down the plan and exit strategy.
- Never attempt to "escape" without a clear plan and the assistance of a trusted person. In many cases when a victim has attempted to leave the home abruptly, she has been harassed, severely injured, or even killed by the perpetrator.

3. Reach Out

- Reach out for help by joining a support group, having counseling on an ongoing basis, or reading about and researching sexual violence and rape. However you do it, reaching out will help you fight against fear and the desire for isolation. You do not have to go through this alone. We are broken through relationships, but we are also healed in safe, loving relationships.
- *Help your client come to an understanding of what it means to trust again. Provide education regarding "safe versus unsafe" people.*

4. Seek God's Healing and Wisdom

- At first, it may be very hard to turn to God for healing. You may be questioning where God has been in the midst of your pain. Find a way to work through this doubt and fear. Pick up a commentary and find verses that remind you of your worth and significance in the eyes of God, such as Psalm 18:7–9; 34:7; 1 Peter 3:12. Ask God to help you work through feelings of guilt, shame, and/or anger. Get involved in a local church and consider joining a small group so that you can be surrounded by a caring body of believers.

BIBLICAL INSIGHTS 6

If out in the country a man happens to meet a girl pledged to be married and rapes her, only the man who has done this shall die. Do nothing to the girl; she has committed no sin deserving death. This case is like that of someone who attacks and murders his neighbor, for the man found the girl out in the country, and though the betrothed girl screamed, there was no one to rescue her.

Deuteronomy 22:25–27

Rape is a serious offense in God's eyes because it twists and corrupts God's beautiful creation of sexual intimacy. Under the Old Testament law, rapists were sentenced to death.

It is biblical to report sexual violence and/or rape and for the offender to be duly punished by the law. Keeping quiet is *not* extending grace; it is failing to recognize one's immense value in the eyes of God.

Despite feelings of guilt and self-blame, rape and sexual violence are *never* the victim's fault. God's Word clearly states that the girl "has committed no sin."

Therefore God gave them over in the sinful desires of their hearts to sexual impurity for the degrading of their bodies with one another. They exchanged the truth of God for a lie, and worshiped and served created things rather than the Creator—who is forever praised. Amen. Because of this, God gave them over to shameful lusts. . . . Furthermore, since they did not think it worthwhile to retain the knowledge of God, he gave them over to a depraved mind, to do what ought not to be done.

Romans 1:24–26, 28

Do you not know that the wicked will not inherit the kingdom of God? Do not be deceived: Neither the sexually immoral nor idolaters nor adulterers nor male prostitutes nor homosexual offenders nor thieves nor the greedy nor drunkards nor slanderers nor swindlers will inherit the kingdom of God.

1 Corinthians 6:9–10

Rape and sexual violence are evil corruptions of the beautiful truths God intended to convey through human sexuality as a picture of Christ and His church. Rather than recognizing that the body is an offering to serve and please one's spouse, the abuser's goal is to control and terrorize the victim to satisfy his own desires. These behaviors degrade and ignore Christ's example—He laid down His life for His bride, the church.

God calls sexual violence "wicked," "shameful," and "depraved" and promises to bring just punishment on the offenders.

The LORD is close to the brokenhearted and saves those who are crushed in spirit.

Psalm 34:18

The Spirit of the Sovereign LORD is on me, because the LORD has anointed me to preach good news to the poor. He has sent me to bind up the brokenhearted, to proclaim freedom for the captives and release from darkness for the prisoners, to proclaim the year of the LORD's favor and the day of vengeance of our God, to comfort all who mourn, and provide for those who grieve in Zion—to bestow on them a crown of beauty instead of ashes, the oil of gladness instead of mourning, and a garment of praise instead of a spirit of despair. They will be called oaks of righteousness, a planting of the LORD for the display of his splendor.

Isaiah 61:1–3

God weeps over the pain and the damaging effects of sin in His children's lives, especially in the area of sexual violence. He created sexuality as a beautiful expression of marital intimacy between a man and a woman; but even more than that, it is

Lifetime Rate of Rape/ Attempted Rape by Race

- All women: 17.6%
- White women: 17.7%
- Black women: 18.8%
- Asian Pacific Islander women: 6.8%
- American Indian/ Alaskan women: 34.1%
- Mixed race women: 24.4%

National Institute of Justice and Centers for Disease Control and Prevention, 1998 a picture of His union with His bride, the church. Sexual violence mars this ideal of intimacy between God and man, grieving the heart of God.

Even in the face of unjust abuse, Jesus Christ can bring freedom from tormented memories, release from feelings of degradation, and comfort to the hurting victim.

Many victims of sexual violence view themselves as ugly, no good, and worthless, but God promises to bring beauty and gladness even out of unimaginable pain.

PRAYER STARTER 7

Heavenly Father, we know Your heart breaks when people are hurt so deeply. Thank You for this person who has come for help and healing. And thank You, Lord, for Your kindness and strength. Give wisdom and courage as she takes the next steps to be honest about the pain. It is so comforting to know You never abandon us and will help this dear person experience Your love and peace in the midst of this storm . . .

RECOMMENDED RESOURCES 8

Fortune, Marie. *Sexual Violence: The Sin Revisited*. Pilgrim Press, 2005.

Langberg, Diane. *On the Threshold of Hope*. Tyndale, 1999.

Meyer, Joyce. *The Love Revolution*. Faithwords, 2009.

Weaver, Andrew, Laura Flannelly, and John Preston. *Counseling Survivors of Traumatic Events*. Abingdon Press, 2004.

Wright, H. Norman. *The New Guide to Crisis and Trauma Counseling*. Gospel Light, 2003.

CDs

Adamson, Tom, and Kathy Adamson. *The Shattering Aftermath of Rape*. Focus On The Family Radio Broadcast.

Dobson, James. *Children of Rape I–III*. Focus On The Family Radio Broadcast.

29 Prostitution and Sexual Exploitation

1 : PORTRAITS

- Trina thought she was doing okay after her first year of prostitution. She was seventeen, lived in her pimp's tricked-out penthouse apartment, and no longer had to fight off her stepdad, who had been sexually abusing her for two years before she ran away to the big city. Then one night she allowed her "john" to tie her up for some kinky sex. When he pulled out his switchblade knife with an eight-inch blade, she screamed in fear, not knowing what he had planned for her.

- Mary was hungry after a long night of lying on her back for the many tricks she had serviced. The sun had come up, and she decided to buy a big breakfast with some of the cash she carried with her. By midmorning she was in the hospital with a bruised body, cut and bleeding face, broken jaw, and missing teeth—her pimp had brutally beaten her for stealing "his money," which she had used for food.

2 : DEFINITIONS AND KEY THOUGHTS

- *Prostitution*, known as the "world's oldest profession," involves *selling one's body for sex and sexual favors*. It can also involve trading sex with someone for drugs or shelter or protection or any number of necessary services to maintain life.

- *Child prostitution* involves paying for sex with minors under age eighteen and is sometimes used to describe the wider concept of *commercial sexual exploitation of children* (CSEC). It was the limitations of the term *child prostitution* that led to the development in the mid-1990s of the term *commercial sexual exploitation of children* as a more encompassing description of specific forms of sexual trade involving children. Nevertheless, "child prostitution" remains in common use and is indeed the wording embedded in international instruments of law.

- The *legality of adult prostitution varies* in different parts of the world. It is legal and heavily regulated in Nevada, some states of Australia, and some European countries, but is punishable by death in numerous Middle Eastern countries.

- The *prostitution of minors is illegal in most countries*. Furthermore, many countries whose citizens most frequently engage in international child procurement, such as the United States, Australia, and European countries, enforce worldwide jurisdiction on their nationals traveling abroad.

- *In every city in America, prostitution rings are organized by pimps who "manage" the women*—sometimes including preteens living and working as sexual slaves—and keep the bulk of their earnings in exchange for shelter and protection from other pimps and dangerous "johns" (*the users of prostitutes and their services*). *Many pimps are dangerous*—abusing drugs and beating their women into servile submission of the worst kind.

- According to one study, the number of *full-time equivalent prostitutes in a typical area in the United States is estimated at 23 per 100,000 population* (0.023 percent), of which some 4 percent are under 18.[1]

- Other studies indicate much *higher rates of child prostitutes*. In 2001, Dr. Richard Estes and Dr. Neil Alan Weiner estimated that in the United States, 162,000 homeless youth are victims of commercial sexual exploitation, and 57,800 children in homes (including public housing) are victims of CSEC. They also estimated that 30 percent of shelter youth and 70 percent of homeless youth are victims of CSEC in the United States and that one-third of street-level prostitutes in the United States are under eighteen years old while 50 percent of off-street prostitutes (those working in massage parlors, strip clubs, and escort services) are less than eighteen years old. According to Estes and Weiner, twelve to fourteen is the average age of entry into prostitution for girls in the United States.[2]

- The length of the working careers of these prostitutes was estimated at a mean of five years. Another study revealed a mean number of 868 male sexual partners per prostitute per year of active sex work, and that the number of men who had prostitutes as sexual partners is seriously underreported.[3] A 1994 study found that 16 percent of eighteen- to fifty-nine-year-old men in a U.S. survey group had paid for sex.[4]

- Street prostitution may be the most common form of sex-for-sale in the United States. Pimps stake out and defend key corners and streets in their communities. Then they parade the girls for passing johns, who drive by and choose a girl that they like. Negotiations are done right on the street, and the girl either gets into the john's car or directs him to a certain hotel/motel that offers rooms for an hour or all night to engage in sex.

- *Brothels* are establishments specifically dedicated to prostitution and are often confined to special red-light districts in big cities. Other names for brothels include *bordello, whorehouse, cathouse,* or *knocking shops*. Prostitution also occurs in *some massage parlors*, and in Asian countries in some *barbershops* where sexual services may be offered as a secondary function of the premises.

- *Escort prostitution* is considered a more high-class form of the business and commonly takes place at the customer's hotel room (referred to as an *out-call*) or at the escort's place of residence or hotel room rented for the occasion by the escort (called *in-call*). This form of prostitution is delivered under the umbrella of *escort agencies*, which ostensibly supply attractive escorts for social occasions. While escort agencies claim to never provide sexual services, very few successful escorts are available exclusively for social companionship. Even where this type of prostitution is legal, the ambiguous term *escort service* is commonly used. In the United States, *escort agencies advertise frequently on the internet*, and advertisements can be readily found on any major search engine and on open forum sites.

3 ASSESSMENT INTERVIEW

Prostitution should primarily be approached as if it were sexual violence and abuse—which in fact is what it is. Being a victim carries stigma, shame, and fear, so young people are not likely to volunteer information about their situation. You can be aware that coercion and violence occur and that these acts can have negative consequences on reproductive health. Through counseling, you can help identify young people who are victims or potential victims and provide services, either directly or through referral. It is important that you listen carefully to the young person when discussing violence. You can establish trust and rapport and create an atmosphere of respect and privacy, elements that may be missing from the lives of young people who are victims of sexual violence.

Questions for a child or young adult who is involved in or was just recently rescued from a prostitution ring:

1. Have you ever been touched sexually against your will?
2. When did it first occur? Is it still going on?
3. Do you feel you are in immediate danger? Are you afraid to go home?
4. Does your partner abuse alcohol or drugs? Are you more likely to be abused during episodes of his drinking or drug taking?
5. Do you use alcohol or drugs to help you cope with the violence?
6. How has this violence affected your daily life?
7. How has it affected your views of sexual relationships today?
8. Have you ever thought of suicide?
9. Do you have a family member or friend you can talk to about this?

4 WISE COUNSEL

Typically, prostitutes do not seek counseling for their problems because they are *suspicious of outsiders and authorities, fear rejection, and fear change.* Prostitutes may fear admitting they have been harmed. They may have difficulty establishing enough control over their own lives to seek counseling, and they may fear that health care and other services will not be available to them because they are prostitutes. Many prostitutes have a *"psychological paralysis"* that involves wanting help but rejecting it at the same time. *However, it has been found that if twenty-four-hour hotlines, counseling, advocacy, and shelter care are made available specifically to prostitutes, these services will be used.* Counseling has been found to help prostitutes recover from sexual trauma and improve their self-esteem.[5]

Often prostitutes fear *violent clients, pimps, and corrupt law-enforcement officers.* Those who engage in street prostitution are also sometimes the targets of serial killers, who consider them easy targets and who use the religious and social stigma associated with prostitutes as justification for their murder. Being criminals in most jurisdictions, prostitutes are less likely than the law-abiding to be looked for by police if they disappear, making them favored targets of predators and serial killers.

It's not unusual for Christians and some feminists to be on the same page regarding prostitution, believing that it is *degrading to all involved and inherently exploitative.* Commercial sex is seen as *a form of rape* enforced by poverty (and often by the pimps' overt violence). Those who believe that prostitution is degrading reject the idea (for different reasons) that prostitution can be reformed and legalized, challenging the false assumptions that women exist for men's sexual enjoyment, that all men "need" sex, or that the bodily integrity and sexual pleasure of women is irrelevant. These ideas, in fact, are what make prostitution an *inherently exploitative, sexist practice.*

One authority asserted that *venereal disease and suicide attempts* are the two greatest health risks for juvenile prostitutes. Fifteen percent of all suicide victims are prostitutes, and 75 percent of prostitutes have attempted suicide. In one study about half of the women reported having sexually transmitted infections.[6] More than 90 percent of women in both street and off-street activities increased their drug or alcohol usage during prostitution.[7] Furthermore, because many prostitutes have been sexually assaulted, they suffer from the *psychological effects of rape and child sexual abuse.* These include rape trauma syndrome, low self-esteem, guilt, and self-destructiveness.

In working with those who have been victims of sexual violence or coercion, it is important to:

- *be sensitive and listen carefully* to the client's needs
- *treat any medical problems*
- *offer a pregnancy test*, if available
- provide information about or services for *STI/HIV screening and treatment*
- offer information about *routine contraceptive use*
- *engage professional intervention*

ACTION STEPS 5

1. Be Patient

- Healing from sexual violence is a long, difficult process, and people will vary in the amount of time required for their healing. Don't put yourself on a time line or tell yourself you should "be over this by now."
- You are courageous to seek help for healing, to talk about your experience, and to bring what was once in darkness into the light.
- *If you are involved in a court matter with this case, focus on the data needed by the court when it is needed and question your client about her willingness and ability to further explore her experiences in the context of counseling.*

2. Grieve Your Loss

- You have been violated. Free yourself to express emotive rage and tears when you are ready.

- *Some clients may go to the opposite, compensatory extreme and are numb, without effect at all as they face their loss. Do not push your client to be emotional if she isn't ready. Feel her pain and walk with her to grieve the loss she has experienced.*

3. Repent When Necessary

- If you entered into prostitution willingly, healing and transformation will happen only if you confess your sins to the Lord and repent of the wrongdoing you caused.

4. Regain Control and Find Support

- Attending a group for survivors of sexual violence or rape can be a healing first step. Share your story with someone you trust. Consider restorative counseling as an aid in regaining control of your life. *A child may benefit from play therapy.*

- Realize how saddened God is by the abuse you have suffered. Jesus understands your pain completely, for He suffered unimaginably in His shameful trial and death on the cross.

- Being believed and being able to say what happened are important first steps in recovery. Your counselor will help you stand strong as you begin to realize that those who victimized you can no longer have any power over you.

5. Set Healthy Boundaries

- Here are some things you need to realize: You have a bright future. You're not a victim but a survivor. You may have lost a lot, but you are not "ruined" for the future. Healing is possible.

- Survivors of sexual abuse need to learn how to practice self-care. One important step is to establish healthy boundaries. Be sure trusted people are aware of your personal boundaries so they can help you stand firm in them.

- *Some people may want to confront their abuser. Others will not or will be unable to do so until they are stronger. Be sensitive to where your client is in the healing process and be careful not to encourage her to engage in any confrontation that would be potentially unsafe.*

6. Consider Counseling and Psychotherapy

- You may need professional guidance to truly deal with the depth of pain that sexual abuse and exploitation have caused. Seek out a counselor with expertise in counseling survivors of sexual abuse.

- *Be ready to refer the client to a counselor or therapist who has expertise in counseling victims of sexual violence.*

BIBLICAL INSIGHTS 6

You intended to harm me, but God intended it for good to accomplish what is now being done, the saving of many lives.

Genesis 50:20

If anyone had good reason for revenge, it was Joseph. His brothers' jealousy provoked them to horrible abuse—selling him as a common slave to be taken away forever (Gen. 37:11–28). Before being raised to power in Egypt, Joseph had lost thirteen years of personal freedom.

Joseph wisely understood that God had overruled his brothers' abuse, making their evil turn out for good. This response of strength and faith can come only from those who trust God to rule—and overrule evil—in their lives.

Sometimes people think they can hide portions of their lives from everyone. They try to hide angry tempers, deep jealousies, or sexual sin. Sexual violence hasn't escaped God's notice. The abuser may have thought he got away with it, but God knows—and God promises to judge appropriately.

Do not take revenge, my friends, but leave room for God's wrath, for it is written: "It is mine to avenge; I will repay," says the Lord. . . . Do not be overcome by evil, but overcome evil with good.

Romans 12:19, 21

God knows all that has occurred in our lives, including the pain, the betrayal, and the brokenness. He was present in the darkness and continues to walk with us when we are coming out into the light. The offenses done to us were done to Him as well—including the shame of being disrobed at the cross.

He promises to repay—vengeance is His and His alone. Our job is to heal and to forgive. Do not let the evil overcome you; do not give the abuser that much power in your life. Overcome the evil by doing good to others and to yourself.

PRAYER STARTER 7

Father in heaven, be the Father of lights and the Father of care and protection to this victim of abuse and prostitution. May she always look to You to stay away from and never be sucked back into that evil system. Walk with her in the journey of healing and redemption that You already can see and have prescribed for her. Bring into her life the people and organizations that will help heal her wounds and champion her as a person deserving respect and care . . .

8 RECOMMENDED RESOURCES

Allender, Dan. *The Wounded Heart: Hope for Adult Victims of Childhood Sexual Abuse.* NavPress, 2008.

Carmichael, Amy. *You Are My Hiding Place.* Bethany House, 1991.

Grant, David, and Beth Grant. *Beyond the Soiled Curtain: Project Rescue's Fight for the Victims of the Sex-Slave Industry.* Onward Books, 2009.

Jewell, Dawn. *Escaping the Devil's Bedroom.* Monarch Books, 2008.

Langberg, Diane. *On the Threshold of Hope.* Tyndale, 1999.

DVD

Wildflowers. AACC Library: DVD training series; to order call 800-526-8673 or visit www.aacc.net.

Pedophilia 30

PORTRAITS 1

- Andy has a secret he finally confides: "No one would understand. I don't even understand it myself." Even though he has never acted on his sexual urges toward children, he feels overcome with guilt and dirty and ashamed because of his desires. He hates himself so much for what goes on in his head that he is considering suicide.

- Lois spent the afternoon at the police station bailing out her husband. On the way home she exclaims, "Child pornography? You should be ashamed of yourself. You make me sick!" Bob just stares out of the car window and says nothing.

- John has struggled with sexual lust for children since he was in high school, but he kept the lid on his desires for many years. When he was forty-five years old—married with two children in high school—he found himself alone with a nine-year-old nephew. He made some suggestive overtures. The boy didn't seem to know what was going on, but he trusted his uncle. In a few minutes, John was having anal sex with the boy, who was screaming in pain. After his orgasm, John threatened the boy not to tell anyone, but a few weeks later, the police arrested John. He was convicted and spent four years in jail. Today he's on the pedophile watch list in his community.

DEFINITIONS AND KEY THOUGHTS 2

- As a medical diagnosis, *pedophilia* (sometimes spelled paedophilia) includes *fantasies, urges, or behaviors that involve illegal sexual activity with a child or children* (generally age thirteen or younger).

- Pedophilic behavior includes undressing the child, encouraging the child to watch the abuser masturbate, touching or fondling the child's genitals, and forcefully performing sexual acts on the child.

- *Some pedophiles are sexually attracted to children only* (exclusive pedophiles) and are not attracted to adults at all. *Some pedophiles limit their activity to their own children or close relatives* (incest), while others victimize other children.

- *Predatory pedophiles* may use force or threaten their victims if they disclose the abuse. *Health-care providers are legally bound to report such abuse of minors.*

- The American Psychiatric Association's publication the DSM-IV-TR provides the following *diagnostic criteria* for pedophilia:

— Over a period of at least six months, recurrent, intense sexually arousing fantasies, sexual urges, or behaviors involving sexual activity with a prepubescent child or children (generally age thirteen years or younger).

— The person has acted on these sexual urges, or the sexual urges or fantasies cause marked distress or interpersonal difficulty.

— The person is at least age sixteen years and at least five years older than the child.[1]

• The diagnosis of pedophilia is *further specified by the sex of the children* to whom the person is attracted, and a specific designation is added if the impulses or acts are limited to incest.

• The causes of pedophilia are not fully known. Some studies suggest a *high correlation between being a victim of pedophilia and becoming a perpetrator*. According to a study of 2,429 adult male pedophile sex offenders in the United States, only 7 percent identified themselves as "exclusive." This suggests that *the majority of pedophiles*—or at a minimum, pedophiles prone to acting on their urges—*are attracted sexually to both children and adults*.[2]

• According to the FBI, 61 percent of rape victims are under age eighteen, and *29 percent are younger than eleven*. Generally accepted academic studies say one out of every four women was sexually molested by an adult before she was eighteen. For men it is one out of ten. Yet only one out of every ten cases of child sexual abuse is reported to law enforcement.[3]

• Most sexual offenders were sexually abused as children; *40–80 percent of pedophiles were raped as children*, observes David Burton, professor at University of Michigan School of Social Work in Ann Arbor. "The large majority of them learn to do what they do. Others we don't understand as well." Often pedophiles target and abuse children who are the same age as the predator when he was first sexually abused. There is much disagreement too about whether child molesters can be treated. Burton says most studies show intense treatment is "phenomenally successful." "We help guys figure out dangerous situations, like being around children, what to do, how to plan and cope with distresses and avoid them."[4]

• While many people guilty of child sexual abuse are pedophiles, *not all persons who struggle with pedophilia have acted on their sexual urges toward children*. In other words, not all persons who experience the urges of pedophilia participate in pedophilic behavior. "It is a need-driven behavior of an individual that can't help themselves," says Ruben Rodriguez, director of the Exploited Children Unit of the International Center for Missing and Exploited Children. "Some people live in the fantasy. Others go beyond the fantasy and have to abuse a child."[5]

3 ASSESSMENT INTERVIEW

1. When did your sexual attraction to children begin?
2. Do you experience sexual attraction to adults as well as children?

3. Have you acted on your urges? If so, when and how? (*See under Wise Counsel for appropriate action if the answer is yes.*) If not, do you fear you may act on your feelings of attraction to children?
4. Have you found anything that helps decrease your sexual attraction to children?
5. Can you identify times and situations when you are more sexually attracted to children?
6. Does anyone, such as your spouse, know about the pedophilic feelings you are experiencing?
7. Have you ever been arrested or charged with sexual abuse or with child pornography?
8. Are any children currently in danger because of your pedophilia? Are you currently acting out your urges?
9. Are you a registered sex offender? If so, what are the specific regulations and prohibitions set for you? How do you feel about this status?
10. Have you ever faced legal action or been arrested for sex crimes? What happened? How did the authorities become involved?
11. Are you willing to participate in a counseling process that may be uncomfortable, difficult, and slow, but one that offers real hope for change?

WISE COUNSEL : 4

Sin affects each of us—no person on earth is immune to the temptations of the world. However, *the pain we cause others by our struggles is not always equal.*

Pedophilia is *essentially a desire to control another person*, and because the victim is a child, he is relatively weak and has limited abilities to resist. The pedophile may use threats to gain the child's silence after the fact.

Perpetrators may try to *convince themselves that their acts are in the child's best interests*, that sex with them demonstrates love, teaches about the beauty of sex, and forms a strong bond of affection. *These delusions must be refuted in counseling.* Pedophilia is one of the most destructive sins a human can inflict on another.

Fantasies play a vital role in the disorder. The *child is pictured as a perfect, pure, and innocent person* the pedophile feels he must possess.

Some sexual sins have negative implications primarily in the family and to the person, but pedophilia has *profound legal and moral consequences.*

According to the National Alert Registry, most pedophiles are *multiple-child offenders.* Even more alarming is the fact that many of these pedophiles are *involved with a number of children on a weekly and even daily basis.* A major problem among many incarcerated pedophiles is that they aren't treated in prison and thus become repeat offenders.

Consult state laws about the duty to report alleged child abuse and to engage Megan's Law if this is necessary.

Even with treatment, most pedophiles are *never completely cured* of their sexual urges toward children. However, *counseling therapy can help* pedophiles reduce their inappropriate sexual urges and help them live a life free of acting on them.

5 ACTION STEPS

The following steps serve as a starting point for pedophilia treatment.

1. Make a Commitment to Act Responsibly

- Healing begins with godly repentance and sorrow. Ask for God's help to keep the following vows.

    — I will never act on the urge to have sex with children.

    — I will work consistently to decrease these urges by refusing to dwell on these sexual fantasies and, instead, purposefully fleeing from them.

    — I will refuse to fantasize about children by learning ways to refocus my thoughts and retrain my mind to replace sexual fantasies with rational thinking.

- If a person struggles with a sexual attraction to children and/or engages in online sexual crimes, he doesn't have to act on those urges. However, to begin a path to recovery, you must engage in consistent counseling treatment with an experienced counselor who has worked with sex offenders.

- *Be prepared to offer a referral to an experienced professional if you have not had experience in counseling pedophiles and sex offenders.*

2. Focus on Healthy Sexuality

- Learn to begin replacing urges toward sexual sin with other activities that do not violate yourself or others. Begin to study and understand God's meaning and purpose for sexuality. Read, study, and meditate on God's Word—His promises and design for sex within marriage.

- *Refer to the recommended resources at the end of this chapter and the Biblical Insights section to provide your client with resources that will lay the foundation for healthy sexual development.*

3. Develop a Plan for Accountability

- Pedophilia is a serious problem because it not only affects you but also causes serious damage to the life of your victim(s). You must become accountable to a mature Christian and trusted friend, pastor, mentor, or support group.

- Because of the serious nature of the problem, it is very important that those who struggle with pedophilia find a support system. This may include an accountability partner with whom you can talk about your ongoing struggles. A support system may include an appropriate therapy or support group, where you can learn more about your own struggles and realize that others face similar challenges.

4. Consider Drug Therapy

- There is often a correlation between depression and pedophilia. Go to your doctor and discuss some of the medical treatments available, which include the following:

  — Depo-Provera: a drug that blocks the hormone progesterone
  — Celexa, Lexapro, Luvox, Paxil, Prozac, and Zoloft: drugs that have met with moderate success in treating pedophilia and depression
  — therapy combined with some type of drug treatment, which has met with some success[6]

Additional notes to the counselor:

- *The continuing reality is that treatment prognosis is especially poor and recidivism is exceptionally high in pedophilia and sex crimes. Many states have had to hospitalize offenders who have served a full prison term but come out as high risk to reoffend because they showed no remorse and made no changes in their attraction to children while in prison. Many churches and pastors have also gotten into serious trouble because they have trusted in the repentant assertions of pedophiles, allowing them into situations with family and children where they have reoffended.*
- *Two tasks are critical when doing any kind of work with pedophiles.*

  1. *Pursue every resource available, including information from experts. Consider the possibility of combined therapies: drugs, individual counseling, and groups.*
  2. *Do everything necessary to protect any at-risk children, even if that means counseling for the separation of the pedophile from his family and others and maintaining that separation for a long period of time.*

Victims of sexual assault are:
- 3 times more likely to suffer from depression than the general population
- 6 times more likely to suffer from posttraumatic stress disorder
- 13 times more likely to abuse alcohol
- 26 times more likely to abuse drugs
- 4 times more likely to contemplate suicide

World Health Organization, 2002

BIBLICAL INSIGHTS 6

People were bringing little children to Jesus to have him touch them, but the disciples rebuked them. When Jesus saw this, he was indignant. He said to them, "Let the little children come to me, and do not hinder them, for the kingdom of God belongs to such as these. I tell you the truth, anyone who will not receive the kingdom of God like a little child will never enter it." And he took the children in his arms, put his hands on them and blessed them.

Mark 10:13–16

God values children tremendously. Jesus rebuked His followers who failed to value them highly enough, and He demonstrated His love by taking them in His arms and blessing them.

It would be better for him to be thrown into the sea with a millstone tied around his neck than for him to cause one of these little ones to sin.

Luke 17:2

This passage is about causing children to sin. Pedophilia crushes a child's spirit and wounds his soul, paving the way for destructive behaviors (both self directed and other directed) in the future.

When you were dead in your sins and in the uncircumcision of your sinful nature, God made you alive with Christ. He forgave us all our sins, having canceled the written code, with its regulations, that was against us and that stood opposed to us; he took it away, nailing it to the cross. And having disarmed the powers and authorities, he made a public spectacle of them, triumphing over them by the cross.

Colossians 2:13–15

God's incredible grace extends to every person and every sin. He accepts our repentant, broken hearts and cleanses us from sin—even the sin of pedophilia and sexual crime.

7 PRAYER STARTER

Heavenly Father, thank You for this person who has shown immense bravery in coming here today. Lord, he wants to walk with You and be an obedient servant, but his urges and attractions are causing him immense problems. Please show him Your greatness and heal him of this affliction. Provide him with the strength, skills, and tools to manage his attractions and live an upright life . . .

8 RECOMMENDED RESOURCES

Arterburn, Stephen. *Healing Is a Choice*. Thomas Nelson, 2005.

Arterburn, Stephen, and Debra Cherry. *Feeding Your Appetites: Take Control of What's Controlling You*. Thomas Nelson, 2007.

Carnes, Patrick J. *Out of the Shadows: Understanding Sexual Addiction*. Hazelden, 2001.

Laaser, Mark. *Healing the Wounds of Sexual Addiction*. Zondervan, 2004.

_____. *L.I.F.E. Guide for Men: A Workbook for Living in Freedom Everyday in Sexual Wholeness and Integrity*. Life Ministries, 2007.

Rogers, Adrian, and Joyce Rogers. *Family Survival in an X-Rated World: A Practical Guide for Guarding Your Heart and Protecting Your Home*. B & H Publishing, 2005.

Course

"Treating Sexual Addiction," Certificate Training Program, Light University/AACC DVD Course; www.aacc.net.

Sexual Harassment 31

PORTRAITS : 1

- "It was pretty cut-and-dried," Monica explained. "My supervisor, in no uncertain terms, said that if I wanted to keep my job, I would have to put out. I refused and I was fired."
- "It seems silly for me to be reporting sexual harassment, but I'm going to do it anyway," John said. "I work in an office of all women, and half the day I feel really uncomfortable. The conversations about sex and men, the names they have for me, and the excessive touching—I can't take another day of it."
- Brenda had been at the company for a few weeks, and during that time she could tell that Alicia, her supervisor, kept her eye on her for unusually long times. She thought Alicia was just a diligent boss, but then Alicia began asking probing questions about her private life. A co-worker told her she thought Alicia was a lesbian, but Brenda didn't want to believe it. When Alicia found out that Brenda was thirty years old and single, she began sending Brenda emails that were a little too friendly in nature and borderline suggestive. Brenda became very uncomfortable when she received a voicemail from Alicia in which she made several comments about her physical attractiveness.

DEFINITIONS AND KEY THOUGHTS : 2

- Sexual harassment occurs when *sexually oriented conduct explicitly or implicitly affects an individual's employment*, interferes with an individual's work performance, or creates an *intimidating, hostile, or offensive work environment*.[1]
- Sexual harassment is a form *of sexual discrimination* that violates Title VII of the Civil Rights Act of 1964.
- Sexual harassment may include one or more of the following:

  — *unwelcome sexual advances*
  — *requests for sexual favors*
  — *verbal conduct* of a sexual nature
  — *physical conduct* of a sexual nature

- Sexual harassment can occur among a variety of people in a variety of circumstances, including but not limited to the following:

— The target may be *male or female.*
— The harasser may be *male or female.*
— The target may be the *same sex or the opposite sex* of the harasser.
— The harasser can be the target's supervisor, an agent of the employer, a supervisor in another area, a co-worker, or a nonemployee.
— The target does not have to be the person harassed but could be *anyone affected by offensive conduct.*
— Sexual harassment may occur *without economic injury to or causing termination of employment* of the target.
— The harasser's conduct must be *unwelcome.*[2]

• In many cases, it is *helpful for the target to directly inform the harasser* that her conduct is unwelcome and request its immediate cessation. Or the target may use any complaint mechanism or grievance system available at the place of employment. Often sexual harassment will cease after an internal complaint is filed.

• According to one official at a U.S. government department, the U.S. Supreme Court has simplified matters concerning sexual harassment by describing *two basic types of unlawful sexual harassment* in the workplace.

Type One: Quid Pro Quo

• The first type of sexual harassment includes a *tangible employment action.* An example of this could be a supervisor who tells a subordinate that she must be sexually cooperative or she will be terminated, passed up for promotion, punished, and so on, and then takes punitive action when the employee does not cooperate. This is referred to as the quid pro quo type of sexual harassment because of its "this for that" nature.[3]

Type Two: Hostile Environment

• Unlike the quid pro quo in which a supervisor imposes an ultimatum, the hostile environment can result from the *unwelcome conduct of supervisors, co-workers, customers, or anyone else* with whom a harassed employee interacts. Behaviors that constitute hostile environment harassment include:

— *threats* to impose a sexual quid pro quo
— *discussion of sexual activities*
— telling *off-color jokes*
— unnecessary or excessive *touching*
— *comments on physical attributes* of an employee
— displaying *sexually suggestive pictures*
— use of *inappropriate nicknames,* such as "Honey," "Doll," or "Babe"
— *threatening or hostile* physical conduct
— use of *crude, crass, and offensive language*[4]

ASSESSMENT INTERVIEW : 3

For the Target of Sexual Harassment

1. When did the sexual harassment begin?
2. What is the nature of the harassment?
3. What did you do to try to end the harassment?
4. Did your attempts to stop the sexual harassment help? Why or why not?
5. Are you still being sexually harassed?
6. Do you feel that you are in physical danger?

For the Supervisor or Sexual Harasser

1. When did the sexual harassment begin?
2. What is the nature of the sexual harassment?
3. Do you understand the legal and ethical consequences of this charge?
4. Has the accusing person talked to you about the problem? If so, what were the results of the conversation?
5. What is the next step in resolving the problem?
6. What can you do to protect future and current employees from sexual harassment from others?

WISE COUNSEL : 4

All human beings are created in God's image and deserve respect. *Sexual harassment, exploitation, and abuse are destructive.* When a person is a victim of this type of injustice, her ability to develop and use her God-given gifts of creativity and wholeness are stifled.

Sexual harassment can occur in several ways. However, no matter how or when it occurs, it *erodes a person's feeling of comfort and safety.* The fact that sexual harassment often occurs at the hand of someone who is supposed to be an advocate (such as a pastor, counselor, teacher, or supervisor) makes the experience even more confusing and painful.

People who complain about sexual harassment must be taken seriously. Perhaps there has been a misunderstanding, and both parties can grow from the process of resolution. But if harassment has occurred, *feelings of betrayal and pain* will be very real for the victim.

In many cases a victim will be *fearful of reporting harassment.* She may be concerned about losing her job, especially if the sexual harasser is her supervisor or someone in a position of higher authority. A victim may also fear being ridiculed, blamed, or called a liar.

The following are general principles for counseling someone who has been sexually harassed:

1. The victim may have very *similar feelings and perceptions as a victim of rape.*
2. The victim *may feel insecure and ashamed* for not being able to prevent the harassment.
3. Almost certainly, the person accused will claim that he has been *grossly misunderstood* and often will *blame the victim* for the problem.
4. The *response of the company* will determine if it is a safe place for the victim to go back to work.
5. Even if the company responds positively to the victim, charges take time to be addressed, and the accused often appeals negative findings, either to the company's human resources department or to the U.S. Equal Employment Opportunity Commission (EEOC). During this long process, *the victim will need reassurance and encouragement.*

It is important to *create a safe environment* for the client to feel respected, believed, and empowered to take control of her life.

Prevention

According to the *EEOC, prevention is the best tool* to eliminate sexual harassment in the workplace. *Prevention begins with employers and managers*, not employees or potential targets of sexual harassment.

Employers and managers are to communicate clearly to employees that *sexual harassment will not be tolerated.* They must create an open environment where sexual harassment, or even potential sexual harassment, can be reported without fear. This can be accomplished in part by establishing *complaint or grievance procedures* and also by taking *immediate and appropriate actions* if and when employee complaints occur.

Reporting Sexual Harassment

If a person believes or suspects she has been a target of sexual harassment, it is appropriate to *report the incident to the management* at the place of employment, or *a charge of sexual harassment can be filed* with the U.S. Equal Employment Opportunity Commission.

To file a charge with the EEOC:

- Charges may be filed in person, by mail, or by telephone. If there is no EEOC office nearby to visit in person, one can call the EEOC toll-free at 800-669-4000 (or call 800-669-6820 for the hearing impaired—TDD) for more information on filing a charge of sexual harassment.
- There are strict time limitations in which charges of sexual harassment or discrimination can be filed. To ensure the ability of the EEOC to act on one's behalf and to protect one's right to file a private lawsuit (should one ultimately need to be filed), be sure to follow any guidelines provided by the EEOC when filing a charge.

For more detailed information, locate an EEOC office near you or go to www
.eeoc.gov.

ACTION STEPS 5

1. Talk Honestly

- You may be asking, *Why me?* You may be experiencing many feelings, such
  as anger at the perpetrator, shame for not being able to stop it, worthlessness,
  and a sense of being used. It's important to talk to someone you trust—a family member, friend, or counselor—to sort through these feelings and receive
  validation. Talk honestly about what has happened to you.

- *Trust and safety are of vital importance. Validate and affirm your client's feelings.
  Help her realize the abuse was not her fault and encourage her to find appropriate ways to express her feelings outside of the counseling office, such as through
  journaling or writing out her story.*

2. Relinquish Self-Blame and Shame

- Develop an understanding of how this harassment happened and realize
  the abuse was not your fault. Work to relinquish blaming yourself and
  feelings of shame.

- What has happened to you is someone else's wrongdoing. You can regain
  control of your emotions and reassume ownership of your personal
  integrity.

3. Consider Joining a Support Group

- It always helps to talk with someone who has shared similar pain and
  receive guidance from the experience of others. In a group setting, individuals comment and discuss their own stories of sexual harassment
  and are able to provide support to each other—as well as advice on how
  to properly report and end the cycle of abuse.

4. Develop a Plan of Action

- Develop a plan of action with your counselor and take the necessary
  steps to ensure that the perpetrator is held responsible for his actions.

5. Pray

- Pray for God's strength to endure and the wisdom needed to properly report
  the abuse. Also trust that God will use this painful experience to bring good
  into your life and allow you to help others.

> In fiscal year 2007, the Equal Employment Opportunity Commission (EEOC) received 12,510 charges of sexual harassment. Men filed 16 percent of them. EEOC resolved 11,592 sexual harassment charges in 2007 and recovered 49.9 million dollars in monetary benefits for charging parties and other aggrieved individuals (not including monetary benefits obtained through litigation).

6 BIBLICAL INSIGHTS

He heals the brokenhearted and binds up their wounds. He determines the number of the stars and calls them each by name. Great is our LORD and mighty in power; his understanding has no limit. The LORD sustains the humble but casts the wicked to the ground.

Psalm 147:3–6

Sexual harassment is a shattering experience that can jolt every aspect of a person's safety and identity, but God is near to the brokenhearted and offers to them His presence, peace, and wisdom. Victims can be assured that someday, somehow God's justice will prevail.

Consider it pure joy, my brothers, whenever you face trials of many kinds, because you know that the testing of your faith develops perseverance. Perseverance must finish its work so that you may be mature and complete, not lacking anything.

James 1:2–4

God can use every experience in our lives—the good, the bad, and the confusing— to shape our character and draw us closer to Him, if we'll let Him. God will even use the traumatic experience of sexual harassment to produce more depth, wisdom, and hope than we've ever known before. Certainly, the abuse wasn't His perfect plan, but by His grace, He turns negatives into positives for those He loves.

If any of you lacks wisdom, he should ask God, who gives generously to all without finding fault, and it will be given to him. But when he asks, he must believe and not doubt, because he who doubts is like a wave of the sea, blown and tossed by the wind. That man should not think he will receive anything from the Lord; he is a double-minded man, unstable in all he does.

James 1:5–8

When harassment begins, the victim is often caught off guard and feels confused. Turning to God in prayer, the Scriptures, and a wise counselor, she can find genuine insight into the path God wants her to follow. The path may not be easy or straight. She may experience a lot of opposition from the perpetrator, and others may not understand why she brought the charge in the first place. But if she trusts God and follows His leading, she can stay strong.

7 PRAYER STARTER

Lord, my friend comes to You today about a traumatic event that has happened to her. She has experienced sexual harassment in the workplace, Lord, and needs Your presence to help her know the correct course of action. She needs to experience Your healing touch, and she needs wisdom to protect herself from further transgressions against her . . .

RECOMMENDED RESOURCES 8

Balswick, Judith, and Jack Balswick. *Authentic Human Sexuality: An Integrated Christian Approach.* IVP Academic, 2008.

Cloud, Henry, and John Townsend. *Boundaries.* Zondervan, 1992.

DeMoss, Nancy Leigh. *The Lies Women Believe and the Truth That Sets Them Free.* Moody, 2001.

Hawkins, David. *Dealing with the Crazy Makers in Your Life.* Harvest House, 2007.

Howard, Linda. *The Sexual Harassment Handbook.* 1st ed. Career Press, 2007; not written from a Christian resource but offers good insight.

Van Vonderen, Jeffrey. *When God's People Let You Down.* Bethany House, 2005.

Wilson, Sandra. *Released from Shame: Moving beyond the Pain of the Past.* InterVarsity Press, 2002.

Wright, H. Norman. *The New Guide to Crisis and Trauma Counseling.* Gospel Light, 2003.

Wright, H. Norman, Matt Woodley, and Julie Woodley. *Surviving the Storms of Life: Finding Hope and Healing When Life Goes Wrong.* Revell, 2008.

PART 4

Gender Identity Issues

32 Homosexuality

1 PORTRAITS

- Jon had kept his secret through junior high and high school. All the guys he knew talked openly and often about their lust for girls in school, but he couldn't stop thinking about the naked guys in the locker room. Now in college, he has heard a rumor that a young man down the hall in his dorm is gay. Soon the two of them got together and began an intense sexual relationship. Jon became a Christian at summer camp when he was twelve, but now he doesn't know what to think about God. His sexual urges seem to overwhelm everything else in his life.

- Kay's parents got divorced when she was a baby, and her father moved to another part of the country, rarely visiting or even calling. Her mother felt guilty and lonely. She smothered Kay with attention throughout her childhood. Kay dated casually when she was in high school, but she felt much more comfortable around her girlfriends. One day Nancy, a new girl in school, asked her to run an errand with her. On the way Nancy drove to a secluded park, stopped the car, and pulled Kay over near her. "I want to kiss you so much it hurts," she whispered. She leaned over and kissed Kay, first tenderly, and then passionately. Kay's emotions exploded. She enjoyed the attention and the sexual attraction, but she felt terribly ashamed and confused. After a week of emotional torture, she confided to her school counselor, "I don't know who I am anymore. Am I a lesbian?"

- Carl began watching porn when he was only eight years old. He became obsessed with sex. By the time he was thirteen, he masturbated several times a day, and when he was in junior high school, he had his first sexual encounter with a girl. Now in college, he's had dozens of partners but can't seem to get enough. Recently he began experimenting with guys too, and he really likes it.

2 DEFINITIONS AND KEY THOUGHTS

- *Same-sex attraction* is a sexual predisposition toward members of the same sex. *Same-sex behavior* is the engagement of any sexual activity between two people of the same sex.

- Probably no other topic elicits *such powerful emotions from people having entrenched and conflicting perspectives* as does homosexuality, especially among the Christian community. Many hold to the biblical view that homosexuality is a perversion of God's design for sex and a distortion of human identity. Others argue that homosexuals "don't have a choice" about their sexual preference, and they lobby for acceptance of the people and their behavior.

- *Identifying the causes of homosexuality* has proven to be a difficult and explosive issue. *Some argue that people choose homosexuality based on the influences of their social environment; others say that homosexuality is genetically predetermined.* At this point, no definitive study has conclusively established the etiology, but several factors seem to contribute.

  — A person's *family background*, and especially one's relationship with the same-sex parent, can shape emerging sexuality in adolescence.
  — *Social interactions*, especially during the formative years, teach and reinforce sexual norms.
  — *Early sexual experiences*—and particularly seductive, abusive, and homosexual experiences—can shape a child's self-concept and perception of sexuality.
  — *Biological causes* have received the most attention in recent years, but ambivalent research results have been advanced as "proving a biological or genetic cause" for homosexuality. Of course, finding a biogenetic cause for homosexuality is compelling to those who espouse a gay lifestyle because it no longer would be considered a choice but a biological imperative and, therefore, not a sinful orientation requiring a spiritual solution.

- The passionate and risky nature of homosexual encounters may make individuals more *vulnerable to various sexually transmitted diseases*, including HIV/AIDS. Young men who have sex with men (MSM) and with a high number of different partners are at extremely high risk for contracting a sexually transmitted infection. According to the CDC, the number of MSM ages thirteen to twenty-four newly diagnosed with HIV is increasing each year and has almost doubled since 2000. The number of infected men increased by 11 percent in 2001 and by 18 percent in 2006.[1]

> More than 68 percent of lesbians report having had a range of mental health problems in the past, including long-term depression and sadness, constant anxiety and fear, and other mental health concerns.
> *Duke Journal of Gender Law and Policy*

ASSESSMENT INTERVIEW 3

1. When did your same-sex attraction begin? How did you become aware of these feelings?
2. Have you acted out your urges? If so, tell me about your experiences.
3. Talk about your relationship with your family of origin. How is your relationship with your mother and father? Were they present in your home when you were a child? Were Mom and Dad actively involved in your life? How did (do) they express affection toward each other? How do they express affection toward you?

4. When was your first sexual experience? What happened? How did it affect you at the time? Have you ever been sexually abused? If so, was it by a same-sex or opposite-sex perpetrator?
5. How have you related to members of the opposite sex? Are you attracted to them? Have you had dating relationships with the opposite sex?
6. Do you fantasize about members of the same sex? How many of these fantasies have come true (or close to true)?
7. Are you currently engaging in sexual relationships?
8. Have you told anyone about your homosexual urges (and behaviors)? How have they responded?
9. What are your hopes and fears about your sexuality?
10. What are your goals for counseling?

4 : WISE COUNSEL

In the controversial realm of homosexuality and sex reorientation therapy, *the counselor's role is easily compromised by demonstrations of shock or extremes of judgment and disapproval.* In fact, most gay individuals are hypersensitive and hypervigilant regarding this dynamic. Stay engaged and express any opinions in a matter-of-fact manner.

As many as 9 million children living in the United States have a gay or lesbian parent, and 25 percent of all lesbian couples are raising children. Twenty percent of these children have considered same-sex sexual relationships even though they have never experienced same-sex sexual attraction.

Duke Journal of Gender Law and Policy

The client has come to you for help (or perhaps has been brought to you by someone else) and is in a very vulnerable emotional state. The person's progress may depend on your ability to make him feel safe and become honest about hurts, fears, and hopes for the future. So while you may be opposed to homosexual behavior, *empathy and understanding are essential* tools at the outset of counseling. *If it is too difficult for you to work with someone struggling with same-sex attraction, you need to refer.* At this time it is extremely important to let your client know you accept him as fully deserving of God's love.

Explore the client's feelings and attitudes about his homosexual urges and behaviors. In many cases, *clients come because they feel confused and ashamed.* (Those who feel satisfied and justified in their homosexuality will rarely if ever come for help.) He may experience *significant anxiety* over his sexual orientation and behaviors, and his fears may cloud his thinking processes. One of the first tasks is to *help him resolve his identity confusion* and decide who he is. Put to him the challenge of answering this crucial question first—a question that will help clarify the identity puzzle: am I in fact gay—which is to embrace a sexual identity—or am I instead a man (or woman or Christian) who is struggling with homosexual attractions and desires?

Avoid "Bible-thumping" at all stages of counseling. Many clients already know the Bible says that homosexuality is sin, and they have avoided coming to a pastor or Christian counselor because they don't want anyone to preach condemnation to them. It is important, however, to draw out what they understand the Bible to say about homosexuality and then discuss what that means to them and where the *dissonance* is. For instance, how do they deal with the Bible's statements? What do they want to accomplish to please God and to know His strength and purpose in life?

Gay clients, particularly men, may be engaged in addictive sexual activity. Sometimes stopping addictive activity will help the client make healthy orientation choices. Many Christian counselors use *an addictions treatment model* in helping homosexuals—and often in the context of group therapy around sexual addictions. This model is based on *several assumptions*, including the possibility of predisposition, the client's desire for change, turning to God for hope and strength, taking a fearless and searching moral inventory of urges and behaviors, genuine repentance, mutual support, and a long-term perspective about change. Like alcoholics or drug addicts, homosexuals may never consider themselves "cured," but by acknowledging their powerlessness over the condition, they begin a process and learn day by day to walk in a way that can lead to a new, healthy lifestyle.

ACTION STEPS 5

Every Christian counselor should be prepared to help the counselee define his goals and move in a constructive direction toward resolving the often confusing ambivalence around identity and sexuality.

1. Identify Personal Goals

- Think about goals you would like to achieve through counseling. Determine what you would like your life to be like at the end of the counseling process. Share these goals with your counselor.

- *Determine if your goals and the client's goals are compatible with your faith and practice. If clients feel affirmed in their homosexual identity and lifestyle and want help to have better relationships with same-sex partners, as one who does not believe that same-sex behavior is right before God, you are probably not the best person to serve as the counselor. Remember, however, that clients may assume that a Christian counselor is rigid and condemning, and they may be defensive until the counselor demonstrates empathy and understanding. Help clients clarify their life goals by offering the stark choice of choosing a gay-affirming posture versus change therapy.*

- *If clients admit their confusion and conflicting emotions about homosexual urges and behaviors and want to change, you can offer a realistic pathway in which they can experience peace, freedom, and joy in Christ, as well as engaging in meaningful relationships with people of both genders.*

2. Explore Your Current Beliefs regarding Sexuality

- Focus on discussing what you have been taught in the past about homosexuality and how this has contributed to your current belief system. What do you consider "normal" and "abnormal"?

- *Many who experience homosexual urges and behaviors come to counseling with a wealth of misinformation about causes, diseases, the definition of "normal" sexuality, and a host of other topics related to the problem. Some have been taught that they've committed a sin God won't forgive, and they feel not only ashamed but hopeless as well. Help the client understand God's design for sexuality, as well as His willingness to forgive and pardon all sin. (See 1 John 1:9.)*

3. Uncover Your Fears and Hopes

- Be honest about your emotions. This is an important step in feeling understood, building trust in your counselor, and moving forward.
- Many people hope that a counselor will give them a quick and easy solution and make them feel better right away. This, of course, won't happen. Homosexuality requires rugged realism about the process and goals for change. Change is possible but often requires hard work and time, and even then, the urges sometimes won't completely go away.
- Homosexuality can be as emotionally explosive in treatment as it is in society, full of raw passion and dark fears. Be transparent about the full range of your feelings.

4. Realize the Importance of Mental Self-Control

- Be open to learning how thoughts and feelings dictate actions. Practice new ways of interpreting and analyzing destructive thoughts and feelings prior to acting on them.
- *The combination of sexual passion and shame causes many homosexuals to be preoccupied, even obsessed, with their sex life and identity. For some, their sexuality is primarily a fantasy world, but this world consumes their lives. It becomes an obsession, and they can't stop thinking about sex. Teach clients to identify thoughts, songs, passages of Scripture, and inspiring messages to focus on and confess aloud, using them to replace their unwanted or intrusive fantasies.*

5. Be Encouraged by Each Step Forward

- Changing identity and a lifestyle is a monumental task. People with other complex issues such as alcoholics, drug addicts, compulsive gamblers, and those with eating disorders have successfully taken steps out of their darkness toward hope and health, and you can do the same.
- Celebrate each step forward you make. Even if you slip, all is not lost. God loves you and He is in the process of helping you change. You can begin to move forward again by repenting, receiving the Lord's forgiveness, and focusing on biblical goals.
- *Provide strong encouragement that the benefits of progress are worth the struggle of moving forward.*

Sexual Identity Therapy

Consider using the Sexual Identity Therapy (SIT) model for counseling to help resolve the critical first issue of identity decision making. Christian psychologists Mark Yarhouse and Warren Throckmorton have developed an excellent counseling model that has been affirmed and recommended by Christian and secular mental health professionals.[2]

6. Consider Participating in Group Support

- The encouragement you will receive in a Christ-centered support group can make a tremendous difference. In an environment of mutual support and accountability, you will hear from others who struggle with similar problems as they make courageous decisions and experience the joys of real change.
- *Provide a referral to a support group in the area for your client or start one yourself.*

BIBLICAL INSIGHTS 6

Therefore, my dear friends, as you have always obeyed—not only in my presence, but now much more in my absence—continue to work out your salvation with fear and trembling, for it is God who works in you to will and to act according to his good purpose.

Philippians 2:12–13

Our obedience to God is a response to His goodness and greatness. We don't just "take Him or leave Him" and obey if we feel like it. All of us have hard choices as we follow Christ, but God promises to work powerfully in us by His Spirit to equip us, change us, and inspire us to keep moving forward.

But when the kindness and love of God our Savior appeared, he saved us, not because of righteous things we had done, but because of his mercy. He saved us through the washing of rebirth and renewal by the Holy Spirit, whom he poured out on us generously through Jesus Christ our Savior, so that, having been justified by his grace, we might become heirs having the hope of eternal life.

Titus 3:4–7

Experimental homosexuality may occur in adolescence or preadolescence and ranges from comparing same-sex genitals to intercourse. Often the phase of experimentation passes, and people become exclusively heterosexual.

When Christ died on the cross, He paid for every sin any human has ever committed—the ones we often ignore, like greed or envy, and the ones that are considered horrible, like murder. There is no sin that's beyond Christ's forgiveness, including homosexuality. If we turn to Him, He pours out His Spirit on us, He forgives us, and He gives us hope and encouragement that life can be much better than we ever dreamed.

You were taught, with regard to your former way of life, to put off your old self, which is being corrupted by its deceitful desires; to be made new in the attitude of your minds; and to put on the new self, created to be like God in true righteousness and holiness.

Ephesians 4:22–24

The process of change requires objectivity and tenacity. It doesn't just happen automatically. In this Ephesians passage, Paul says it's like changing clothes. We take off our old behaviors and thoughts; then our minds are renewed by the Scriptures, and we put on new, healthy, positive behaviors that honor God. To change clothes we have to be intentional about what we take off and put on. It's the same way with changing our lifestyle.

7 | PRAYER STARTER

Father, You are wise and strong. My friend is struggling with his desires, and he wants to change. Lord, You offer hope that change is possible. Give wisdom about the steps that can be taken to replace old fantasies with new, healthy thoughts. Provide courage for him to take the steps he needs to take and to keep moving forward when he feels discouraged . . .

8 | RECOMMENDED RESOURCES

Carnes, Patrick J. *Out of the Shadows: Understanding Sexual Addiction*. Hazelden, 2001.

Charlton, Randolph, and Irvin D. Yalon. *Treating Sexual Disorders*. John Wiley and Sons, 1997.

Clinton, Tim, Arch Hart, and George Ohlschlager. *Caring for People God's Way*. Thomas Nelson, 2009.

Dallas, Joe, and Nancy Heche. *The Complete Christian Guide to Understanding Homosexuality: A Handbook for Helping Those Who Struggle with Same-Sex Attraction*. Harvest House, 2009.

Klein, Walter. *God's Word Speaks to Homosexuality*. Wine Press, 2007.

Laaser, Mark. *Healing the Wounds of Sexual Addiction*. Zondervan, 2004.

_____. *L.I.F.E. Guide for Men: A Workbook for Living in Freedom Everyday in Sexual Wholeness and Integrity*. Life Ministries, 2007.

Stott, John. *Same Sex Partnership? A Christian Perspective*. Baker, 1998.

White, John. *Eros Defiled*. InterVarsity Press, 1977.

Yarhouse, Mark, and Stanton Jones. *Ex-Gays? A Longitudinal Study of Religiously Mediated Change in Sexual Orientation*. InterVarsity Press, 2007.

DVDs

Davis, Scott. *The Question of Homosexuality: A Conversation for Youth about Same-Sex Attraction*. Harvest House, 2009.

Laaser, Dr. Mark, Dr. Patrick J. Carnes, and Dr. Daniel Amen. *Freedom Begins Here: Diagnosis and Treatment of Sexual Addiction*, 2005.

Gender Identity Disorder 33

- Sam was named after her father and has always been "Daddy's favorite." "That's not to be confused with 'Daddy's little girl,'" she says. "I hate being a girl," she protests. "I'm more boy than girl."
- Pat had a normal childhood, but around the age of thirteen, he started feeling that something was wrong. Now, at sixteen years old, he isn't developing physically like the other boys, and socially he's being picked on more and more. One classmate commented about Pat, "What is he? He walks, talks, and even looks like a girl!"
- Once called Danny, Danielle has been taking hormone treatments for the last year to develop secondary sex traits common for women. "Hips and breasts—that's a good first step," Danielle says. "As soon as I can afford it, I'm getting the surgery to become a woman. I've been a woman my entire life on the inside. Now I'll finally be a woman on the outside too."

DEFINITIONS AND KEY THOUGHTS 2

- *Gender identity disorder* is a diagnosis given to persons who meet a certain number of clinical criteria related to *feelings of discontent regarding their biological sex* and *identification with the opposite sex*. The disorder is more prevalent in males (who want to be women) than among females (who want to be men).
- According to the American Psychiatric Association and the *Diagnostic and Statistical Manual of Mental Disorders IV* (DSM-IV-TR), the *following criteria must be met* before a person can be given the official diagnosis of gender identity disorder:

  — There must be evidence of a strong and persistent cross-gender identification.
  — This cross-gender identification must not merely be a desire for any perceived cultural advantages of being the other sex.
  — There must also be evidence of persistent discomfort about one's assigned sex or a sense of inappropriateness in the gender role of that sex.
  — The individual must not have a concurrent physical intersex condition (e.g., androgen insensitivity syndrome or congenital adrenal hyperplasia).

231

— There must be evidence of clinically significant distress or impairment in social, occupational, or other important areas of functioning.[1]

- The DSM-IV-TR also provides diagnostic criteria for gender disorders that do not meet the criteria for the diagnosis of general gender identity disorder. The following criteria are sufficient for a diagnosis of *gender identity disorder in children* as well as for *gender identity disorder not otherwise specified* (GIDNOS). For the former diagnosis, criteria must be identified before a person is eighteen years of age.

  — Intersex conditions (e.g., androgen insensitivity syndrome or congenital adrenal hyperplasia) and accompanying gender dysphoria.
  — Transient, stress-related cross-dressing behavior.
  — Persistent preoccupation with castration or penectomy without a desire to acquire the sex characteristics of the other sex, which is known as skoptic syndrome.[2]

- *Adults with gender identity disorder often*:

  — desire to live as a person of the opposite sex
  — pursue a sex reassignment operation
  — dress and act in ways that are indicative of the opposite sex
  — become socially isolated or ostracized
  — develop moderate to severe depression
  — develop moderate to severe anxiety

- Gender identity disorder in children is often *reported as "having always been present,"* and people with the disorder do not remember a time when they were satisfied with their gender. However, other people with the disorder report that symptoms *began in adolescence or adulthood* and seemed to grow in intensity over time.

- Issues regarding gender identity can manifest in a variety of ways. For example, some people may *cross-dress*, while others may pursue *sex-change surgery*.

- *Gender identity disorder in children* may be seen in a number of traits. They may:

  — express a desire to be the opposite sex
  — find their genitals or indicators of their current gender gross and unwanted
  — engage in activities and play more appropriate to the other sex
  — believe they will grow up to become the opposite sex
  — often experience rejection by their peers
  — become isolated and shy
  — develop moderate to severe anxiety
  — present low self-esteem
  — drop out of school

- Among children, *the disturbance is manifested* by any of the following:

  — A boy may assert that his penis or testes are disgusting or will disappear, assert that it would be better not to have a penis, have an aversion toward rough-and-tumble play, and reject male stereotypical toys, games, and activities.

  — A girl may reject the gender-typical practice of urinating in a sitting position, assert that she has or will grow a penis, state that she does not want to grow breasts or menstruate, or have a marked aversion toward normative feminine clothing.

- In pathological cases, *children deviate from the normal model* of exploring masculine and feminine behaviors. Such children *develop inflexible, compulsive, persistent, and rigidly stereotyped patterns of same- or opposite-sex identity and behavior*. On one extreme are boys who become excessively masculine in a compensatory way. The opposite extreme is seen in effeminate boys who reject their masculinity and rigidly insist that they are really girls or that they want to become mothers and bear children. Such males frequently avoid playing with other boys, dress in girls' clothing, play predominantly with girls, try out cosmetics and wigs, and display a stereotypically feminine gait, arm movements, and body gestures. Although much less common, *some girls may similarly reject traditionally feminine roles and mannerisms* in favor of masculine characteristics. Professional intervention is required for both extremes of gender behavior.

- *Not all transsexuals* (those who dress or act as people of the opposite gender) *have gender identity disorder*. Transvestic fetishism is another clinical condition (categorized as a paraphilia) and is described in the next chapter.

- Generally speaking, *homosexuals do not have gender identity disorder*. The majority of homosexuals identify strongly with their biological gender. Homosexuality is distinctive in that it involves a sexual *attraction to persons of the same gender*.

ASSESSMENT INTERVIEW 3

1. How long have you experienced concerns about your gender identity?
2. In what ways has your issue with gender affected your life?
3. Do you have a support system of close friends or family? Tell me about them.
4. Have you involved yourself with any support group for the issues you are facing?
5. What are you hoping to gain or change through counseling?
6. In addition to gender identity issues, are you experiencing significant depression? If so, in what ways is this affecting you?
7. In addition to gender identity issues, are you experiencing significant anxiety? If so, in what ways is this affecting you?
8. Have you struggled (or do you now struggle) with depression, substance abuse, or thoughts about harming yourself? If so, tell me about it.

4 WISE COUNSEL

Individuals suffering from gender identity disorder experience a *conflict between their actual gender and the gender they feel they are*. For example, a client who is biologically male may identify more with being a woman, feeling like a woman trapped in a man's body. Many individuals struggling with gender identity disorder are *biologically normal*—they were born physically in one sex or the other. However, in rare circumstances, people are born with genitalia and *other external, physical traits that are confusing to them*, which can lead to gender identity disorder. Explain to your client that, in such cases, *abnormal physical traits do not sidetrack God's plan* for her life and sexual identity.

This disorder is *quite confusing and discouraging* to the person who suffers from it, and social rejection is a common occurrence. Substance abuse, clinical depression, and suicide attempts are common contributing problems. In addition, people who struggle with gender identity disorder often *feel debilitating shame* because they are well aware of being very "different" and they don't fit in with their peers. It's not unusual for these people to hide their desires and live in a secret world—until they can find someone who affirms their sexual identity or loves them enough to accept them the way they are. Many keep their condition secret and get married, hoping marriage will cure their problem.

Children learn gender-appropriate behavior at home, but quite often they *experiment with items and behaviors commonly used by the opposite sex*. For example, a little boy may put on his mother's lipstick, or a little girl may play with her brother's toy truck instead of her doll. Typically, children grow out of this kind of behavior with no problems. However, *when this behavior becomes pathologically obsessive and rigid*, gender identity disorder can occur.

5 ACTION STEPS

Treating gender identity disorder can be a slow and complicated process. Better recovery outcomes are associated with early diagnosis and treatment. Encourage your client to begin with the following steps.

1. Talk about Your Personal Views regarding Your Biological Sex

- Begin to examine your current way of thinking to find any half-truths that may be contributing to your core belief system. What do you believe are the positive aspects of your gender? What do you see as the negative aspects of your gender?
- *Help your client to identify any negative thinking regarding her gender. For example, a male suffering from gender identity disorder may say, "Men are pigs. They are crude, crass, and uncaring. Unlike me, men are athletic and sportsmanlike. Men*

don't enjoy art and fashion." Point out the misstatements or half-truths—many men are not crass, aren't particularly athletic, and enjoy art.

2. Begin to Identify with Others of Your Sex

- If you desire change, you must step out and begin to find ways to relate with those who share your biological sex.
- *Provide more examples and creative solutions to aid the client in identifying things she has in common with others of the same biological sex.*

3. Discuss Discomfort with Your Physical Appearance

- Always remember, even though a person's external appearance may be different from the average person of a particular sex, genetically the person is always fully male or fully female. Physical appearance as an indicator of gender is secondary.
- Some people with gender identity disorder have genitalia and secondary sex characteristics consistent with their biological sex (meaning they have normal physical development). However, others may have either ambiguous genitalia or a hermaphroditic physical condition. Discuss with your counselor your feelings toward your biological sexual features.
- *For the client who has abnormally developed genitalia, genetic testing may be helpful. Confirming a person's gender based on genetics and considering outward biology as only secondary can be effective tools in reframing thoughts about gender identity.*

BIBLICAL INSIGHTS 6

For You formed my inward parts; You covered me in my mother's womb. I will praise you, for I am fearfully and wonderfully made; marvelous are your works, and that my soul knows very well. My frame was not hidden from You, when I was made in secret, and skillfully wrought in the lowest parts of the earth. Your eyes saw my substance, being yet unformed. And in Your book they all were written, the days fashioned for me, when as yet there were none of them.

Psalm 139:13–16 NKJV

People who struggle with gender identity disorder experience tremendous inner conflict and adversity in relationships. They need God's love, grace, and care. They need to be reminded that God hasn't abandoned them in their struggle, that He has fashioned them and ordained each day of their lives, and that He will continue to work in their lives to help them carve out a strong, healthy self-concept.

For we are His workmanship, created in Christ Jesus for good works, which God prepared beforehand that we should walk in them.

Ephesians 2:10 NKJV

God has a plan for the life of every believer. He is the Creator of all and has prepared a job for each of us to do in His name. We are uniquely special and dearly loved—made with a specific purpose. He knows the identity of each one of His children and desires us to trust Him in all His ways.

I cry aloud with my voice to the LORD. . . . I pour out my complaint before Him; I declare my trouble before Him. When my spirit was overwhelmed within me, You knew my path. . . . For there is no one who regards me; there is no escape for me; no one cares for my soul. I cried out to You, O LORD; I said, "You are my refuge, my portion in the land of the living. Give heed to my cry. . . . Bring my soul out of prison, so that I may give thanks to Your name."

Psalm 142:1–7 NASB

David was clearly distressed and troubled when he cried out to the Lord in this manner. He knew the only One who could save him from the pain in his life was God. Many who struggle with gender identity issues feel alone. They think no one understands and no one cares. Often they experience intense fear about expressing their feelings to others, knowing that judgment or rejection may be just around the corner. As Christian counselors, it is our duty to provide comfort, encouragement, and understanding of God's unconditional love, helping our clients understand that He will be the refuge they need.

7 : PRAYER STARTER

Lord, thank You for my friend and her willingness to talk today about this sensitive issue. It is an issue not everyone understands, God, so please walk with her and show her Your understanding as she learns more about Your plan for her life. Thank You for Your wisdom and strength . . .

8 : RECOMMENDED RESOURCES

Balswick, Judith, and Jack Balswick. *Authentic Human Sexuality: An Integrated Christian Approach*. IVP Academic, 2008.

Dallas, Joe. *Desires in Conflict: Hope for Men Who Struggle with Sexual Identity*. Harvest House, 2003.

Eldredge, John. *Wild at Heart: Discovering the Secret of a Man's Soul*. Thomas Nelson, 2006.

Eldredge, John, and Stasi Eldredge. *Captivating: Unveiling the Mystery of a Woman's Soul*. Thomas Nelson, 2005.

James, David E., IV. *God's Truth about Gender: Unraveling the Lies of Modern Human Sexuality, Behavior and Identity*. VMI Publishing, 2008.

Paulk, Anne. *Restoring Sexual Identity: Hope for Women Who Struggle with Same-Sex Attraction*. Harvest House, 2003.

Transvestic Fetishism 34

PORTRAITS 1

- Roger is a real man's man. But he has a secret that would shock his guy friends. He has a secret stash of women's silk underwear, and he puts a pair on almost every day.

- When Jim was a child, playing with his older sister, she would dress him as a girl. As he grew older, Jim never stopped enjoying dressing in women's clothing, and now he finds it both entertaining and sexually gratifying.

- Carl doesn't just pass for a woman; he's often the prettiest "woman" in the room—tall, dressed to kill, with a husky yet sexy female voice to boot. And he is thrilled by how many men come on to him and just dies laughing at the shock on their faces when they finally discover that "she is a he."

DEFINITIONS AND KEY THOUGHTS 2

- A person experiencing a *transvestic fetish* is one who derives sexual gratification from *dressing in clothing made for persons of the opposite gender*. The *vast majority of those with a transvestic fetish are men* who dress and behave as women—as many popular movies portray. Authorities surmise that the statistics are tilted toward men because in Western culture females can wear men's clothing without anyone taking notice.

- Related terms for a transvestic fetish are *transvestism* (the practice of a transvestic fetish) and *transvestite* (one who has a transvestic fetish).

- The practice of a person with a transvestic fetish can range from dressing *partially in clothing of the opposite gender* to *dressing fully in opposite-gender clothing*, wearing cosmetics, and speaking or using mannerisms of the opposite gender. Some transvestites appear to be of the opposite gender to the degree that *they cannot be distinguished as transvestites*.

- The American Psychiatric Association categorizes transvestic fetishism *as a paraphilia*—a sexual disorder characterized by socially inappropriate sexual conduct (other paraphilias include exhibitionism and voyeurism).

- People who are transvestites *should not be considered homosexual*, though some homosexuals are also transvestites. According to the *Diagnostic and Statistical Manual IV* (DSM-IV-TR), most men who dress as women are heterosexual.

- Transvestic fetishism *usually begins in adolescence* when boys begin to experiment with the clothing or cosmetics owned by their sisters or mother.
- In some cases, transvestic fetishism begins earlier *if a mother dresses her son as a girl.* This practice is often associated with the mother's anger toward men, preference for little girls over boys, or in some cases hatred of the male gender.

3 ASSESSMENT INTERVIEW

1. When did you begin cross-dressing? What thrill do you get out of it? How has it progressed up to now?
2. From whom is this a secret? What would it do to your relationship with these people if they knew?
3. Where do you practice cross-dressing? Who joins you in it?
4. Are you involved in any risky sexual behaviors in conjunction with cross-dressing?
5. What would be some benefits of stopping this behavior? What are your fears about stopping?
6. What are your goals for counseling?

4 WISE COUNSEL

To the secular world, transvestic fetishism might be considered an ethical, personal, sexual preference. However, dressing as a member of the opposite gender to obtain sexual gratification is *a perversion and a denial of God's design for sexuality.*

Though transvestic fetishism is an aberrant sexual practice and classified as a paraphilia, *it isn't a criminal activity* because transvestites don't force their sexual appetites onto other people.

In most cases *transvestites don't initiate or want counseling,* but their spouse or significant other may be so distressed that she comes for help. Your role is to provide wisdom and direction for the distressed person and hopefully open lines of communication so the transvestite will come for help too.

An encyclopedia of mental disorders makes the following points about the *treatment of transvestic fetishism*:

- The use of aversion therapy, and particularly the use of electric shock therapy, has been largely unsuccessful in treatment of transvestic fetishism.
- People with fetishes have also been treated by using a form of behavioral therapy known as "orgasmic reorientation." This therapy attempts to help people stop experiencing arousal by transvestic behavior and learn to respond sexually to a different and more appropriate set of sexual stimuli. This also has had limited success.
- Most persons who have a transvestic fetish never seek treatment from professionals. A preoccupation with cross-dressing is viewed as essentially harmless

to other persons, since transvestism is not associated with criminal activities or forcing one's sexual preferences on others.[1]

ACTION STEPS : 5

1. Find a Motivation for Change

- It's difficult to change a habit or behavior without motivation. Take a moment to evaluate every area of your life and current level of functioning. How are you doing in your relationships with others? Identify any reasons you commonly use to justify this behavior and discuss them with your counselor.
- Try to understand how your behavior is affecting your relationships and consider changing for the sake of those you love.

2. Discover God's Plan for Sex

- God has created mankind for relationships. He has given each individual a desire for sexuality within his or her biological makeup. And every human is genetically created fully male or fully female. Begin to explore and develop an understanding of the plan God has for you within the sex of your genetic design. Discuss with your counselor the unique personality traits you possess and how you were created with a special purpose in this life.
- Focus on your God-given uniqueness and think about how God wants you to have an impact on His kingdom.
- *Help your client learn new coping mechanisms for resisting the urge to dress in women's clothes, how his thoughts affect his emotions, and how negative emotions can lead to sexually deviant behaviors.*

3. Trust God

- God loves you just the way you are! Trust Him and His plan for your life. Lean on Him for strength to overcome the desire to engage in transvestic behaviors. Pray for His divine intervention and healing. He will never leave you or forsake you. He will be your refuge and strength when you are weak.

4. Seek Accountability with a Mentor or Trusted Friend

- With the help of your counselor, locate a mentor or trusted friend with whom you can confide. Ask him to help you remain accountable to commitments you make toward change and to encourage you along this journey of healing.
- *Be ready to explore your client's list of possible mentors and friends. Discuss the difference between safe and unsafe people. Make sure the person your client picks as an accountability partner understands the importance of confidentiality and*

trust. Find out if he is willing to ask your client the hard questions while loving and encouraging your client to stand strong.

6 : BIBLICAL INSIGHTS

Therefore, prepare your minds for action; be self-controlled; set your hope fully on the grace to be given you when Jesus Christ is revealed. As obedient children, do not conform to the evil desires you had when you lived in ignorance. But just as he who called you is holy, so be holy in all you do; for it is written: "Be holy, because I am holy."

1 Peter 1:13–16

The measurement of our lives isn't what our society permits (or what it thinks is amusing). Ultimately we answer to God alone, and one day we will give an account to Him for our behavior. This realization reframes our choices and helps us clarify our direction in life. It also helps us understand that any obsession or compulsion can easily become an idol that we worship instead of worshiping the one true God.

Since you call on a Father who judges each man's work impartially, live your lives as strangers here in reverent fear. For you know that it was not with perishable things such as silver or gold that you were redeemed from the empty way of life handed down to you from your forefathers, but with the precious blood of Christ, a lamb without blemish or defect. He was chosen before the creation of the world, but was revealed in these last times for your sake. Through him you believe in God, who raised him from the dead and glorified him, and so your faith and hope are in God.

1 Peter 1:17–21

Change is hard, but we begin with the strong assurance of God's wonderful forgiveness. We look back at the cross and see that Jesus paid the price for all of our sins. When we realize how much He has forgiven us, we'll want to please Him with every fiber of our lives.

Finally, be strong in the Lord and in his mighty power. Put on the full armor of God so that you can take your stand against the devil's schemes. For our struggle is not against flesh and blood, but against the rulers, against the authorities, against the powers of this dark world and against the spiritual forces of evil in the heavenly realms. Therefore put on the full armor of God, so that when the day of evil comes, you may be able to stand your ground, and after you have done everything, to stand.

Ephesians 6:10–13

The struggle with cross-dressing, like every other difficulty in our lives, is a spiritual battle, and we need to make sure we put on our armor of faith to fight and win. When we forget this truth, we are easily blindsided by the enemy's accusations and temptations.

PRAYER STARTER : 7

Dear God, thank You for making sex and for making us sexual beings. God, my brother has been finding sexual gratification by dressing as a person of the opposite sex. Please show him the way to change and be with him as he recovers from this sexual problem. Thank You for Your forgiveness, wisdom, and strength . . .

RECOMMENDED RESOURCES : 8

Carnes, Patrick J. *Out of the Shadows: Understanding Sexual Addiction*. Hazelden, 2001.

Laaser, Mark. *Healing the Wounds of Sexual Addiction*. Zondervan, 2004.

_____. *L.I.F.E. Guide for Men: A Workbook for Living in Freedom Everyday in Sexual Wholeness and Integrity*. Life Ministries, 2007.

DVD

Laaser, Dr. Mark, Dr. Patrick J. Carnes, and Dr. Daniel Amen. *Freedom Begins Here: Diagnosis and Treatment of Sexual Addiction*. 2005.

PART 5

Sexual Issues in Parenting and Family Life

35 Raising Sexually Healthy Children

1 PORTRAITS

- Bob stood with his older sister and informed his parents, "I have something to tell you, and I don't think either of you will like it." He looked at his sister, and she nodded for him to proceed while his parents waited silently. Bob hemmed and hawed and finally blurted out, "I'm in love with another man, and we are going to move in together." As his parents looked on quizzically, Bob said, "Don't you get it, I'm gay . . . and I think I've been this way for a long time."

- Stella came home for the weekend with her new college roommate, and both her parents were surprised and pleased she had made such a close friend in so little time since the school year began. That night Stella's mom burst into the room to tell her about the news she had just heard on TV about a violent incident at the university. She was shocked to find Stella and her new friend naked together and locked in a steamy sexual embrace.

- Reb and Robin decided to travel to their daughter's apartment at the local state university one gorgeous fall day, thinking the two-hour drive would be enjoyable. They waited an inordinately long time at the door, and when Darcy opened it, she looked guilty about something. Coming inside they saw Darcy's boyfriend lying on the couch and heard their daughter say that he had spent the night there because they had drunk a little too much the night before. Though Robin seemed to accept the story, Reb was convinced his daughter had not slept alone.

2 DEFINITIONS AND KEY THOUGHTS

- Raising *sexually healthy children* from *a biblical perspective* means to raise *heterosexually oriented kids who look forward to and choose to wait until marriage before they become sexual*—then they stick to and *remain sexually and emotionally faithful to their spouse* for as long as they are married.

- This definition probably seems fairly narrow to a lot of people in this sexually obsessed age we live in, but it is consistent with God's prescription for healthy sexual living. If that is so—and it is a quite testable proposition—it means that *any deviation from God's standards invites trouble and will result in unneeded pain and suffering that grieves God.*

- *Kids spell love t-i-m-e.* There is no substitute for every hour, minute, and second of quality time parents spend with their children. Kids need heavy doses of their parents, every day if possible, and they need the modeling and the direct instruction that only a parent can give about creating a healthy marriage and maintaining good sexual relations. Hence, families need to spend not only more time together, but time together in which parents are *discussing sexual issues openly*, not giving out commands and sounding like just another TV commercial.

ASSESSMENT INTERVIEW 3

The following questions will help you assess how well the family you are counseling is doing in terms of spending quality and quantity time together.

1. Does your family have a weekly family fun time and a family devotion time? How about time for discussion of family values and rules? Would you consider scheduling one hour for each every week?
2. Do you need ideas of things to do during family time? What kinds of things could you imagine doing with the family? What activities do you, your spouse, and your kids all enjoy?
3. Are you concerned about the sexual values, behavior, and images concerning sex that are influencing your children every day? What specific concerns do you have about them?
4. How much time do you spend with your children each week? When you are with your kids, do you focus on accomplishing something or just being with them? Do your kids have time with you without commands? Will you have a family time during which cell phones, television, and other distractions are eliminated?
5. Do you pray with your family?
6. How much time do you spend each day talking with your family?
7. Are you able to talk about sex? Would you like to talk about sex with your children? Have you tried to have "the talk" in the past? How did it go?
8. Do you as parents display your love for one another in front of your children? Does/would that make you feel uncomfortable?
9. Do you usually feel too tired for family time? What else is getting in the way of having family time? Are you able to put work aside to focus on the needs of your family?
10. If you go by how you spend your time, what is most important in your life right now? What in life is more important than a strong relationship with your family?

WISE COUNSEL 4

First, families need to *set aside time for family fun*. That is, scheduled times for the entire family to enjoy the presence of each other while engaging in *an interactive group activity*. This is different from a family sitting together watching a movie, and this is different from a family being together while each person "does his or her own thing," such as playing personal video games, reading books, doing homework, or listening to an iPod. Stephen Covey calls this a "collective monologue," which is not particularly useful in building family bonds.

Family devotion time is an important opportunity for a family to maintain their spiritual wellness and to create a bridge to all sorts of discussions about issues. The main purpose of the family gathering is to *worship God and study His Word.* This can take the form of singing, praying, Scripture reading, and discussion of spiritual or religious topics.

Some people think that scheduling family times is impersonal and unspontaneous. However, scheduling it *ensures that it happens* and is a surefire way to track the time the family spends together. Many working parents find it easier to schedule family time in their planners as a "crucial meeting." That way nothing can push it out of the way.

Contrary to popular belief, building family bonds is not just about quality time—it's also about the quantity of time. It's about praying with your kids before bedtime, getting drinks of water in the middle of the night, and listening to kids' dreams the next morning over breakfast. Relationships are built during unexpected moments of togetherness, as well as after hours and hours of just being together.

When families spend time together in this way, parents will be able to *talk with their children about sex in ways that are not threatening or embarrassing.* Thus raising sexually healthy children should flow very naturally. Before talking to their kids about sex, however, it's essential that parents think first about *what they believe and what they model.* Sexuality is a beautifully designed aspect of identity; as such, it is important for parents to examine their beliefs about sexuality in light of God's Word. In today's world, the liberal influence of the media through television, movies, and music can easily foster a loose view of sexuality. And for divorced and single parents, being involved in a new romantic relationship reveals to the children a parent's attitude about sexuality. Children will be quick to pick up on discrepancies between what their parents say and what they do.

Compared with abstainers, sexually active adolescents are more likely to use substances, have lower academic achievement and aspirations, and experience poorer mental health.

American Journal of Preventive Medicine, 2004

5 ACTION STEPS

1. Show Affection to Each Other

- Don't be afraid to let your children see a *public display of affection between Mom and Dad.* Kiss, hug, compliment, hold hands, and so on. Kids may fuss about how you need to stop that "yucky kissing stuff" or jokingly tell you to "get a room," but in the long term they will remember that Mom and Dad were attracted to one another and committed to *only each other* for life.

- Make it a priority to set aside time weekly or at least biweekly to "date" each other. This will keep your attraction and connectedness to one another alive and vibrant.

2. Talk with Your Kids (Age Appropriately) about Sex

- Be sure to talk with your kids about sex, taking into consideration their age and what they are ready to hear. Because of the increasing influence of the media from an early age, sooner is better than later. Don't wait until your kids are in middle school health class! As a parent, you have the right—and the responsibility—to be the first one to explain the gift of sex that God has created. Your kids won't get that perspective on TV or from their friends. When you discuss sex, keep it low-key. Allow your kids time for reflection and perhaps they'll even ask a question. There are many great books and video series available that will assist in developing open communication between kids and parents regarding sex and sexuality. Avoiding "the talk" will only encourage your child to have it elsewhere—at school, among peers, and so on.
- Develop a plan for how and when to have "talks" with your children. Your counselor can provide you with research and referrals to resources that will aid in making this an effective and memorable conversation. *See the recommended resources listed at the end of this chapter.*

> Early sexual debut has been shown to lead to subsequent depressive symptoms, especially in female adolescents who debuted prior to age 16 and whose relationships ended.
>
> *American Journal of Sociology, 2007*

3. Share God's Word about Love, Sex, and Relationships

- Be prepared to share specific passages of Scripture that express God's design and plan for sexual purity in relationships and marriage. It is always important to be able to give reasons for your convictions. This will provide a solid foundation your children can stand on when temptation comes.

BIBLICAL INSIGHTS 6

But you must continue in the things which you have learned and been assured of, knowing from whom you have learned them, and that from childhood you have known the Holy Scriptures.

2 Timothy 3:14–15 NKJV

Timothy had been learning the Bible from childhood. Christian parents have the God-given responsibility to raise their children to know and love God and His Word. The teaching parents provide their children will be embedded in their minds, giving them a strong foundation on which to build.

In the same way, the Spirit helps us in our weakness. We do not know what we ought to pray for, but the Spirit himself intercedes for us with groans that words cannot express.

Romans 8:26

As parents, a conversation with our children regarding sex and relationships can be hard and often anxiety provoking. Wondering when and how to approach this subject can leave many parents feeling confused and even fearful. It is so comforting to know that God is strong when we are weak. He will be faithful to intercede on our behalf and will provide the peace needed to conduct a Spirit-filled conversation children so desperately need to hear from their parent(s).

Therefore, I urge you, brothers, in view of God's mercy, to offer your bodies as living sacrifices, holy and pleasing to God—this is your spiritual act of worship. Do not conform any longer to the pattern of this world, but be transformed by the renewing of your mind. Then you will be able to test and approve what God's will is—his good, pleasing and perfect will.

Romans 12:1–2

If a young person is to be sexually pure and spiritually mature, she must be willing to sacrifice selfish desires. The vision parents should hold up to their children is one of proper worship of God. This involves a willingness to sacrifice any personal wishes, passions, and sexual desires that are displeasing to a holy God. By modeling this attitude for their children, parents play a vital role in their children's lives, instilling in them a vision for holiness that is worth fighting and sacrificing for.

7 : PRAYER STARTER

Thank You for these parents who have come today, Lord. They want to raise their children well; they want to be good parents, especially in raising sexually healthy children. Right now, they feel they don't quite know which way to turn. Show them the way, Lord. Show them, especially, that the love they have for their children is a pale shadow of the love You have for them all as their heavenly Father . . .

8 : RECOMMENDED RESOURCES

Chirban, John T. *What's Love Got to Do with It: Talking with Your Kids about Sex.* Thomas Nelson, 2007.

Jones, Stan, and Brenna Jones. *God's Design for Sex,* a series of four books. NavPress, 2007.

Laaser, Mark. *Talking to Your Kids about Sex.* WaterBrook, 1999.

McDowell, Josh. *Why True Love Waits: The Definitive Book on How to Help Your Kids Resist Sexual Pressure.* Tyndale, 2004.

Stoop, David, and Jan Stoop. *The Complete Parenting Book: Practical Help from Leading Experts.* Revell, 2004.

Sexually Active Kids and Teens **36**

PORTRAITS 1

- John and Cynthia had enjoyed a wonderful relationship with their daughter Sara, who was in the eighth grade. She had been an exemplary child and student. Recently, though, Sara had been acting a bit strange. She rarely made eye contact with her parents and was always rushing off to events and studies instead of talking with them. John thought it was "just a phase" she was going through, but Cynthia wasn't so sure. Weeks later Cynthia had a conversation with the mother of one of Sara's best friends, and the mother asked if Sara was using birth control. "Birth control?" Cynthia almost shouted at her. "What in the world for?" In the next few minutes, she learned far more about Sara's sexual behavior than she could have imagined.

- Kim was a single mother who was doing the best she could do to raise her two sons. Life was a struggle for her. Kim's older son, Jason, was a top athlete in high school, and he was known as a stud in every way. Some of Kim's friends asked her if she minded him having a reputation of "laying nearly every cheerleader at the school." She laughed nervously but was horrified that anybody saw her son that way. She had suspected it but had never let it really sink in.

- Dana called her husband, Pete, to tell him that the principal at the high school wanted to meet with them immediately. When they arrived, the principal informed them that their son and his girlfriend had been caught performing oral sex in the parking lot during a class break.

DEFINITIONS AND KEY THOUGHTS 2

- A *sexually active child* is a teenager or a preteen who is engaging in illicit sexual behavior—including pre-intercourse and arousal behaviors, such as viewing pornography or performing oral sex—with other teens or adults and is neither emotionally mature nor physically protected from the negative consequences of such behavior.

- Of the 18.9 million new cases of STIs (sexually transmitted infections) each year, 9.1 million (48 percent) occur among fifteen- to nineteen-year-olds. *Although fifteen- to twenty-four-year-olds represent only one-quarter of the sexually active population, they account for nearly half of all new STIs each year.*[1]

- The Guttmacher Institute reports:

— *Nearly half (46 percent) of all fifteen- to nineteen-year-olds in the United States have had sex at least once.*

— By age fifteen, only 13 percent of teens have ever had sex. However, by the time they reach age nineteen, *seven in ten teens have engaged in sexual intercourse.*

— Most young people have sex for the first time at about age seventeen but do not marry until their middle or late twenties. This means that young adults are *at risk of unwanted pregnancy and sexually transmitted infections for nearly a decade.*

— *Teens are waiting longer to have sex* than they did in the past. Some 13 percent of females and 15 percent of males age fifteen to nineteen in 2002 had had sex before age fifteen, compared with 19 percent and 21 percent, respectively, in 1995.[2]

- The majority (59 percent) of sexually experienced teen females had a first *sexual partner who was one to three years her senior.*[3]

- Young people who claim to be Christians *experience sexual activity at slightly less but at nearly the same rate* as the overall population of teenagers.

- The *sexual pressures on young people* today are enormous. *Music, movies, and access to sexually explicit internet sites* multiply the effects of normal hormonal urges and the normal developmental stage of adolescent experimentation.

- Some Christian parents view their children's sexual experimentation as *the worst thing that could happen to them*—the parents, that is—because it makes them look like "bad parents" to their friends.

- Quite often the *mother and father of a sexually active young person have very different perspectives and values* about their child's sexual behavior. If they don't find common ground, the teenager will *play them against each other* in the triangle and push family rules and adult behavior to the outer extremes.

3 ASSESSMENT INTERVIEW

These questions are directed to one or both parents.

1. How and what did you learn about your child's sexual behavior?
2. How long has it been going on? How many partners has he had?
3. How did you (or each of you) respond when you found out?
4. How did your child respond when he was caught?
5. Tell me about your values regarding sexuality. How were your values developed? What was your sexual experience when you were your son's age? How does that experience color your expectations for your child now?
6. What is your hope for your son at this point?
7. (*For the couple*) On what points do you agree as to a course of action? At what points do you disagree?
8. Describe the status of your relationship with your child now.

9. Even as you establish consequences, what are some ways you can communicate love, forgiveness, and acceptance? What difference do you think that will make?

10. What consequences are you considering? How can you make them effective?

11. What is your plan for keeping your communication with your son meaningful, especially regarding sex?

WISE COUNSEL 4

Research has shown that the more education children or teens have about sex the less likely they will be to experiment or act out. *Parents must talk, talk, talk to their children about sexual behavior and values*, normalizing the subject of sex in the household—even while laughing about it at times—and creating an expectation that discussions about sex are normal and to be expected. Parents know such conversations are happening within their child's peer group, so they should make them happen at home as well.

Parents need to *talk in an age-appropriate way* about their values regarding sex from early in the child's life. Even if the child is a teenager and the parents have never talked with him about sex, it's not too late to start.

As parents respond to their child's sexual behavior, it may be helpful for them to *remember their own sexual history* as the context for their values for their child's sex life. This reflection may give them insight, patience, and resolve for the actions that need to be taken.

Discuss biblical teaching and stories that *reinforce godly values and behavior*. Parents should share examples of blessings in their life as a result of following God's standards for sexuality. Encourage them also to be willing to talk about the consequences they have experienced for not obeying God's commands about sexual purity.

Consider the relationship between the mother and father to *note similar or different attitudes and approaches* to the child's behavior. One of the most important steps in the process is to help the parents come to a consensus about the path they need to follow. If they can't agree, the child will probably try to pit them against each other to gain control of them and the situation.

One of the biggest lessons to be learned and imparted when kids are acting out sexually is forgiveness. *God's grace covers every sin*, even when our kids do something that potentially wrecks their lives. Forgiveness, though, doesn't mean there shouldn't be discipline for past sins and boundaries in the future. *We give forgiveness unilaterally, as Christ forgave us, but trust must be earned by consistently responsible behavior.*

The parents need to *share their frustrations, fears, and anger* about the situation with the counselor. Perhaps they're blaming each other; perhaps they're withdrawing. Understanding each other's feelings and perspective is crucial to establishing good communication with the teenager.

Parents need to avoid the extremes of passivity (giving up) and harsh, out-of-control reactions. Instead, they need to speak calmly to their child about their hopes and fears, God's plan for sexuality, the potential natural consequences of the behavior (pregnancy and STIs), and the existing natural consequences (the erosion of trust because of his choices and deception). Parents need to communicate *the long-term view of the child's future* (education, career, and family) that can be derailed by pregnancy, abortion, or disease. *Painting a strong hope for a glowing future* keeps the conversation from focusing only on past sins and punishment, and it allows the parents to reinforce their dreams for their child.

Parents need to understand that *the explosion of hormones* is very real for adolescents, and the reasoning center of their brains (the frontal cortex) won't catch up until their early twenties. At that point, reason will often trump urges, but until then, parents need to play a key role in helping the child *set limits* and *maintain* them when with friends.

Many parents feel *horrified and shocked* when they learn of their child's sexual actions. They think about the sweet, compliant child they have known and they wonder, *Who is this kid?* It is time to get real and to understand that their child's peer group is talking and maybe exploring sexual issues and boundaries. Adolescence is a time of change—physically, emotionally, relationally, and hormonally—and *sexual temptations abound in every school and almost every group of friends*.

When parents are surprised by their child's behavior, they generally *lash out or withdraw from the child*, but instead, they need to *increase the quality of their relationship*. If they talk only about the sin and punishment, they may drive their child into the arms of others. It's a good time to shower their child with unconditional affection, hugs, affirmation, and comments about what their child is doing right. Opening a dialogue about the parents' and the child's values, hopes, fears, and dreams can be a positive step in learning to understand each other.

5 : ACTION STEPS

1. Talk

- The primary tool for combating teenage promiscuity is open, honest communication between you and your kids. Use examples from your own life of sexual temptations as a youth to open the dialogue with your children.

- *In the counseling session, encourage the parents to share their frustration, anger, and hurt over the revelation of their child's sexual actions. Also invite them to reflect on their own sexual history, especially when they were their child's age, and compare that time to today's world with its incredible sexual temptations and pressure. Use this conversation to help the parents understand each other's perspective and reactions to the child's behavior.*

2. Teach

- Use nonreactive, respectful dialogue with your child to impart biblical values and the necessary skills for healthy relationships: respect instead of manipulation, boundaries instead of coercion or giving in, and living by Scripture rather than peer pressure.

- Many young people believe they are invincible or "bulletproof." Take time to explain to your child God's plan for sexual activity in marriage as well as the risks of teenage pregnancy and STIs.

3. Have Tough Love

- Consequences for teen sexual promiscuity must be considered and prayed through very carefully. In most activity involving children's misbehavior, natural consequences (such as running out of spending money) work well, but in the realm of sexuality, natural consequences can be severe and enduring, such as pregnancy and STIs.
- Involve your son or daughter in the negotiation of consequences, including the severity and the duration of the discipline.
- Consider *logical* or *imposed* consequences that are enforceable. Avoid those that aren't. Appropriate consequences may include:

  — Permanently put a block or filter on the computer at home and the child's computer to prevent access to sexually explicit sites.
  — Permanently restrict access to social sites that invite or allow sexually explicit dialogue and personal photos.
  — In junior high and high school, set limits about girls dating boys who are more than a year (or perhaps two) older.
  — Enforce a reasonable curfew that can possibly be less restrictive as trust is built and talk becomes more expansive.
  — Do not allow the child to spend the night at the homes of those who don't share your values or, perhaps, even to go to those homes at all.
  — For a reasonable period, restrict access to cars, cell phones, funds, and other conveniences as enforceable and painful consequences for misbehavior.

- Don't create unenforceable consequences. For example, trying to shield your child from his sexual partner may be impossible to enforce in a school setting where students have classes together.
- Go over the list above with your counselor and come up with a plan. Discuss the plan with your child and invite his participation in finalizing it. This helps your child own the plan, which is a strong motivation for him and will encourage you too.

4. Listen and Ask Questions

- Explore the history of your child's behavior, including his sexual behavior. Was sex a one-time event? Is there a pattern of sexual experiences with one person or with multiple partners?
- *Often the powerful combination of adolescent individuation, resentment over parental authority, and shame cause a deep rift in a teenager's relationship with*

253

his parents. Try to uncover topics and times when communication was healthy and open and help the parents use these as stepping-stones to build the relationship.

5. Expect Resistance

- Some kids explode in anger from the moment they are caught, but others are full of remorse in the early stages of disclosure. Sooner or later teenagers will resist the restrictions on their freedom, and you need to be prepared to stand firm in the consequences you've established.
- Look beyond your child's immediate behavior and moods. While you shouldn't be blind to the reality of your child's sin, realize that sexual compromise isn't your child's identity. Discipline in the context of love.
- *Help parents anticipate this resistance by asking questions about how they'll respond when it happens.*

6. Encourage Purity

- Regardless of your child's past sexual involvement, encourage him to begin actively pursuing purity. Teach purity as a positive *vision* for marriage. While it's easy for teens to get hung up on their past sexual mistakes, challenge your child, even if he is currently sexually active, to make a decision for purity starting today. Encourage your child to make a vow to abstain from sex until marriage and to join groups at church and at school that have done so. This may include wearing a ring or necklace that publicly communicates this vow.

6 BIBLICAL INSIGHTS

Train a child in the way he should go, and when he is old he will not turn from it.
Proverbs 22:6

This passage doesn't guarantee children will always return to the Lord but that they will consider the parents' teaching when they are in crisis and things are not working. It refers to both our sin nature that responds to temptation and the God-given "bent" each child has and each parent needs to notice, name, and nurture. Even when they are most disappointed in their child's behavior, parents can affirm, "You did well at . . ." or "You're really good at . . ."

Flee from sexual immorality. All other sins a man commits are outside his body, but he who sins sexually sins against his own body. Do you not know that your body is a temple of the Holy Spirit, who is in you, whom you have received from God? You are not your own; you were bought at a price. Therefore honor God with your body.
1 Corinthians 6:18–20

We live in such a sex-saturated culture that it's easy to miss God's perspective about sex—that it is His wonderful gift to be experienced in the safety and security of marriage. As Christians, we need first to understand that we belong to God. He loves us and knows what's best for us and our children, and sexual abstinence (or a reaffirmation of abstinence) before marriage is His will because it protects the cherished relationship of a husband and wife.

Bear with each other and forgive whatever grievances you may have against one another. Forgive as the Lord forgave you. And over all these virtues put on love, which binds them all together in perfect unity.
Colossians 3:13–14

Discipline without forgiveness is harsh, but grace can eventually melt even the hardest heart. In setting consequences for a sexually active child, we need to use equal measures of discipline, forgiveness, hope for the future, and affection.

Hear, O Israel: The LORD our God, the LORD is one. Love the LORD your God with all your heart and with all your soul and with all your strength. These commandments that I give you today are to be upon your hearts. Impress them on your children. Talk about them when you sit at home and when you walk along the road, when you lie down and when you get up. Tie them as symbols on your hands and bind them on your foreheads. Write them on the doorframes of your houses and on your gates.
Deuteronomy 6:4–9

Even if parents have failed to impart God's truth to their kids until now, they can begin at this important juncture in their relationship with their children. Kids don't appreciate a stale Bible thumping, but they may be surprisingly open to their parents' sharing their hearts, their own experiences of hope and failure, and their pursuit of an authentic faith in God. With Him, there's always hope for change.

PRAYER STARTER 7

Father, these parents care deeply about their child. You care even more, and You have a bright future for this child. We know that You are willing to use everything—even our sin—to teach us life's most valuable lessons. Thank You for Your grace. Give these parents wisdom to set clear consequences, love to see beyond their child's sinful behavior to a bright future, and perseverance to keep pursuing Your path through change . . .

RECOMMENDED RESOURCES 8

Chapman, Gary. *Anger: Handling a Powerful Emotion in a Healthy Way*. Northfield, 2007.
_____. *The Five Love Languages of Teenagers*. Moody, 2000.
Clinton, Tim, and Gary Sibcy. *Loving Your Child Too Much: Raise Your Kids without Overindulging, Overprotecting or Overcontrolling*. Thomas Nelson, 2006.

Dobson, James. *The New Hide or Seek: Building Self-Esteem in Your Child*. Revell, 2001.

Laaser, Mark. *Talking to Your Kids about Sex*. Random House, 1999.

Meeker, Meg. *Epidemic: How Teen Sex Is Killing Our Kids*. LifeLine Press, 2002.

_____. *Your Kids at Risk: How Teen Sex Threatens Our Sons and Daughters*. Regnery, 2007.

Oliver, Gary, and Carrie Oliver. *Raising Sons and Loving It! Helping Your Boys Become Godly Men*. Zondervan, 2000.

Rainey, Dennis, and Barbara Rainey. *Parenting Today's Adolescent*. Thomas Nelson, 2002.

Scherrer, David L., and L. Klepacki. *How to Talk to Your Kids about Sexuality*. David C. Cook, 2004.

Teenage Pregnancy 37
and Parenting

PORTRAITS : 1

- Kay had blossomed into a young beauty during eighth grade, and everyone noticed the new "high school girl" at the lake that summer, especially Ted. He was entering his senior year in high school, and Kay was very flattered that this senior stud was paying attention to her. Early in the new school year, Kay was shocked when she realized she was pregnant. Ted denied having anything to do with it and told her to get out of his life.

- Kimmy had been sneaking out at night with her best friend, Twyla, and the two were shadowing a punk gang of troublemakers for a number of weekends. One night the gang surrounded and raped them, threatening to kill them if they ever told anyone. Six weeks later, when Kimmy was found to be pregnant as a result of the rape, the girls could keep the secret no longer.

- Since she had begun menstruating, Jill had wanted nothing else but to have babies and be a mother. Raised by her single mother, who had borne her at fifteen, Jill figured she could "milk the system" the same way her mother had, having babies whom the state would support. Though only sixteen, she began sleeping with the twenty-five-year-old married man who lived in the apartment next door, determined to have his next child.

DEFINITIONS AND KEY THOUGHTS : 2

- Teenage sex often leads to *teen pregnancy—children having children and becoming parents while still living at home with their own parents.* While many teens now abort their babies, many give birth and commit to raising the child with or without the father, or they give the child up for adoption.

- *Single parenting*—and most teen parents are single parents—involves *taking responsibility for parenting one's child without the benefit of the other parent or a spouse,* usually as a result of abandonment or the other parent's inability because of his age. Each year in the United States, nearly *750,000 teenagers fifteen to nineteen become pregnant.* The rate of teenage pregnancy has dropped 36 percent since its peak in 1990; however, it is still a significant social issue.[1] Today in the United States there are 13.6 million single parents, and those parents are responsible for raising 21.2 million children (approximately 26 percent of children under twenty-one in the United States).[2]

- There are *few things more difficult* than being a young single parent. One of the biggest problems faced by teenage mothers is the increased economic pressure that comes with providing for a child. *Often financial need forces teenage moms to set aside educational goals to provide for their baby's basic needs.* In fact, statistics show that *seven of every ten teen mothers will drop out* of high school.[3]

- Many single moms continue to live at home, enlisting the help of their parents in raising their child. However, some parents react to the news of their daughter's pregnancy by kicking her out of the house, creating an even more stressful situation for the mom-to-be. Regardless of living arrangements, *the demands of life as a single parent are 24-7.* Changing diapers, feeding the baby, fixing meals, cleaning house, paying bills, holding down a job, and possibly even attending school can be draining and overwhelming. Nearly half of all teenage moms receive welfare,[4] but even with government assistance, *raising a child on your own is very difficult.* Teen mothers earn an average of 5,600 dollars per year during the first thirteen years of parenthood.[5]

> One of every 5 females will have given birth by age 20.
> *Urban Institute, 2003*

- *In most cases, the baby's father is absent from the life of the teenage mother.* The deterioration of fatherhood in America is considered one of our most serious social ills. Nearly 40 percent of children fall asleep in homes where their fathers are not present. Fatherlessness is associated with crime, suicide, teenaged pregnancy, drug and alcohol abuse, and incarceration. Moreover, the National Commission on Children found that nearly half of all children in disrupted families have not seen their fathers at all in the past year.[6]

- For most teenage moms, the lack of emotional support from the baby's father coupled with financial pressures and increased responsibility can seem overwhelming. While parenting a newborn is difficult as a couple, running "solo" can be lonely, frustrating, and discouraging. So it's essential for the single mom to *build a network of friends who are willing to listen to her concerns, support her, and invest in her new family.* Taking care of a needy baby makes it harder to maintain friendships, but deep, honest relationships are critical to staying psychologically healthy and not getting overwhelmed. With the love and support of caring friends, raising a baby as a teenage mom is not only doable but also rewarding.

3 ASSESSMENT INTERVIEW

Asking the following questions may help you get a better idea of how the single teen parent is coping (or will cope) with the task of raising a child alone.

1. What options are you considering for the baby? (*In today's world, there are many options for a pregnant teen: carrying the baby to term, placing the baby up for adoption, or abortion. Ask this question to decipher an honest read of what the pregnant teen is thinking.*)

2. Do you have any questions about pregnancy and abortion? (*Do not assume that she has been informed about her options. A teenager's brain is not fully*

developed, and her ability to think through actions and consequences to those actions is limited. Most teenagers think only about the present.)

3. What kind of support system do you have? Are your parents around? Do they (will they) help out with raising your child?

4. How will you provide emotional support to your child? Will your child have a healthy influence from persons of the opposite gender?

5. *If the counselee already has a child*: How long have you been a single parent? Describe a typical day or week for me.

6. Is the other parent ever involved with your child? Is his involvement disruptive or helpful to your child?

7. How are you taking care of yourself as a single parent? When was the last time you went out with friends to have fun? Who cares for the child when you are out?

8. How difficult is it for you right now as a single parent?

9. What are your plans for your future? What about marriage? Are you considering college? How are you planning to sustain your family financially?

WISE COUNSEL 4

To the expectant mother, the option of abortion often seems like a "quick fix" that will make the problems and stresses go away. Help your client *explore her alternative options, including carrying the baby to term and adoption*. While a teen mom is often influenced by her boyfriend or her parents in making a decision, communicate to your client the importance of researching the available options and *making an informed personal decision that will be best for her and her baby*. Having a baby is not a death sentence! While the pregnant teenager can easily view a pregnancy as "ruining" her life, you can guide your client in seeing God's providence and love, even in an unexpected pregnancy. (See Action Steps below to help her process options such as placing the baby for adoption.)

The discovery of a baby on the way can wreck the world of a teenager, so it is critical to help a teen mom find answers to the questions she is grappling with, such as, How can I tell my parents? What do I do about my boyfriend? Can I stay in school? Can God ever forgive me? Will my life ever be "normal" again? *Listening to and validating your client's feelings are important first steps*; then help her find answers to her questions. Don't be hesitant to talk frankly about the struggles she is experiencing and lead the teenager in finding practical solutions to her anxieties and concerns.

> Seven of every 10 teen mothers will drop out of high school.
>
> *U.S. Census Bureau, 2000*

If your client chooses to keep her baby, help her realize the value of the newly formed family. Regardless of the birth father's level of involvement in the baby's life, it's important for the single mom to understand that *she and her baby constitute a family*.

The key to successful single parenting is the *recruitment of "substitute parents" who will be committed to becoming a part of the new family*—parents, aunts and uncles, friends, neighbors, Big Brothers or Sisters—anyone trustworthy who will commit to assisting the baby to grow up as healthy and well-adjusted as possible. Getting involved in a local church and attending a support group with other single moms are good ways to gain *meaningful encouragement and practical support*.

As her child gets older, *a young mother may find it particularly challenging to parent a boy by herself*. If the father is not present, a mom should try to find quality male influences for her child through a grandpa, uncle, Boy Scout leader, coach, and others. While mothers have a natural tendency to want to protect their kids, it is important for the single mom to let her son "play rough" with the boys sometimes. She needs to establish what is clearly right and wrong, while giving her child some measure of autonomy.

5 : ACTION STEPS

1. Be Honest about Your Anxieties and Fears

- Having a baby can be scary, especially for a single mom! Anxiety, fear, anger, frustration, self-blame, and a host of other emotions may have been part of your first response to the news of your pregnancy. Find a safe person—a friend, family member, teacher, or counselor—to talk it out with. Put words to the fears, questions, and worries on your mind. You don't need to be strong or "pull yourself together." Just be real.

2. Choose to Live in God's Forgiveness

- Regardless of the circumstances under which the baby was conceived, realize that God extends free and complete forgiveness as you seek Him, despite your mistakes (or in the case of rape, the wrongful behavior of someone else). Living in guilt, self-condemnation, or shame is not just unhealthy, it's unbiblical.
- God's love for you is not based on what you do or don't do. In fact, there is nothing you could ever do to change the way He cares about you as His daughter. Even if unexpected, every child is a gift from God—a child to be cherished and loved.

3. Investigate All the Available Options

- You may be feeling extremely overwhelmed with the prospect of having to raise a baby on your own, and you may think that your only option is an abortion. This simply isn't so. Throughout the United States there are nearly three thousand crisis pregnancy centers staffed by volunteers who want to give you true alternatives and who will lovingly help you learn about available options.
- Your counselor will help you find a crisis pregnancy center or look in the Yellow Pages under the heading "Abortion Alternatives" or call, toll-free, 1-800-848-LOVE.
- *Have a list of crisis pregnancy centers on hand as a referral source for the client.*

4. Build a Support Network

- Being a teenage mom is tough but far from impossible. You can raise a child, but don't try to do it on your own. Ask for the support and counsel of people you look up to. Don't let the fact of your unexpected pregnancy cause you to withdraw from your family, church members, and friends because you feel ashamed. God has blessed you with the miracle of a little life inside, and to sustain that little life, you need the help and support of people who love you. Don't try to make the journey alone.

5. Develop a Parenting Plan

- Most teen parents live in the household of their family of origin, but living with your parents does not mean that you can check out as a parent yourself. You will need to think through your new role as a parent as well as a child living in your parents' home. Take some time to discuss with them your changing role and what is expected. You will need to talk about:

  — the rules that you will need to follow

  — what is negotiable and what is not (for example, curfews might be negotiable)

  — setting aside family times that will be honored consistently (a particular night of the week or breakfast or dinner together)

  — chores and household tasks (who does what, what is required, when must the chores be completed?)

  — who will take care of the baby (where and when?)

  — how school and/or work will fit into the picture

  — who will cover what expenses

- *Parenting plans will vary based on the age of the teen parent and other issues involved. Have the whole family talk together and share ideas. They should try to incorporate everyone's ideas into the plan. Even the youngest members can have input, but the parents are responsible for the final say.*

BIBLICAL INSIGHTS 6

There is therefore now no condemnation to those who are in Christ Jesus.
Romans 8:1 NKJV

While it's easy to condemn ourselves when we feel we've done something very wrong, God's Word says that, because Jesus has taken our condemnation, we as His followers are free. Living free means accepting the reality that God is the one who controls our lives and provides for us. Rather than comparing ourselves with others, God wants us to see ourselves through His eyes—free from condemnation!

If we confess our sins, He is faithful and just to forgive us our sins and to cleanse us from all unrighteousness.

1 John 1:9 NKJV

God's Word addresses sin here simply and clearly: confess it, and God forgives it. No ambiguity whatsoever! As a believer, it's easy to overcomplicate the Christian life with rules, expectations, and dos and don'ts. But the promise of Scripture is that God is ready and willing to forgive our sins and that no sin is too big for Him to forgive!

I will instruct you and teach you in the way which you should go; I will counsel you with My eye upon you.

Psalm 32:8 NASB

Being a single mom is hard work and often confusing, but according to the psalmist, we don't have to figure everything out on our own. In this promise in Psalm 32, we realize that God wants us to bring our needs to Him. As the all-sufficient and all-knowing One, there's no problem that He doesn't know the answer to. And far from being abstract and distant, God is revealed in this passage as a loving and reliable Father. God says, "I will," because with Him there's no question. He will always come through—He will always answer His children.

Behold, children are a heritage from the LORD, the fruit of the womb is a reward.

Psalm 127:3 NKJV

You made all the delicate, inner parts of my body and knit me together in my mother's womb. Thank you for making me so wonderfully complex! Your workmanship is marvelous—how well I know it. You watched me as I was being formed in utter seclusion, as I was woven together in the dark of the womb. You saw me before I was born. Every day of my life was recorded in your book. Every moment was laid out before a single day had passed.

Psalm 139:13–16 NLT

Children are precious to God, even when born in unexpected circumstances. A baby's life is a miracle that God created, and taking care of that life should be of primary importance to a parent. Psalm 139 shows God's love and care for every baby. Even though, when the baby is in the womb, we can't see him or her, God knows all the intricate details—eye color and type of hair, as well as the hopes, dreams, aspirations, and passions the child will have one day. Every single day of a baby's life is written out in God's mind, and every one of those days is filled with His grace.

For I am convinced that neither death nor life, neither angels nor demons, neither the present nor the future, nor any powers, neither height nor depth, nor anything

Each year nearly 750,000 teenagers between the ages of 15 and 19 become pregnant. The rate of teenage pregnancy has dropped 36% since its peak in 1990.

About 9% of all children (6.6 million) lived in a household that included a grandparent. 23% of children living with a grandparent had no parent present.

12% of Hispanic children and 14% of Black children lived with a grandparent, while 6% of White non-Hispanic children lived with a grandparent.

Centers for Disease Control and Prevention, 2000

else in all creation, will be able to separate us from the love of God that is in Christ Jesus our Lord.

Romans 8:38–39

Nothing can separate us from Jesus if we are His child, not even an unexpected pregnancy or being a teenage mom, not the rejection of a boyfriend or the misunderstanding of friends. Nothing can change the love God has for us because not only did He create us, He also redeemed us. His love for us isn't conditional. Paul says that nothing in all of creation can change that.

PRAYER STARTER 7

Lord, I don't think there is a job in the world more difficult than being a single parent. This teenage mom needs an extra blessing from You if she is going to survive the road that lies ahead. Be with her and her child, at all times, in all things . . .

RECOMMENDED RESOURCES 8

Clinton, Tim, and Gary Sibcy. *Loving Your Child Too Much: Raise Your Kids without Overindulging, Overprotecting or Overcontrolling.* Thomas Nelson, 2006.

Frisbie, David, and Lisa Frisbie. *Raising Great Kids on Your Own: A Guide and Companion for Every Single Parent.* Harvest House, 2007.

Graham, Ruth, and Sarah Dormon. *I'm Pregnant . . . Now What? Heartfelt Advice on Getting through Unplanned Pregnancy.* Gospel Light, 2004.

Howe, Michele. *Going It Alone: Meeting the Challenges of Being a Single Mom.* Hendrickson, 2000.

Leman, Kevin. *Single Parenting That Works: Six Keys to Raising Kids.* Tyndale, 2006.

McDowell, Josh, and Ed Stewart. *My Friend Is Struggling with an Unplanned Pregnancy.* CF4K, 2009.

Richmond, Gary. *Successful Single Parenting.* Harvest House, 1998.

38 Incest

1 : PORTRAITS

- Jean had never told anybody what happened when she was growing up. She had hoped if she never talked about it, it would go away. After all, it had only happened once. She had never told her parents because she didn't think they would believe her. She had avoided her uncle as often as she could after that. Now it didn't seem to make sense to talk about how he had sexually abused her.

- Bill was so confused but refused to tell anyone about his divorced, alcohol-abusing mother for fear they would be separated. When Mom was distraught at night, she would call on Bill to come to bed with her and nuzzle and caress her breasts until she "felt better." Even though he was now fifteen, this had gone on for so many years that it seemed normal to the young man.

- Don and Judy noticed their daughter Carrie had been more clingy, and she protested vehemently when they left for a night and put Grandpa in charge. "What is going on with her?" they wondered. A week later their oldest daughter, Marie, came to them and told them that Grandpa had been sexually abusing her for years and was now doing the same thing to her younger sister, Carrie. Don was shocked beyond words. His wife broke down and through her tears said, "I thought this was all over with my dad."

2 : DEFINITIONS AND KEY THOUGHTS

- Incest is defined as *sexual contact or behavior intended for sexual arousal that goes on between persons who are closely related* in family systems, such as between parents and children, siblings, children and grandparents, and first cousins. *Illegal incest involves any family sex between an adult and a minor child.*

- Incest usually takes the form of *an older family member sexually abusing a minor.*[1]

- In the last twenty years, child abuse (including incest) has been given more attention. Still, incest remains *one of the most underreported crimes* in the United States. Often the victim conceals the truth about incest due to feelings of guilt and shame and fear of the abuser.[2]

- Incest is a *particularly destructive* form of sexual abuse because the abuse occurs at the hand of someone the victim is supposed to be able to trust.

- Persons who were victims of incest *have a higher incidence* of depression, anxiety, post-traumatic stress disorder, borderline personality disorder, substance abuse, and sexual dysfunctions.[3]

- Most incidents of *incest between siblings* involve those of opposite sex: 74 percent. The incidence of same-sex siblings is 26 percent, with 16 percent between brothers and 10 percent between sisters.[4]

- Incest occurs in families that are financially well off, as well as in homes of low socioeconomic status. Incest happens to persons of *all races and ethnicities.*

- A study of a nationally representative sample of state prisoners serving time for violent crime revealed that *20 percent of their crimes were committed against children,* and three-fourths of prisoners who victimized a child reported the crime took place in their own home or in the child's home.[5]

- Victims of *incest are often very reluctant to reveal what has occurred.* Many young incest victims are told by the perpetrator that what is happening is a "learning experience" and an older family member does it in every family. *Incest victims may fear they will be disbelieved, blamed, or punished if they tell what has occurred.*

ASSESSMENT INTERVIEW 3

Many therapists have been attacked legally in recent years for conducting interviews that have been judged to be overly directive or suggestive of the defendant's guilt. Therefore prosecutors have added trained interviewers to their staff who use anatomically correct dolls and conduct indirect interviews with mostly open questions.

If there is a chance that your client's case will end up in court, please make referral for such legally sensitive interviewing to be done elsewhere and inform the courts, lawyers, and anyone else that you intend to interview and work only for therapeutic goals and purposes. Indicate your intention to assert privilege with all your therapeutic communications and case notes.

The following assessment is done for therapeutic purposes only, even if this information may become part of the court record, and assumes that the interviewee is at least twelve years of age or older. You may want to have a parent or guardian present to assist the process. Interviewing abused children is a unique and legally sensitive art that requires special training and experience. All such cases should be referred to an expert in this area of counseling.

1. What has happened that has brought you here today?
2. Is this the first time you or your family has sought help?
3. Tell me about your family. How are things going at home?
4. Tell me about your past. Have you had any painful or unusual things happen—even a long time ago? How long did this go on?
5. Can you tell me who was doing that to you? (*If the person seems reticent, explain that you need to know to help him, others who might be abused, and the abuser. In addition, if your client is a minor and still in contact with the abuser, immediate reporting action may need to be taken.*)
6. Do you know if others in your home are being abused?

7. What problems are you currently having as a result of what happened? (*Listen to how the abuse affected the person. No two people are alike in the story or the consequences of incest. Be aware that incest victims tend to minimize the impact of the abuse.*)

8. Tell me how you feel about what has happened to you. (*The client needs to have permission to feel his true emotions.*)

9. Do you feel responsible for the abuse? Do you feel responsible for keeping it a secret?

10. What was told to you about what might happen if this secret ever came out? (*Reassure the client that he is not alone and that he is not responsible for the abuse.*)

11. What do you believe about yourself—are you a mostly good or mostly bad person? (*Uncover unhealthy beliefs that have developed as a result of abuse. For example, what does he think about himself that he would allow this abuse to continue?*)

12. What do you believe about the person who did these things to you? (*Listen for rationalizations, such as, "He couldn't help it; he was drunk." These defenses have helped the client cope but have also made him less capable of seeing himself as a true victim of abuse.*)

13. Have you ever tried to stop the abuse? What happened?

14. What would you like to have happen as a result of our meeting today? What do you need so you will heal from this?

15. Whom have you told about this? How did that person respond?

16. Where do you think God has been in all of this?

4 : WISE COUNSEL

People who have experienced incest have had their *most sacred boundaries violated in a tragic way.* Healing from incest involves restoration of healthy boundaries and of trust. The counseling process must be gentle and not contribute to an unintentional wounding or shaming of the person. Follow the client's lead as he tells his story and use careful prodding to move on from any silences, but don't force the victim to tell what he may not be ready or able to disclose. Reassure him that *the incest was not his fault.*

Incest is perhaps the *most terrifying way one human can harm another,* as it destroys the central relationship that should be a source of deep care and protection from harm. Children look to their parents and extended family for information about who they are, how the world is, and who God is. When incest happens in a family, *a tragic corruption of those images* takes place.

In the recovery from incest (either as a child or as an adult who looks back on the trauma), it is important for the person to rethink the nature of God and to understand that God is not like the person who hurt him, but instead is good, loving, and kind—the opposite of the evil that was done to him.

One of the questions often asked by someone who has experienced incest is "Why me?" Sometimes *feelings of worthlessness* result from incest.

As the counselor, you need to *keep your own anger against the perpetrator in check* to provide a safe environment for the client to truly share his feelings.

Sexual behavior with a minor under eighteen years of age is a criminal offense, whether the sex was consensual or not. This behavior must be reported to appropriate authorities if you are a mandatory reporter in your state. Consult state laws about the duty or discretion to report.

The standard practice when working with sexual abuse victims is to inform the client about the limits of confidentiality at the beginning of the counseling process. To maintain their trust and show uncommon respect, it is also a good practice to notify your clients ahead of time that you must report and that you hope your reporting does not cause them to refuse further care, and you are completely willing to continue your work together.

ACTION STEPS 5

1. Talk about the Abuse

- The first step to healing is to talk it out. Find someone you trust—a pastor, teacher, or counselor who is not part of the problem—and talk honestly about what has happened. Getting out of an abusive situation requires help, and talking is the first step in getting connected with the people who know what to do.

  — Abuse is treatable and you will be a survivor.
  — You are not responsible for the abuse, only for your recovery.
  — Express, accept, and be prepared to deal with your thoughts, behavior, and feelings (even the irrational ones!).

- *Be careful not to retraumatize the person with your questions about the abuse. Trust and safety are of vital importance. Rule out any suicidal risk, depression, or medical concerns—especially if the incest or rape was recent. Assess also the nature of and length of the incest—its degree of severity and its history. Sometimes the person is seeking help for other problems that actually stem from sexual abuse.*

2. Give Yourself Time to Heal

- Healing from rape or incest is a long, difficult process, and people vary in the amount of time they require for healing. Don't put yourself on a time line or tell yourself you should "be over this by now."
- *Be sensitive and assess your client's current emotional state and his ability to discuss the abuse on a more specific level. Praise your client for the courage it takes to seek help, tell his story, and bring what was once in darkness into the light.*

3. Grieve

- You have been violated, and emotive rage and tears are normal and need to be expressed. Allow yourself to experience and process emotion, rather than holding it in.

- *Some clients may go to the opposite, compensatory extreme and be numb, without effect at all in the face of their loss. In such cases, don't force clients to cry or feel sad before they are ready. Let yourself feel the necessary pain with them and walk with them to grieve their loss.*

4. Learn to Regain Power

- Begin to learn how to stand up for the abused child within you. Recapture your power, voice, and control that the perpetrator took from you. Use the power of Jesus, who understands completely your pain, as He too suffered unimaginably in His shameful trial and death on the cross.

- Being believed and being able to tell your story of abuse are important first steps. Allow your counselor to help you stand strong, have a voice, and be empowered over the one who has exerted power over you.

- *Some people may want to confront their abuser. Others will not or will be unable to do so until they are stronger. Be sensitive to where your client is in the healing process.*

5. Attend a Support Group

- Healing is a journey. Experts who work with survivors of incest know the power of empathy and sympathy in the healing process. You do not have to go through this alone. Utilize the expertise and willingness of others to walk with you prayerfully, offering the support you deserve.

- Attending a group for survivors of sexual violence can be a positive healing step. By sharing your story with others who have experienced a similar kind of pain, you can grow as well as help others to grow—simultaneously.

- *Be ready to provide a list of referrals to local Christian professionals who have experience in counseling survivors of sexual abuse and incest as well as support groups that meet in your area.*

6. Set Healthy Boundaries

- As an abuse survivor, your personal boundaries were severely violated, which most likely left you confused and wondering what is healthy and normal. An important step is to establish healthy boundaries and be able to communicate these boundaries in an assertive and positive manner.

- Learn to differentiate between safe and unsafe people and what is appropriate and what is not appropriate regarding physical and verbal interactions with others.

Additional notes to the counselor:

- *Continue reassuring your client that healing will take place. Sessions may get tougher as you delve into his past, but encourage him throughout the process to remain consistent and strong.*

- *You may need some professional guidance to truly deal with the depth of pain that incest has caused your client. It is not wrong or a sign of weakness to seek out further professional help or consultation from a counselor with some expertise in counseling incest survivors. Make sure to obtain written consent from your client when speaking to third parties.*

BIBLICAL INSIGHTS 6

You intended to harm me, but God intended it for good to accomplish what is now being done, the saving of many lives.

Genesis 50:20

If anyone had good reason for revenge, it was Joseph. His brothers' jealousy provoked them to horrible abuse—selling him as a common slave to be taken away forever (Gen. 37:11–28). Before being raised to power in Egypt, Joseph had lost thirteen years of personal freedom.

Wisely, Joseph understood that God had overruled his brothers' abuse, making their evil turn out for good. This response of strength and faith can come only from those who trust God to rule—and overrule evil—in their lives.

Do not take revenge, my friends, but leave room for God's wrath, for it is written: "It is mine to avenge; I will repay," says the Lord. . . . Do not be overcome by evil, but overcome evil with good.

Romans 12:19, 21

God knows all that has occurred in our lives, including the pain, the betrayal, and the brokenness. He was present in the darkness and continues to walk with us. The offenses done to us were done to Him as well—including the shame of being disrobed at the cross.

He promises to repay—vengeance is His and His alone. Our job is to heal and to forgive.

Do not let the evil overcome you; do not give the abuser that much power in your life. Overcome the evil by doing good to others and to yourself.

Nothing in all creation is hidden from God's sight. Everything is uncovered and laid bare before the eyes of him to whom we must give account.

Hebrews 4:13

Sometimes people think they can hide portions of their life from everyone. They try to hide angry tempers, deep jealousies, or sexual sin.

Sexual violence hasn't escaped God's notice. The abuser may have thought he got away with it, but God knows. And God promises to judge appropriately.

7 PRAYER STARTER

Oh, God, Your heart breaks when people are hurt so badly. Thank You for this person who has come for help and healing from You. And thank You, Lord, for Your kindness and strength. Give wisdom and courage as he takes the next steps to be honest about the pain. You never abandon us, and You will help this dear person experience Your love and peace . . .

8 RECOMMENDED RESOURCES

Allender, Dan. *The Wounded Heart: Hope for Adult Victims of Childhood Sexual Abuse.* NavPress, 2008.

Frank, Jan. *Door of Hope.* Rev. ed. Thomas Nelson, 1995.

Langberg, Diane. *On the Threshold of Hope.* Tyndale, 1999.

Thompson, Shonda. *Don't Retain the Ashes: Breaking through the Secrecy of Incest.* Tate Publishing, 2008.

Thrasher, Mary. *Finding Hope in the Valleys of Life.* Moody, 2002.

Singles and Sexuality **39**

PORTRAITS :**1**

- Amanda, a twenty-nine-year-old single Christian, has set high standards for the man she hopes to marry. She has made a list of qualities she is looking for in a spouse, and though she has been on a number of dates, no relationship has lasted beyond six months, except for one in her early twenties that lasted two years. She has a great career and many solid friendships with other women, but often she finds herself feeling lonely and dreaming of the day she can finally start a family. With friends and family nudging her to settle down and her own awareness of her biological clock ticking away, Amanda is growing angry with God that she is still single.

- Darleen looked furtively at the ring she still wore from high school. She had promised to remain sexually pure until marriage, believing that God would bless her if she honored His code of sexual abstinence until she found her life's partner. Now she is in college and in love with a young man she hopes to marry, but she's conflicted over his invitation for sexual intimacy and exploration. She wonders why he has not even mentioned marriage in the future.

- Ralph had been divorced for two years when he began dating again. However, as he started dating, he realized the desire to be sexual with the women he was dating was too overwhelming to control. He convinced himself that it was just sex, not love, with "no strings attached." However, his "no strings attached" mentality has caused more emotional damage to the women he has dated than he ever imagined it would. Torn between the sexual desires and not wanting to hurt anybody, he has now turned to pornography and has even thought about engaging a prostitute.

DEFINITIONS AND KEY THOUGHTS :**2**

- Single Christians *struggle between a sexualized culture* that promotes sex without marriage in many different ways and a *church that calls them to remain celibate until marriage.* For many, it is a difficult and consuming conflict.

- Since the Bible limits sex to marriage, many singles have attempted to *narrow the definition of sex to refer only to sexual intercourse.* Hence, many consider oral sex "not really sex." Yet, since *oral sex intends to bring the recipient to orgasm* and since a *sexually transmitted disease can be caught through oral sex,* it must be considered wrong if done outside of marriage.

- Anal sex, even homosexual relations, could be considered nonsexual in this "only intercourse" definition. Therefore *one must be very careful how sex is defined* and what is considered okay.
- The term *"hooking up"* has as many definitions as it does people who do it. From teenagers to single adults, "hooking up" can refer to any sexual activity as simple as kissing or French kissing to oral sex with friends, acquaintances, strangers, or a dating partner.
- *Contributing factors for singles having sex outside of marriage include*:

1. Justifying it by saying everyone is doing it.
2. Engaging in sex with the man or woman you are "in love with" because your attitude is that you're "probably going to marry him or her anyway."
3. A permissive sexual culture in which sex outside marriage, even bisexual and homosexual relations, is touted by the media as exciting and your human right to enjoy.
4. High numbers of divorced individuals.
5. The culture's increased acceptance of cohabitation.
6. The permissive message that is often sent to the children of divorce that cohabitation is okay.
7. The use of drugs and alcohol, especially among college students. When mixed with sex, this combination can have lifelong negative effects and is a major reason for the increased rates of date rape, STDs, and unexpected or unwanted pregnancy.

3 : ASSESSMENT INTERVIEW

Be careful how you approach the client in counseling, as most young singles will be sensitive to a condemning attitude and will likely tune you out if that's what they hear. A better approach is to draw out their own beliefs and whether they have violated their own moral code. It is likely that the presenting problem will have little or nothing to do with sexual misconduct, but when they talk about their depression, anxiety, or "relationship problem," it may open the door for further discussion and influence.

Also for your counseling approach, consider other factors that relate to the individual's relationship status. That is, is she young, single, and looking for marriage? Is she a young business professional not looking for marriage but struggling with sexual thoughts and desires? Is she divorced and looking for another relationship? Consider the context and work from there. Different issues will certainly arise based on these factors. For instance, many young singles experience anger with God that they are still single; they wrestle with fantasies of being married. Many young women have self-esteem issues, while longing to feel beautiful and desired by men. Those in dating relationships may struggle with self-control. And others are caught up in a culture of "hooking up" with friends, strangers, and acquaintances. Divorced individuals have a different mind-set because they have already been in consummated marriages and are missing the sexual intimacy that accompanied that relationship. Feelings of loneliness, rejection, and isolation are very common.

General Questions

1. What is your personal belief about sex outside of marriage? How are you doing with living up to your own expectation of yourself in this area?
2. Do you have a boyfriend or someone with whom you are sexually intimate? Have you broken your own moral code when it comes to sexual intimacy? If so, how?
3. Are you discussing or thinking about marriage with this person?
4. Do you have feelings of shame and guilt after engaging in sexual practices because they break your own moral code? What steps have you taken to resolve this dilemma?
5. When was the first time you had sex? How often do you have sex? Are you sexual with just one person or with more than one?
6. Do you always enjoy sex? If not, why do you do it?
7. Do you always use protection when you have sex? Do you believe it has always been effective? Should we set you up for STD testing, just to be on the safe side?
8. Do you plan your sexual activity ahead of time or does it just happen?
9. Do you believe that your behavior is right and healthy or do you want to change it?
10. If you want to change, what strategies have you tried? How well have they worked?
11. Have you ever been pressured into having sex? What would you do if it happened again? Have you ever thought that you were raped? *If the client was raped, ask:* How has being pressured into sex affected your attitudes and feelings about sex?
12. Is there any relationship between love and sex? If so, what is the relationship?
13. Do you think God can forgive you for your sexual wrongdoing? What are your thoughts about God at this stage? Is He big enough—powerful enough—to release you from the hold that this person/drive/situation has on you?
14. What do you think you should do now? If you could draw a picture of an ideal living situation a year from now, what would it be?

Rule-Out Questions

1. Were you forced to have sex? If so, when did this take place? (*If the person is a minor, the rape must be reported.*)
2. Is there any possibility that you are pregnant? If so, what are your thoughts about what you are going to do?
3. Sexually transmitted diseases can be caught through oral sex as well as intercourse. Have you engaged in unprotected oral sex or intercourse? (*If so, the person needs a medical exam immediately. If infected, the person should contact every person she has been with, at least within a particular window of time, so they can be tested.*)
4. Are you feeling depressed? Have you ever considered the link between your sexual behavior and depression? Have you considered harming yourself? Do

you have a plan? (*Be prepared to get help. Contact 800-273-TALK or visit www .suicidepreventionlifeline.org and follow recommended procedures.*)

5. Have all of your sexual encounters been heterosexual? If not, how long have you been having sex with someone of the same gender?

6. If you have engaged in homosexual activity, has this been continual or just experimental? (*If homosexuality is an issue, see the chapter on homosexuality.*)

4 : WISE COUNSEL

Whether our sexuality has brought us intimacy in our relationships or led us into pain and despair, we are created as sexual beings in God's image. Genesis 2:24–25 shows God's design for man and woman to be united as one flesh. This sexual union occurred *before* mankind fell into sin. Thus, *people were created to be free to share their body openly with their spouse, delight in each other sexually,* and *honor God with their pleasure.*

The Bible says, "For out of the heart proceed . . . fornications. . . . These are the things which defile a man" (Matt. 15:19–20 NKJV). Often when somebody is living in sexual sin, it is because of the person's inability to control her sexual desires. These sexual desires, if for the opposite sex, are natural and need not be punished, *but they do need to be understood in light of the person's current season of life—singleness.*

Healing is possible after infidelity and sexual wrongdoing. To begin the healing process, the individual will need to *understand what caused the sexual acting out.* This will require a thoughtful, sometimes long look at the sexual pattern that has developed. *Renewing a level of relationship with God again is transformative and essential.* It starts by first confessing any sexual sins and then learning to discern and tell the truth to herself and others to whom she will become accountable. It will also be necessary for the healing individual to *take time for restoring and enriching relationships on a nonsexual basis.* The restoration process involves identifying and reestablishing what was good about building friendships. The enriching process involves *learning and implementing new skills and behaviors* to strengthen relationships.

Many people experience shame because they contracted an STD from illicit sexual contact. Treatment, then, must be *tailored to the specifics of each person's case,* addressing the issues of grace, forgiveness, forgiving others, and restoring broken trust. Since the client is single, make recommendations about *abstinence* and discuss the *power for ministry* of celibate living.

5 : ACTION STEPS

1. Realize the Beauty and Purpose of Sexuality

- Sexual desire and intimacy form an expression of love and commitment between a husband and wife. The Bible says, "There is more to sex than mere skin on skin. Sex is as much spiritual mystery as physical fact" (1 Cor. 6:16 Message). Often media and movies portray sex as an exciting adventure, but any attempt to satisfy sexual needs outside of marriage will only hurt you in the long run. Masturbation, pornography, or other forms of sexual behavior outside of marriage can strip sex of the beauty and mystery God intended and ultimately distance you from the "sensitivity" of the Holy Spirit (Eph. 4:19) and heart of God. Any sexual activity outside of marriage has the very strong potential of some form of emotional, physical, and/or spiritual consequences.

- *Gently correct any misinformation the client may have about sexuality and sexual behavior, and explain that sex can be part of a healthy sex life if it is experienced as a gift from God in the context of marriage. Any obsessive preoccupation and life-quenching shame because of sexual activity outside of marriage should be addressed. If the client has repented and begun to take steps toward healing and celibacy, God has forgiven her and she no longer needs to live in the shame of the behavior. Healthy sexuality can be restored.*

2. Build Solid Relationships

- Invest yourself in intimate friendships with people of your gender and surround yourself with people who will really care about you and hold you accountable for a pure thought life. A preoccupation with sexual activity may stem from a lack of healthy nonsexual relationships, and pornography and sexual fantasizing can isolate you more.

3. Make a Commitment to Act Responsibly

- Even if you struggle with sexual attraction, *you don't have to act on those urges.* Sexual feelings are not a choice but a God-given gift, and you should not feel guilty for having these urges.
- Pray and ask God for the power to:

  — not act on sexual urges through masturbation or pornography
  — run from situations of sexual temptation
  — refuse to fantasize about sex by refocusing your thoughts on another topic

4. Fight for Purity

- Don't expect to be able to say no in the passion of the moment. Decide beforehand what you will and will not do.
- Set specific boundaries for interaction in a romantic relationship, including:

  — whether or not you will be alone in a car or apartment together
  — what forms of physical touch you will allow
  — where you will and won't go on dates (bars, clubs, and wild parties don't encourage purity)

- Pray every day for the power to remain pure and ask God to sanctify and prepare you for good sexual relations in marriage.

275

5. Seek Accountability and Support

- You can maintain sexual purity, even while dating someone you love and hope to marry. Ask a friend or mentor to hold you accountable and ask you regularly about what's going on in your relationship . . . and your mind.

- Also consider attending a therapy or support group, where you can learn more about your struggles and interact with others who are facing similar challenges. Above all, be honest. Lying won't help you stay pure.

6 BIBLICAL INSIGHTS

But I say this as a concession, not as a commandment. For I wish that all men were even as I myself. . . . But I say to the unmarried and to the widows: It is good for them if they remain even as I am.

1 Corinthians 7:6, 8 NKJV

Paul, in the context of ministry and freedom to minister, considered being single ("as I myself") to be far more valuable than being married. Marriage, in this context, was to be pursued only if sexual self-control was a problem that could not be resolved. Single Christians have the greatest freedom to travel and minister the gospel—serving God as their primary focus and goal.

But if they cannot control themselves, they should marry, for it is better to marry than to burn with passion.

1 Corinthians 7:9

Paul exhorts Christians to marry rather than burn with passion. The self-control that he advocates adds stability to the life of the single person rather than the instability of constantly battling sexual desires.

But it happened about this time, when Joseph went into the house to do his work, and none of the men of the house was inside, that she caught him by his garment, saying, "Lie with me." But he left his garment in her hand, and fled and ran outside.

Genesis 39:11–12 NKJV

Lust has no godly goal or logic. Sometimes you can't talk someone out of doing wrong—you just have to get out of the way. Joseph knew only one answer to this moral challenge: view it from God's perspective. He concluded that violating his sexual integrity would be a "great wickedness" and "sin against God" (v. 9).

Sexual sin hurts our relationship with God and can destroy relationships with others. Joseph realized that he had no choice but to run!

So God created human beings in his own image. In the image of God he created them; male and female he created them. Then God blessed them and said, "Be fruitful and multiply. Fill the earth and govern it."

Genesis 1:27–28 NLT

We are created in the image of God and made to exult in each other's physical attractiveness. In Genesis 2:24–25 the Bible describes the love Adam and Eve shared together, their commitment to one another, and the freedom and safety they experienced as "one flesh" in a soul relationship. When a man and a woman become one in marriage, the bond of physical intimacy strengthens their relationship. Within the bonds of marriage, God approves of and encourages sexual pleasure and ultimately procreation.

PRAYER STARTER 7

Dear Lord, thank You that my friend is seeking help. Please help her see Your plan for sexuality and, more importantly, Your plan for her life as a single person. Help her learn new strategies to handle temptation. We know that once we ask for Your forgiveness, we have it. We praise You for this reality and thank You for Your forgiveness. Please be with her every step of the way as she seeks to preserve purity in the days to come . . .

RECOMMENDED RESOURCES 8

Anderson, Neil T., and Dave Park. *Purity under Pressure.* Harvest House, 1995.

Arterburn, Stephen, Fred Stoeker, and Mike Yorkey. *Every Man's Battle: Winning the War on Sexual Temptation One Victory at a Time.* Harvest House, 2005.

Ethridge, Shannon. *Every Woman's Battle: Discovering God's Plan for Sexual and Emotional Fulfillment.* WaterBrook, 2003.

Hammond, Michelle McKinney. *Why Do I Say "Yes" When I Need to Say "No"?: Escaping the Trap of Temptation.* Harvest House, 2002.

Perkins, William. *The Naked Truth: Sexual Purity for Guys in the Real World.* Zondervan, 2004.

Smalley, Michael and Amy. *Don't Date Naked.* Tyndale, 2003.

Video Series

Feree, Marnie. *Female Sex Addiction.* American Association of Christian Counselors Life Enrich Video Series, 2003.

Laaser, Mark. *Male Sex Addiction.* American Association of Christian Counselors Life Enrich Video Series, 2003.

40 Elder Sex

1 : PORTRAITS

- Empty nesters Richard and Beth Ann sit at separate sides of the couch in the counselor's office. "How can I feel close to my wife when she's cut me off from sex?" Robert begins. "How can I be intimate with him sexually when we haven't been intimate emotionally for years?" Beth shoots back.

- All her life Hannah's very religious but now dead mother told her that sex is dirty business. Hannah has never experienced any enjoyment during sex, and now it's even worse. "I thought I had this stuff resolved thirty years ago. Now my husband complains that I approach sex as if my dead mother were sitting on my shoulder and whispering poison into my ear."

- Hal lay in bed, fully awake in the middle of the night—his head was spinning and his gut was churning. He gazed over at the beautiful young woman sleeping naked next to him, and his heart groaned. *What am I going to do now? How would my wife and children respond if they saw me like this?* Guilt shot through him as he recalled how the sexy young woman—thirty-two years his junior—had come on to him in the bar of the hotel where he was staying for a week while attending to business in a far-away city. It had been a long but successful week, and he had been ready to relax. *The sex we had was incredible,* he thought, but he could already tell that the aftermath was going to be nearly impossible to manage. *What am I going to do now?*

2 : DEFINITIONS AND KEY THOUGHTS

- *As God created it, sexual intimacy is an essential and beautiful aspect of marriage.* Biblically the purpose of sex is threefold: procreation (Gen. 9:7), intimacy (2:24), and pleasure (v. 25). In the older years of marriage, however, sex can easily become a hassle.

- A recent study reported in the *Journal of Sex Research* discovered that "*14 percent of men and 26 percent of women in the longest relationships had had no sexual intercourse in the last year.* The reasons for this abstention were rooted in lack of sexual desire, as well as illness, including erectile dysfunction, causing problems in sexual performance."[1]

- Reporting on their research, Osmo Kontula and Elina Haavio-Mannila found, surprisingly, that in many cases older couples viewed their marriage as happy, and were also equally *happy with the physical closeness and touching* that they experienced with their partner. The quality of the relationship had not suffered, although it had lasted more than 40 years, and sexual activities were less frequent than before. The decrease in sexual activity did not make them unhappy because *they did not consider sex very important in their relationship.*[2]

- *While sex is important to a marriage relationship, it is by no means the foundation.* In later years, closeness and intimacy can be maintained even in the wake of health problems and lack of sexual desire. Accepting that diminishing sexual appetites are a normal part of aging, a couple can still continue to enjoy each other sexually and rest in the solidity of their relationship. In fact, diminished sex among elders can be balanced out by *quality* over *quantity* in making love. After years of sexual experience together, a well-seasoned couple knows what most pleases the other.

- *Even among older married couples, their marriage still provides the highest levels of sexual pleasure and fulfillment for men and women.* Just as with younger marrieds, intercourse is more frequent among older couples in happier marriages.

- More than *60 percent of older Christian couples* struggle with some type of sexual dysfunction in their marriage.[3]

- Mary Ann Mayo and Dr. Joseph Mayo provide this data and these wise insights about elder sex:

  When connubial bliss is discontinued by an older couple more often than not it is due to illness. There are *plenty of sexy seniors in the 70 to 90s age range who continue an active love life.* Among those who are over 60 years old with partners, 80 percent report being sexually active.[4]

- There are two truths to keep in mind. The first is that *difficulty with sexual functioning cuts across all age groups* and is not due solely to the fact that we get old. The second is that *from midlife, sexual problems increase for both men and women.* This second truth has led to the conclusions that the problems must be hormonal and they can't be fixed. Like death and taxes, when you enter the last third of your life, it seems that the good times have rolled right past you and what's left is a poor substitute for what used to be. However, these assumptions concerning old age are not always true. It *is* possible for elder couples to enjoy good times together, including times of sexual intimacy.

ASSESSMENT INTERVIEW 3

With an older couple there are three important issues: Are they experiencing sexual problems? Do they have a clear idea of God's design for sex? And do they believe that sexual decline is inevitable with age, or do they think that sex can be the best it has ever been for them? Asking the following questions may help you get a more complete picture, but when pursuing this subject, a helper must always be highly tuned to a couple's consent and where their sexual communication boundaries lie.

1. Are both of you pleased with your sex life? What works and what doesn't?
2. Do you understand that God's design for sex—now that procreation is a moot issue—still includes intimacy and pleasure? How strong is your spiritual intimacy? How strong is your emotional intimacy? How strong is your sexual intimacy?
3. Do you both feel you are having enough sex? Have you tried some things to increase your sexual fulfillment and pleasure? Has it worked?
4. Are you dedicated to improving your emotional and sexual fulfillment as a couple? Have any medical or other obstacles gotten in the way of your emotional or sexual intimacy?
5. Are there any serious sexual problems? When did you start noticing these changes? What have you done to correct this problem? Is that a priority in coming to counseling?

4 : WISE COUNSEL

David and Claudia Arp have done extensive research on couples in "second-half marriages" and have compiled the *top ten concerns* in the empty-nest years.[5]

1. conflict
2. communication
3. sex
4. health
5. fun
6. recreation
7. money
8. aging parents
9. retirement planning
10. children

The top three issues in the empty nest—*conflict, communication, and sex*—are also the major problem areas for younger couples.

To experience long-lasting passion in marriage, couples must focus their sexual times together on *delighting in each other's body*. Arousal, intercourse, and orgasm do not measure sexual satisfaction, but they result *when the pleasure of one's partner is the focus*.

However, pleasure should not be the sole focus of sex in marriage; *marital intimacy and mutual happiness* must also be top priorities. In pursuing these goals, the couple has to accept their differences as a man and a woman: *the husband's more predictable constancy* and *the ever-changing complexity of the woman*. Then sex will be more interesting, less goal oriented, less pressure filled, and more deeply satisfying, even in the later years of a marriage.

ACTION STEPS : 5

1. Have a Thorough Medical Evaluation

- Not only may an acute or chronic medical disorder be interfering with an older couple's sexual life, but if they don't know about it, the problem is not being treated. You should both have a thorough medical examination to rule out any physical problems that could interfere with your sex life.

2. Refocus on Intimacy and Friendship

- Being intentional in your marriage is critical, especially since raising your kids through the teenage years has likely robbed you of time together. Be intentional about rebuilding intimacy and friendship. Make memories together. Go on hikes, camping trips, walks in the woods, concerts, shopping expeditions—do the things that you did when the two of you first got together years ago. Not only does such intentionality build the bonds of intimacy and oneness, but it also has the potential of rekindling the passionate love that may have been pushed aside through the parenting years.

3. Pursue Mutual Goals

- Though you have reached the empty-nest years of your relationship, your goals for your sex life should remain the same as in earlier years: mutual fulfillment and mutual pleasure. Your counselor will help you find new ways to pursue these goals of intimacy in an empty-nest home.

4. Talk about Concerns

- From time to time all couples need to clear the air. They need to discuss openly the physical and emotional changes they are experiencing as well as the issues that have gone with them through all the stages of their marriage—all couples have perpetual concerns that will always be around with no final solutions. Learn how to accept the things that will not change and resolve those issues that can be resolved. Change, when handled wisely, can enhance an empty-nest marriage. The key is to step back and understand your spouse's point of view as well as voice your own.

- One way to clear the air is to practice active listening—taking turns being the speaker and the listener. The goal is to understand and validate the other spouse's perspective. You don't have to agree, but you do need to listen to understand the other's viewpoint.

> The greatest complaint about sex among older couples: increased libido and decreased sexual response.
>   Many couples drift away from sexual activity in their older years, but sex has been shown to promote:
> - better sleep habits
> - less stress
> - more happiness
>   Despite health problems, comfort and self-acceptance make for great sex in older couples.
>
> AARP the Magazine, 2008

- As couples hit the empty-nest years, many find their roles changing. Don't be surprised if this happens in your relationship, and learn how to accept and enjoy your new role.
- *Many couples need help in knowing how to handle new roles as their relationship changes over the years. Begin helping your clients redefine their roles as individuals and as a couple.*

5. Re-ignite Your Love

- The empty-nest and later years of life are a great time for couples to revitalize their love life. Focus on both the emotional and the physical sides of love the way you did when you were first married. Enjoy the freedom you have to be alone together, doing whatever you choose to express your love to each other.
- Empty-nest couples need to understand how their bodies change and how this may affect the pace of lovemaking. At this stage of life, your love life may be described as a delightful stroll rather than a race or sprint. Do what feels right for both of you. Also, as physical health and stamina come more and more into play, you both may need to take the role of initiator from time to time. Talk about your expectations and be willing to experiment and be creative.

6 : BIBLICAL INSIGHTS

Since you have in obedience to the truth purified your souls for a sincere love of the brethren, fervently love one another from the heart.

1 Peter 1:22 NASB

When husbands and wives commit to one another on their wedding day, they vow to love each other until the day that one or both partners depart from this earth. A sincere and committed union is formed. In 1 Peter, we are challenged to love one another fervently from the heart. When spouses show this kind of committed love to one another, there is no challenge too hard to overcome.

Drink water from your own cistern, running water from your own well. Should your springs overflow in the streets, your streams of water in the public squares? Let them be yours alone, never to be shared with strangers. May your fountain be blessed, and may you rejoice in the wife of your youth. A loving doe, a graceful deer—may her breasts satisfy you always, may you ever be captivated by her love.

Proverbs 5:15–19

No matter what happens along the journey of aging, husbands and wives can experience a deep and satisfying sexual relationship. The act may change due to physical challenges, but the spirit remains the same—full of passionate desire and fresh excitement!